QUICK GUIDES:

For a helpful way to review for comprehension, see the Quick Guides located throughout the text and listed in the detailed table of contents:

QUICK GUIDE 4   LISTENING TO A CLIENT SYSTEM

As you listen to a client system, ask yourself the following questions:

- What brings the client system here today?
- How does the client system describe the situations, and what meaning do these situations have for them?
- What will life look like when the situation is better?
- What strengths and talents do they have?
- What are their expectations of me?
- What do they want to happen in their work with me?
- What can we accomplish together?

Julie Birkenmaier is an Associate Professor in the School of Social Work at Saint Louis University. Dr. Birkenmaier's practice experience includes community organizing, community development, and nonprofit administration. Her research and writing focuses on community development, financial capability, financial credit, and asset development. Along with Marla Berg-Weger, she also co-authored *The Practicum Companion for Social Work: Integrating Class and Field Work* (3rd edition).

Marla Berg-Weger is a Professor in the School of Social Work at Saint Louis University. Dr. Berg-Weger's social work practice experience includes public social welfare services, domestic violence services, mental health, medical social work, and gerontological social work. Her research and writing focuses on gerontological social work and social work practice. She is the author of *Social Work and Social Welfare: An Invitation* (3rd edition). Along with Julie Birkenmaier, she co-authored *The Practicum Companion for Social Work: Integrating Class and Field Work* (3rd edition). She is the past president of the Association of Gerontology in Social Work and currently serves as the Chair of the *Journal of Gerontological Social Work* Editorial Board Executive Committee and is a fellow in the Gerontological Society of America.

Martha P. Dewees, Associate Professor Emerita of the University of Vermont, made her way into social work through counseling and then focused on mental health work at the state psychiatric facility. Her inclusion on the faculty at the University of Vermont provided the impetus for looking at social work practice through the lenses of human rights, social justice, strengths, and social construction.

www.routledgesw.com

Alice A. Lieberman, The University of Kansas, Series Editor

An authentic breakthrough in social work education . . .

New Directions in Social Work is an innovative, integrated series of texts, web site, and interactive case studies for generalist courses in the Social Work curriculum at both undergraduate and graduate levels. Instructors will find everything they need to build a comprehensive course that allows students to meet course outcomes, with these unique features:

- All texts, interactive cases, and test materials are **linked to the 2008 CSWE Policy and Accreditation Standards (EPAS).**

- **One Web portal with easy access** for instructors and students from any computer—no codes, no CDs, no restrictions. Go to www.routledgesw.com and discover.

- **The Series is flexible and can be easily adapted for use in online distance-learning courses as well as hybrid and bricks-and-mortar courses.**

- Each Text and the Web site can be used **individually** or as an **entire Series** to meet the needs of any social work program.

TITLES IN THE SERIES

Social Work and Social Welfare: An Invitation, Third Edition by Marla Berg-Weger
Human Behavior in the Social Environment, Third Edition by Anissa Taun Rogers
Research for Effective Social Work Practice, Third Edition by Judy L. Krysik and Jerry Finn
Social Policy for Effective Practice: A Strengths Approach, Third Edition by Rosemary K. Chapin
The Practice of Generalist Social Work, Third Edition by Julie Birkenmaier, Marla Berg-Weger and Martha P. Dewees

The Practice of Generalist Social Work

Third Edition
by Julie Birkenmaier and Marla Berg-Weger, Saint Louis University, and Martha P. Dewees, University of Vermont

To access the innovative digital materials integral to this text and completely FREE to your students, go to www.routledgesw.com/practice

In this book and companion custom website you will find:

- Complete coverage of the range of social work generalist practice within the framework of planned change, encompassing engagement, assessment, intervention, and evaluation and termination—for work with individuals, families, groups, organizations, and communities. This edition features expanded coverage of practice with individuals, families, groups, organizations, and communities.

- Consistent and in-depth use of key theoretical perspectives and case examples to demonstrate essential knowledge, values, and skills for generalist social work practice. But the text does not overwhelm the student reader with a plethora of nuances of intervention and other skills that will occur in a variety of practice settings and roles. *Instead, this book presents clearly the core competencies for general social work practice.*

- Six *unique*, in-depth, interactive, easy-to-access cases, which students can easily reach from *any* computer, provide a "learning by doing" format unavailable with any other text(s). Your students will have an advantage unlike any other they will experience in their social work education. One case, Brickville, is brand new to this book. Go to www.routledgesw.com/cases to see each of these cases on the free website.

- In addition, *four* streaming videos relate to competencies and skills discussed in the book at the three client system levels—individuals and families, groups, and communities. The videos depict social workers demonstrating skills discussed in the chapters, and offer instructors numerous possibilities for classroom instruction. In the video for the new case, "Brickville," a social worker combines individual and family practice skills with multicultural community engagement as he works with an African American family about to be displaced by redevelopment and facing multiple stressors. Go to http://routledgesw.com//sanchez/ engage/video, http://routledgesw.com//

riverton/engage/video, and http://routledgesw.com//washburn/engage/video, and http://routledgesw.com//brickville/engage/video to see *each* of these videos that are included within *each* of the web-based cases.

- At least 10 exercises at the end of each chapter provide you with the means to insure that your students can *demonstrate their mastery* of the theoretical frameworks, skills, and core competencies of generalist social work practice as presented *not just* in the text, but in the free web-based cases as well. Instructors can choose from among the approximately 5 exercises that relate to relevant practice issues, and 5 relate specifically to one of the on-line cases.

- A wealth of instructor-only resources also available at www.routledgesw. com/practice provide: full-text readings that link to the concepts presented in each of the chapters; a complete bank of objective and essay-type test items, all linked to current CSWE EPAS standards; PowerPoint presentations to help students master key concepts; a sample syllabus; annotated links to a treasure trove of social work assets on the Internet and teaching tips on how to use them in your practice sequence of courses.

- A clear focus on generalist social work practice, informed by the authors' decades of real-world practice experience, at *all* levels of engagement and intervention.

ADAPTING THE THIRD EDITION TO YOUR COURSE NEEDS

CUSTOM OPTIONS FOR THE TEXT ARE AVAILABLE: if an instructor or social work program wishes to assign *only a portion* of the text for a micro-level practice course, or a course focused on group practice, they may do so. Smaller units of the text are available in modular formats from the publisher. Please contact orders@taylorandfrancis.com if you would like to pursue this option.

The Practice of Generalist Social Work

Third Edition

Julie Birkenmaier
Saint Louis University

Marla Berg-Weger
Saint Louis University

Martha P. Dewees
University of Vermont

Routledge
Taylor & Francis Group

NEW YORK AND LONDON

Third edition published 2014
by Routledge
711 Third Avenue, New York, NY 10017

and by Routledge
2 Park Square, Milton Park, Abingdon, Oxon OX14 4RN

Routledge is an imprint of the Taylor & Francis Group, an informa business

© 2014 Taylor & Francis

The right of Julie Birkenmaier, Marla Berg-Weger and Martha P. Dewees to be identified as authors of this work has been asserted by them in accordance with sections 77 and 78 of the Copyright, Designs and Patents Act 1988.

Second edition published 2011 by Routledge

Trademark notice: Product or corporate names may be trademarks or registered trademarks, and are used only for identification and explanation without intent to infringe.

Library of Congress Cataloging in Publication Data
The Library of Congress has cataloged the one-volume edition as follows:
Dewees, Martha.
   [Contemporary social work practice]
   The practice of generalist social work / by Julie Birkenmaier, Marla Berg-Weger, and Martha Dewees. – [Third edition].
      pages cm. – (New directions in social work)
   Includes bibliographical references and index.
   1. Social service. 2. Social service–United States.   I. Birkenmaier, Julie.   II. Berg–Weger, Marla, 1956-   III. Title.
   HV40.D534 2014
   361.3'20973--dc23
   2013020892

ISBN: 978–0–415–73177–5 (pbk)
ISBN: 978–1–315–84960–7 (ebk)

Typeset in Stone Serif
by RefineCatch Limited, Bungay, Suffolk, UK

BRIEF CONTENTS

DETAILED CONTENTS

PREFACE

MAJOR CHANGES TO THE THIRD EDITION

Like the previous editions, this new edition of *The Practice of Generalist Social Work* provides detailed coverage of the knowledge, skills, values, competencies, and practice behaviors needed for contemporary generalist social work practice. Using a strengths-based perspective, students are given a comprehensive overview of the major areas relevant for social work practice, including: theoretical frameworks; values and ethics; expanded coverage of communication skills for all client systems; and extensive coverage of practice with all client systems through all phases of the change process. *The Practice of Generalist Social Work* offers a comprehensive discussion of practice with individuals, families, groups, communities, and organizations within the concepts of planned change, encompassing engagement, assessment, intervention, evaluation, and termination. Students have the opportunity to learn about generalist practice through in-depth case studies, examples, and exercises integrated throughout the text.

This edition expands greatly on the previous edition to provide all the material necessary and relevant for a two or three course sequence. This third edition provides additional contemporary case studies and applications of theory and knowledge for all client system levels. New exhibits provide in-depth information relevant to practice, summarize pertinent facts from the chapter, and give practical examples of the application of key chapter content. The Quick Guides provide students with brief guidelines for practice and sample documents used in practice. These expanded resources contain up-to-date individual, family, group, community and organizational guidance for the beginning practitioner. New and expanded end-of-chapter exercises, and online supplemental material, including videos, podcasts, and other web-based resources with teaching tips give the instructor additional avenues to challenge students to integrate and expand on chapter content.

For the new editions of all five books in the New Directions in Social Work series, each addressing a foundational course in the social work curriculum, the publisher has created a brand-new, distinctive teaching strategy that revolves around the print book but offers much more than the traditional text experience. Quick Guides within the text offer students guidance for their field experiences. Book-specific websites are accessible through the series website, www.routledgesw.com, and offer a variety of features to support your integration of the many facets of an education in social work.

At www.routledgesw.com/, you will find a wealth of resources to help you create a dynamic, experiential introduction to social work for your students:

- Companion readings linked to key concepts in each chapter, along with questions to encourage further thought and discussion.

- Six interactive fictional cases (three new for this edition) with accompanying exercises that bring to life the concepts covered in the book, readings, and classroom discussions.

- A bank of exam questions (both objective and open-ended).

- PowerPoint presentations, which can serve as a starting point for class discussions.

- Sample syllabi demonstrating how the text and website, when used together through the course, satisfy the 2008 Council on Social Work Educational Policy and Accreditation Standards (EPAS).

- Quick Guides from the books offered online for students to copy and take into the field for guidance.

- Annotated links to a treasure trove of articles and other readings, videos, podcasts, and internet sites.

ORGANIZATION OF THE BOOK

The following paragraphs serve to briefly introduce each of the chapters included in this book with emphasis on the updated content. All chapters have updated and expanded end-of-chapter exercises that use online resources.

Chapter 1

Understanding Social Work Practice provides an overview of social work practice by grounding students in the purpose of social work, social work competencies, types of client grouping, and the practice framework of engagement, assessment, intervention, termination, and evaluation. A discussion of the ethics that guide social work practice, licensure of social work, client populations that social workers work with, and the tensions in social work provides students with real-world information about the profession. Students are also introduced to major theoretical perspectives for social work practice, including the ecosystems, social justice, human rights, strengths, and postmodern perspectives. In this third edition, Chapter 1 features five new exhibits and two new quick guides to highlight key content and summarize material, including a summary of social work approaches.

Chapter 2

In contrast to a straightforward overview of values and ethics, **Applying Values and Ethics to Practice** provides a brief history of social work ethics and the NASW *Code of Ethics* (2008), then contrasts the *Code of Ethics* with the International Federation of Social Workers' Ethical Statement, and also discusses the limits of ethical codes. A discussion of the intersection of ethics and the law gives students information about the interplay between the two, followed by a discussion of ethical dilemmas and processes for resolving them. Extensive discussion about common practice dilemmas gives students exposure to situations that they may encounter in practice, followed by an emphasis on risk management. Expanded coverage of ethics violations and state sanctions round-out the discussion. New content in Chapter 2 includes expanded coverage of ethics violations and state sanctions.

Chapter 3

Individual Engagement: Relationship Skills for Practice at All Levels provides students with the characteristics of core relationships qualities, as well as a description of the specific skills for dialogue with clients at all system levels, including coverage of common communication pitfalls. As the helping relationship includes the dimension of power, the chapter provides extensive coverage of sources of power within relationships, and provides guidance on the use of power through a case study of "Jasmine and the Social Worker." Practical questions guide students toward active listening. Students are also provided with strategies and skills for promoting social justice and human rights within helping relationships. New content in this third edition includes an exhibit on nonverbal behavior guidelines, a quick guide that helps students discover their listening skills, and content about using children as translators.

Chapter 4

Social Work Practice with Individuals: Assessment and Planning includes a focus on the assessment and planning process within the global environment in which practicing social workers live and practice. The chapter begins with a discussion of the history of assessment and moves to an overview of theoretical approaches to social work practice, both classic and contemporary (strengths, narrative, and solution-focused). The application of evidence-based practice approaches is highlighted. The need for practice knowledge and behaviors in the area of diversity within the assessment and planning phases emphasizes the need for cultural competence. The chapter concludes with a discussion of the relevant skills and practice behaviors in the assessment and planning phases of the social work intervention process, including skills needed for strengths-based, narrative, and solution-focused approaches, documentation, and self-care for the social worker. This edition offers more content on narrative and solution-focused approaches, documentation, self-care, and suicide risk assessment with vulnerable populations with more examples on applications of knowledge and theory.

Chapter 5

Social Work Practice with Individuals: Intervention, Termination, and Evaluation introduces students to key areas of social work practice that will impact virtually every dimension of their professional lives. With an emphasis on theoretical perspectives, students learn to apply various intervention, termination, and evaluation practice behaviors. Traditional and contemporary social work roles are highlighted and discussed. Documentation and record-keeping for social work interventions is explained. Interventions with individuals are also framed within an empowerment practice approach. Framed within theoretical perspectives for understanding diversity, students are offered an overview of the skills required to be a culturally competent social work practitioner. New features in Chapter 5 include additional content on cognitive behavioral treatment and expanded content on motivational interviewing, documentation, and empowerment.

Chapter 6

Social Work Practice with Families: Engagement, Assessment, and Planning The chapter begins with a history of social work practice with families, grounded within a systems framework. Theoretical perspectives, including narrative and solution-focused, are discussed within the context of the engagement and assessment phases of interventions with families with emphasis on empowerment. Students encounter a broad range of family constellations as they read about contemporary family social work. Practice behaviors and skills are presented for achieving engagement and assessment with families and documentation strategies are included. This newest version of Chapter 6 offers more content on documentation, empowerment, and more in-depth discussion about solution-focused and narrative assessment and planning.

Chapter 7

Social Work Practice with Families: Intervention, Termination, and Evaluation conceptualizes generalist social work practice interventions with families. Continuing with the theoretical perspectives discussed in Chapter 6, this chapter develops interventions with families using strengths and empowerment, narrative, and solution-focused approaches. Skills and practice behaviors for intervening, terminating, evaluating, and documenting family-focused interventions are discussed in detail. New to this edition is more in-depth content on empowerment and resiliency, and extended exploration of narrative and solution-focused family interventions.

Chapter 8

Social Work Practice with Groups: Engagement, Assessment, and Planning provides students with up-to-date perspectives on social work practice with groups. The chapter opens with an overview of the role of groups within our communities and profession followed by a historical and contemporary perspective on the use of groups for change. The dimensions of group practice are presented within the framework of theoretical perspectives (i.e., narrative and solution-focused). Planning for group interventions, including the engagement and assessment of group members, is emphasized from a practice behaviors perspective along with the importance of cultural competence in the group setting. With this edition, Chapter 8 now includes expanded coverage on cultural competence in group work.

Chapter 9

Social Work Practice with Groups: Intervention, Termination, and Evaluation Developing and implementing interventions with various types of groups is the emphasis of this chapter. Continuing the framing of skills and techniques within theoretical perspectives, the use of evidence-based interventions with groups is introduced using the strengths, narrative, and solution-focused frameworks. Models for group intervention are described along with an in-depth examination of the roles, skills, and practice behaviors required for carrying out a group-level intervention. Termination and evaluation of group interventions are also covered. New to Chapter 9 is additional content on narrative group work, social worker roles, group member behaviors, and evaluation.

Chapter 10

Social Work Practice with Communities: Engagement, Assessment, and Planning introduces students to the concept of community. The chapter defines and discusses types and functions of communities. Students learn about various theoretical perspectives, including contemporary perspectives for community practice. Engagement and assessment concepts, including community-based analysis, evidence-based practice, and community needs assessments, are extensively discussed. Examples of types of needs assessments, surveys used in needs assessments, and needs assessment summaries provide additional practice guidance. Community practice skills are thoroughly covered, as are the implications of global interdependence for community practice in the United States. This edition contains expanded content on needs assessments, including types, examples, and surveys used to collect needs assessment data.

Chapter 11

Social Work Practice with Communities: Intervention, Termination, and Evaluation builds on the engagement and assessment content of Chapter 10 to present strategies and techniques for community practice. Using the insights gained about practice at the individual, family, and group levels, this chapter expands the students' awareness of social work practice with communities through a discussion of today's trends and skills for intervention, including community social and economic development, and community organizing. Included in this discussion is coverage of international community practice. Examples of public and private efforts to promote evidence-based community practice assist students in applying the material. Additional guidance on advocacy efforts and asset based development are presented. Students also learn the knowledge and skills needed for termination and evaluation of community practice. The third edition offers a host of examples of contemporary community interventions, with a special focus on community development and community organizing examples, as well as quick guides that offer students concrete tools to use in community interventions, termination, and evaluation.

Chapter 12

Social Work Practice with Organizations: Engagement, Assessment, and Planning covers a challenging client system for beginning practitioners—the organization. Students learn a wealth of practical and theoretical aspects of organizations, including a discussion about the purpose and structure of organizations, power relations within organizations, and social work within host organizational settings. The chapter provides discussion about the elements of an internal assessment of organizations, to include organizational culture, and external assessments as well. Material about organizational policy advocacy and nonprofit partnerships help guide practice. The many new, recent examples of organizational engagement and assessment provide students with contemporary illustrations of key content in Chapter 12. Three new quick guides offer handy tools to assist students in their efforts to contribute to organizational engagement and assessment work.

Chapter 13

Social Work Practice with Organizations: Intervention, Termination, and Evaluation uses the foundation built in Chapter 12 to discuss approaches, perspectives, and models for intervening with organizations. This chapter provides extensive coverage of the relationship between theoretical perspectives and organizational change, as well as a practical framework for thinking about generating change and the needed knowledge for a social work generalist in this endeavor. Termination and evaluation of change efforts within organizations, including a discussion about the role of the generalist practitioner in this process, help students see their potential role in a change effort with organizations. Content about the challenges of implementing organizational change, and persuasion skills to assist in these efforts, provide direction for the practitioner. In this edition, Chapter 13 has expanded content that includes examples of intervention at the organizational level that includes developing and refining new programming, as well as the associated challenges.

INTERACTIVE CASES

The website www.routledgesw.com/cases presents six unique, in-depth, interactive, fictional cases with dynamic characters and real-life situations. Three of them—the RAINN, Hudson City, and Brickville cases—are entirely new to this edition of the series. Your students can easily access the cases from any computer. The cases provide a "learning by doing" format unavailable with any other book, and the experience will be unlike any other your students will experience in their social work training.

Each of the interactive cases uses text, graphics, and video to help students learn about engagement, assessment, intervention, and evaluation and termination at multiple levels of social work practice. The "My Notebook" feature allows students to take and save notes, type in written responses to tasks, and share their work with classmates and instructors by e-mail. Through these interactive cases, you can integrate the readings and classroom discussions:

The Sanchez Family: Systems, Strengths, and Stressors   The 10 individuals in this extended Latino family have numerous strengths but are faced with a variety of challenges. Students will have the opportunity to experience the phases of the social work intervention, grapple with ethical dilemmas, and identify strategies for addressing issues of diversity.

Riverton: A Community Conundrum   Riverton is a small Midwest city in which the social worker lives and works. The social worker identifies an issue that presents her community with a challenge. Students and instructors can work together to develop strategies for engaging, assessing, and intervening with the citizens of the social worker's neighborhood.

Carla Washburn: Loss, Aging, and Social Support   Students will get to know Carla Washburn, an older African American woman who finds herself living alone after the loss of her grandson and in considerable pain from a recent accident. In this case, less complex than the Sanchez family case, students can apply their growing knowledge of gerontology and exercise the skills of culturally competent practice at the individual, family, and group levels.

RAINN Based on the first online hotline for delivering sexual assault services, this interactive case includes a variety of exercises to enable students to gain knowledge and skills related to the provision of services to persons in crisis. With a focus on social work practice at all levels, exercises provide insight into program services and evaluation, interactions with volunteers and clients, and research.

Hudson City: An Urban Community Affected by Disaster A natural disaster in the form of Hurricane Diane has hit Hudson City, a large metropolitan area on the northeastern coast of the United States. This interactive case will provide students with insights into the complexities of experiencing a disaster, including the phases of the human response to disaster and the social work role in responding to natural disasters.

Brickville A real estate developer has big plans to redevelop Brickville, an area of a major metropolitan area that has suffered from generations of disinvestment and decay. The redevelopment plans have stirred major controversy among community residents, neighborhood service providers, politicians, faith communities, and invested outsiders. This case is a "community case" in which a "family case" is embedded; the case is multi-layered and detailed. Students will be challenged to think about two levels of client systems, and the ways in which they influence and are influenced by one another.

IN SUM

We have written this book with the purpose of providing you and your students with the information needed to learn the knowledge, skills, values, competencies, and practice behaviors that are required for a competent and effective generalist social work practice. The multiple options for supporting your teaching of this content are intended to help you address the diverse range of student learning styles and needs. The design of this text and the instructor support materials are aimed at optimizing the experiential options for learning about generalist practice. We hope this book and the support materials will be of help to you and your students as they embark on their journey toward social work practice.

ACKNOWLEDGEMENTS

We would like to thank the many colleagues who helped to make this book and previous editions possible. To Alice Lieberman, we are grateful for your innovation and vision that has resulted in this series and the web-based supplements that bring the material alive. We appreciate the camaraderie and support of the authors of the other books in this series—Rosemary Chapin, Anissa Rogers, Judy Kryzik, and Jerry Finn. A special thank you to Anissa Rogers and Shannon Cooper-Sadlo, and Andrea Seper whose creativity makes the exercises, test questions, and PowerPoint slides enticing and easy to use. We want to thank the group who participated in the production of the video vignettes: actors John Abram, Patti Rosenthal, Beverly Sporleder, Sabrina Tyuse, Kristi Sobbe, Myrtis Spencer, Phil Minden, Katie Terrell, and Shannon Cooper-Sadlo and videographers, Tom Meuser and Elizabeth Yaeger. A special thanks goes to Sue Tebb, for her careful review and invaluable feedback, and Andrea Seper, graduate student assistant, for her extensive assistance with this edition and supplemental materials. Thanks also goes to social work graduate student assistants, Michelle Siroko and Luxiaofei Li, for their help with research, writing and editing. We also want to thank:

Toni Johnson	University of Kansas
Lara Vanderhoof	Tabor College
Chrys C. Ramirez Barranti	Sacramento State University
Kameri Christy	University of Arkansas
Robin Bonifas	Arizona State University
Bill Milford	Thomas University
Martha Haley-Bowling	Ferrum College
Mary Clay Thomas	Mary Baldwin College
Armon Perry	University of Louisville

for their reviews of the book as it was evolving. Finally, we are most appreciative to the staff of Routledge for their support and encouragement for making this book a reality. It takes a village . . . .

ABOUT THE AUTHORS

Julie Birkenmaier is an Associate Professor in the School of Social Work at Saint Louis University, Missouri. Dr. Birkenmaier's practice experience includes community organizing, community development, and nonprofit administration. Her research and writing focuses on financial capability, financial credit, community development, and asset development. With colleagues, she co-edited *Financial Capability and Asset Development: Research, Education, Policy and Practice*. With Marla Berg-Weger, she also co-authored the textbook, *The Practicum Companion for Social Work: Integrating Class and Field Work* (3rd edition).

Marla Berg-Weger is a Professor in the School of Social Work at Saint Louis University, Missouri and Executive Director of the Geriatric Education Center. Dr. Berg-Weger holds social work degrees at the bachelor's, master's, and doctoral levels. Her social work practice experience includes public social welfare services, intimate partner violence services, mental health, medical social work, and gerontological social work. Her research and writing focuses on gerontological social work and social work practice. She is the author of *Social Work and Social Welfare: An Invitation* (3rd edition). With Julie Birkenmaier, she co-authored the textbook, *The Practicum Companion for Social Work: Integrating Class and Field Work* (3rd edition). She is the Past President of the Association of Gerontology in Social Work and currently serves as the Chair of the *Journal of Gerontological Social Work* Editorial Board Executive Committee and is a fellow in the Gerontological Society of America.

Martha P. Dewees, Associate Professor Emerita of the University of Vermont, made her way into social work through counseling and then focused on mental health work at the state psychiatric facility. Her inclusion on the faculty at the University of Vermont provided the impetus for looking at social work practice through the lenses of human rights, social justice, strengths, and social construction. These are reflected in her previous publications and in the first edition of this book.

CHAPTER 6

Social Work Practice with Families: Engagement, Assessment, and Planning

The social work profession and the family have traveled a long distance together, sometimes in close companionship and sometimes on divergent paths, only to meet once again on the same road. Our profession began in the company of the family and has returned to it once again.

Ann Hartman and Joan Laird, 1983

Key Questions for Chapter 6

(1) What competencies do I need to engage with and assess families? (EPAS 2.1.10(a) & (b))

(2) What are the social work practice behaviors that enable me to effectively engage and assess families? (EPAS 2.1.10(a) & (b))

(3) How can I use evidence to practice research-informed practice and practice-informed research to guide the engagement and assessment with families? (EPAS 1.2.6)

(4) How do the perspectives and experiences from my present family and/or family of origin impact my engagement with and assessment of client families?

FAMILY IS THE EARLIEST, MOST BASIC, AND, SOME SAY, most challenging small group one can experience during a lifetime. It is also probably the most powerful in shaping who we become. For some, family means home, safety, and acceptance. For others, family means violence and danger. Some people may feel important and cherished with family or never quite good enough or even useless. Others may feel swallowed up in their family's dysfunction, or may long for, and bask in, the wholeness of unconditional support. Most of us experience a mix of feelings in between these. Family is a complicated enterprise, and many of us harbor some of its tensions that make us both joyful and troubled. Virtually all members of society have experienced some kind of family, and most have ideas (or dreams) of the qualities that an ideal family could or should possess.

This chapter explores the concept of family—definition, meaning, and place within the contemporary social context—and the process of engagement and assessment with families. We will also look at theoretical perspectives for working with traditional and contemporary family structures as well as dynamics, skills, and tools for working with the range of families. This chapter will also guide you through challenges and strategies for understanding the impact that family issues can have on your clients and you.

FAMILIAR PERSPECTIVES AND SOME ALTERNATIVES

The enormous and rapid changes in social rules in most Western countries have led many to contend that the "traditional" family has been lost. A traditional vision of the ideal U.S. family portrays a nuclear group consisting of two heterosexual adults and two or perhaps three children. The father supports the family economically, and the mother supports it emotionally. There are clear roles, rules, and jobs that each member undertakes. If the mother also works outside the home, she is still free to participate in the kindergarten car pool, do the laundry, entertain friends, and "be there" for her husband and children. A more contemporary version of the father makes him increasingly sensitive to the feelings and needs of his wife and children, but his work still takes priority. In contrast, the National Association of Social Workers (NASW) (2007a, para. 3) provides this definition of the contemporary family: "two or more people who assume obligations and responsibilities generally conducive to family life." This inclusive perspective on the family embraces parents who are divorced, separated, unmarried, grandparents, gay, lesbian, bisexual, transgender, or questioning, adoptive, and fostering, along with couples who have no children, partnered couples, and families caring for older adult members. Social workers must use practice approaches that recognize the diversity of family constellations (Hull & Mather, 2006). For example, to avoid assumptions and confusion, the social worker should ask the client to describe and define her or his family unit (Wood & Tully, 2006) rather than make assumptions, based on household composition. Given the changing nature of the family and the fluidity of membership in some families, it is important to ask each member of the family, "Who do you consider to be part of your family?" A follow-up question may then be, "Of these people, who is biologically and/ or legally related to you?" For instance, a client's "aunt" may not be a legal or biological family member but is considered by the client to be a part of her or his family.

Those with nostalgic older visions of family are appalled at what they see today as a lack of morality in many young families. There is distress about young adults who live together with no permanent commitment. Single women often choose to become parents and do not suffer the social stigma so prevalent only a few generations earlier. Parents who are gay, lesbian, bisexual, transgender and questioning (LGBTQ), who earlier had to conceal their sexual identities, are joyfully parenting children, and many are serving as foster and adoptive parents in conjunction with state child protection agencies. In the past, LGBTQ individuals were not even given the option to foster or adopt children; now they are recruited by these organizations. Although these developments in our U.S. cultural norms are lamented by some, fear of change may overshadow the research about new, more inclusive family and parenting arrangements. We will take a more in-depth look into this issue later in the chapter.

Nonetheless, there are real issues in the surrounding context of the contemporary family that create concerns for social workers. The U.S. divorce rate of 52 percent for men and 44 percent for women (U.S. Census, 2010b) is closely related to the ever-growing number of children who live in a single parent-headed household with incomes below the poverty level. The percentage of children who live in poverty with a single mother has reached 32 percent, while single father-headed households experience poverty rates of only 16 percent (U.S. Census, 2011a). Some believe that commitment to the stability and endurance seems to have vanished. While the number of unmarried teen parents is slowly declining (31.2/1000 teen females in 2010, down from 34.2/1,000 teen females in 2008) (Hamilton, Martin, & Ventura, 2012), the rate of births to teen parents of color continues to be high (36–47 births/1,000 teen mothers) (Hamilton et al., 2012). The associated legacies of perpetuated poverty, increased family violence, and health and mental health issues, and a sense that two generations—the child and the child's child—have sacrificed much of their potential, provide little hope for the future. Clearly, the change in predominant family compositions has required changes in service delivery, and impacts society. The widening of the income equality gap and economic pressures resulting from the recent economic recession has created additional challenges for families that impact their well-being. The result of such change has been serious societal issues with which society and social work must grapple.

There are other ways to look at family. In keeping with this book's focus on multiple realities, we will explore the experiences of an array of family constellations to expose illusions about the family and develop a more balanced perspective. This chapter will discuss the experiences of both traditional and nontraditional families. Consider Exhibit 6.1, which describes the experience of family for countless people who have been marginalized, that is, who have lived in the margins of our culture and others.

HISTORICAL ANTECEDENTS FOR FAMILY SOCIAL WORK

The social work profession has a long history of working with families, shaped by the context of the times. In community mental health centers and youth agencies, hospitals and schools, and welfare and child protection efforts, social workers work to strengthen families. Collins, Jordan, and Coleman (2013) encourage social work students interested in working with families to explore this area of practice using the following list of questions:

- What is the purpose of family social work?

- How does family social work differ from family therapy?

- How can I work effectively with families who are different from my own family?

- What is my role as a family social worker?

- How will I know what factors contribute to the family's difficulties?

- How should I work with an entire family and with all members in the same room at the same time?

- How will I know what questions to ask family members? What do I say to the family?

- How do I engage all the members of the family, particularly if they seem resistant, feeling blamed, uncommunicative, or overpowered by another member?

- What should I do if family members get angry at me or another member of the family?

- What do I need to know to help families change? What knowledge will help the families begin to change?

- What skills will I need when there are young children in the interview? Older children?

- What can I do to protect individual family members when the rest of the family is attacking or blaming?

- How do I help families that are paralyzed by a crisis to rise about it and solve their problems?

- What do I need to know about family social work when working with families of different ethnic, racial, or sexual orientation backgrounds?

- What skills are needed for prioritizing the family's problems and then for each of the phases of work with families (pp. 1–2).

Why is there such a concern for the maintenance of the family? What does our culture expect the family to do, and how do we think the family should work? Although there are many possible responses to these questions, two particular perspectives are examined that seem to have special relevance for social workers today—the family as a functioning unit and the family as a system.

©: Harry Hu, courtesy of Shutterstock® images

EXHIBIT 6.1

Family: Views from the Margins

- What we may consider now to be the ideal family has never actually flourished in any culture for any length of time: Children have historically been considered commodities that enhanced the economic status of their fathers, who owned them, and their value was often equated to the amount of work they did. Childhood as a time to be nourished and cherished is a relatively new and narrowly prescribed phenomenon of Western culture and some nations in the East. The United Nations instrument "The Rights of the Child" reflects the need for considering children as genuine people and not possessions. In contrast, in parts of the United States, children are prostitutes, drug dealers, and hired thieves. In much of the world they are all these and also soldiers.

- Ideal conceptions of the family have historically served to restrict and diminish the role of women as categorical caretakers. Many women throughout history have been required to abandon their dreams and have also been seen as property to be exploited. Men, too, are assumed to fit into tightly proscribed roles that may not be compatible with their identities or goals.

- In many families of the past, infant and childhood mortality was high and parents may have died by their early 40s. Such circumstances produced a crisis for remaining family members, resulting in placements with distant relatives, community members, or in orphanage care. The idealistic notion of earlier times places blinders on the realities of disease, early death, and other forms of danger that surely shaped the overall experience of family.

EXHIBIT 6.1

Continued

- It is still the family, even in contemporary U.S. society, that is the primary force for socialization and nurturing of children and support of the community. As an example, the families of children experiencing mental illnesses still provide most of the care and nurturing of their adult children, in spite of federal and state programs designed to assist them.
- The definition of family as rigidly restricted to biological and legal ties and hetero-sexual partners or adoption has always marginalized and scapegoated significant numbers of people who have meaningful and productive relationships and who make significant contributions to the community, the socialization of children, and the general economic and social order.
- More contemporary notions of family have liberated both men and women to develop and carry out the roles of child caretaking, economic provision, management, personal development, and health care in a way that does not deny their individual aspirations and talents; the same principles hold for gay, lesbian, bisexual, and transgender families with biological or adopted children.
- Contemporary families have greater biological control over the number and timing of pregnancies and can plan family composition in a way that is consistent with their financial capacities and other internal demands (for example, one partner is in school or another is committed to the care of a parent). Women are now more able to exercise control over their reproduction, and make decisions about their future.

Family as a Functioning Unit

A concrete way to think about the importance of the family is to explore the societal expectations of the family. The following functions are among those that are typically viewed as critical to the contemporary maintenance of families:

- Provide the material and economic necessities for sustenance and growth.
- Offer members emotional security, respect, safety, and a place for appropriate sexual expression.
- Provide a haven for privacy and rest.
- Assist, protect, and advocate for members who are vulnerable or who have special needs.
- Provide support for members' meaningful connection and contribution to community life.
- Facilitate the transmission of cultural heritage.
- Provide a socially and legally recognized identity.
- Create an environment in which children can be nurtured and socialized.

The responsibilities reflected here emphasize not only the functional roles of individual family members and their needs and identities but also the connection to their communities and the overall societal environment. This compilation is not prescriptive; that is, it does not specify *how* children should be nurtured but allows for individual and cultural interpretation. Rather than seeking individual or family dysfunction, the exploration of these tasks in various areas of family life tends to highlight strengths as well as areas for improvement. In that respect, this set of functions serves as a useful guide for assessing the degree to which societal expectations are met in any particular family.

While families serve a critical function in society, we must recognize they have needs which may not be met, thus requiring the involvement of a helping professional. Needs may be categorized in many different ways, but one strategy is to consider the family as a system with a practical purpose. Building on the work of Kilpatrick and Cleveland (1993), Kilpatrick (2009) presents a strategy for classifying family needs by levels, including:

Level 1—basic survival. Needs are in the areas of food, shelter, medical care.
Level 2—structure and organization. Needs center on setting limits and safety concerns.
Level 3—space. Needs relate to issues of privacy, access, and boundaries.
Level 4—richness and quality. Needs exist in areas of inner conflict, intimacy, and self-actualization (p. 4).

Taking into consideration the type and level of need, the social work assessment and intervention process can be focused within a conceptual framework that encompasses both context of those persons with whom you work (i.e., family/community, couple/dyad, and individual) and orientation of the intervention you choose with the family. Will the intervention have a focus on behavioral/interactional change, experiential aspects of clients' thoughts and feelings, or historical, emphasizing family-of-origin issues (Kilpatrick, 2009, p. 10)? Incorporating these complexities of the family system into your social work intervention can help to gain insight into the way in which the family functions, their needs, and the most effective strategies for helping them to reach their desired goals.

Family as a System

Because social work focuses on interactions among people and between people and the environment, the profession enthusiastically adopted systems theory in the 1970s. **Systems theory** posits that a system involves a series of components that are highly organized and dependent upon each other in an orderly way. In the profession, this conceptualization is applied to the multiple levels of practice (individual, group, family, organization, and community). The systems perspective remains influential in social work theory in spite of a growing number of critiques that suggest it is too rigid and tends to place the social worker outside of the work. Nevertheless, systems theory holds continuing authority in many views of structural arrangements, particularly the family. Three elements of systems theory are particularly important:

- Change in one component

- Subsystems and boundaries

- Family norms

Change in One Component   Possibly the most powerful idea in the systems theory for social workers is that change in one part of the system will affect all other components. Social workers, therefore, seek to learn about aspects of a client's environment, including family functioning. For example, knowing that a child's father has just been sent to prison is useful information when exploring reasons for that child having angry outbursts or sullen withdrawals in school. In another example, a mother being physically abused by her intimate partner is likely to have repercussions on her daughter's fragile health. Social workers often find such connections intuitive and useful. Still, you will want to guard against seeing such a situation as automatically producing one type of response. In systems theory, one set of actions can predict multiple sets of reactions. For example, the child whose father goes to prison may respond by being more attentive to her or his mother or by working harder in school. As another example, consider the family in which the primary wage earner becomes unemployed. This event can create a ripple effect within the family. While one of the adolescent children may seek employment to help the family, another may demonstrate anger that her or his perceived needs will not be met.

Subsystems and Boundaries   Another dimension of systems theory that is relevant to social work is the concept of subsystems. **Subsystems**, or components of a system that also have interacting parts, provide a mechanism for organizing relationships and planning ways to engage with them. In systems theory, the individual is a subsystem of the family, the family is a subsystem of the community and the community is a subsystem of the culture. A family may also be a subsystem of more than one larger system, or of differing systems, so you must be thoughtful about making unqualified judgments regarding the place that an individual or group occupies within the system. For example, in a blended family, there may be members who consider themselves part of the family and community from the previous marriage. Social workers have the opportunity to support and facilitate such healthy transition relationships for client systems. Exhibit 6.2 depicts the components of a family system.

In thinking about the concept of family, social workers often distinguish between the subsystem of the parents and the subsystem of the children. The relationship between these subsystems is reflected in the types of **boundaries**, or limits that separate the systems that the family constructs. If the children are included in all decisions the family makes, the boundaries are **permeable**, meaning that information and interchange goes easily across them. However, permeable boundaries can be taken to the extreme of **diffuse boundaries**, which means that boundaries are too loose and that parents should assume more decision-making authorities to maintain appropriate boundaries between them and their children.

Appropriate boundaries between the subsystems of parents and children may vary considerably depending on culture, the times, background, and/or the boundaries within which the parents themselves were reared. While you may consider a boundary to be inappropriate if a mother who uses her pre-teen daughter as her primary confidante, particularly related to her relationship with the child's father, other families may view this as acceptable. Can you cite examples in your own family in which these boundaries are similar or different from those of your friends or other extended family members? Further, consider the way in which your experience with your own family might relate to families with whom you will be working.

Family Norms   Most families establish **family norms**, or rules of conduct, that are related to boundaries and subsystems. These can be similar to the norms described in Chapter 7, in application to groups, but have an additional complication in

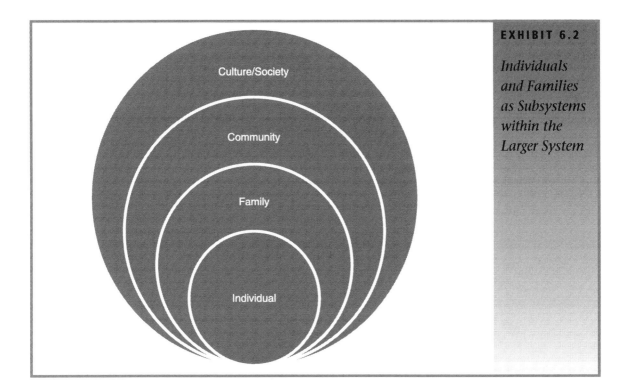

EXHIBIT 6.2

Individuals and Families as Subsystems within the Larger System

families in that they are often held as sacrosanct and not negotiable. Family norms may also never be articulated, despite the fact that all members of the family are clear about them. This implicit aspect of norms can make them difficult to address and challenge, so much so that family members may not even realize that there are rules; nevertheless, everyone understands the allowable behavior of family members. For example, all the members of a family may understand that no one will enter into a dispute with Dad at the dinner table, or that everyone will attend religious services, or that all of the children will go out of state to college. Some of these rules apply to everyday boundaries and may simply make some mundane things a lot easier (for example, if a door is closed, one is not to enter without knocking). Other such rules may signal secrets that are taboo or too difficult to talk about or that perpetuate unjust or oppressive situations, such as all the female children know not to find themselves in the same room alone with Grandpa, or no one asks Mom how she got a bruise on her face.

In applying a systems analysis to family norms, a social worker may recognize that interrupting the family's patterns of behavior or relationship by breaking a rule is, in fact, feasible and desirable. For example, a social worker may point out that one of the children spoke out one day about the bruises on Mom's face. This disclosure led to the mother talking about the violence which began the process of empowerment and decreased family violence. Yet, this process might also result in violence directed at the child who raised the issue in the first place; therefore, the social worker would not likely encourage a child to take such an action without support and protection. Family norms in such cases are often very powerful and need to be carefully evaluated before any family member is put at risk.

Implications of Family Systems Theory for Generalist Practice

Along with the notion of function, two specific dimensions reflected in family systems theories have influenced generalist social work practice with families. The first is family structure, and the second is intergenerational patterns. In many respects these represent a classic approach to Western ideology of the family and have influenced the responses of many social service policies and agencies. You may discover that these ideas have shaped your thinking also. As a basis for considering family structure and intergenerational patterns, consider the following practice principles for social work assessment and intervention with families that have evolved from a systemic perspective (Logan, Rasheed, & Rasheed, 2008, pp. 184–185):

1. Family is considered within a "context" that is comprised of multiple systems.
2. Rooted in the basic systemic foundation, the family "is more than the sum of its individual parts," all of which serves to function as a unique system.
3. A change within one part of the family system creates change in the entire system.

4. Viewing the family as a unique system provides the practitioner with the opportunity to focus on the issues that present challenges to the entire system.
5. A systemic-focused assessment and intervention provides a view of the family as a complex system.
6. Behaviors are viewed as a product of the multi-faceted system and not the result of one individual or action.
7. A systems perspective that promotes a strengths-based perspective frames the family assessment within the context of the environment in which they live.
8. Family members, particularly those in minority groups, are viewed within the context of their family system as well as the larger societal system.
9. Family function may be impacted by the legal, social, and economic biases and discrimination that affect families with members who are considered to be in cultural, racial, ethnic, religious, or sexual minority groups.

Family Structure   The relationship among the generations of a family, especially between the subsystems of children and parents, is the **family structure**. One of the early scholars in defining models for family interventions, Minuchin (1974) posits that the boundaries between children and parents should be clear and that parents should be in charge of major decisions as they also carry out appropriate caretaking functions. The difficulties that families experience are usually thought to be a result of blurring the boundaries between these two subsystems.

Some family boundaries may be so diffuse that the result is **enmeshment**, which suggests that family members are too close, have few distinctions in role or authority, and enjoy little autonomy or independence (Nichols, 2011). As an example, consider the family in which the adult children share virtually every life experience with their mother, seldom make decisions without consulting one another and her, and are emotionally dependent on one another. In an enmeshed family, a routine life experience, such as a job change or change in dating relationship by one member of the family creates strong reactions by others in the family.

On the other hand, if the boundaries between family members are too rigid, the family is thought to be **disengaged**. In this situation, the subsystems are so separated that there is little sense of family identity, and parents are apt to relinquish much of their caretaking role as they pursue their own interests and the children pursue their own. In a disengaged family, a significant job change or a divorce in the family may be barely acknowledged by other family members.

When you read about or work with young people who seem to have little or no effective connections with their families, and have experienced school or legal problems, you may wonder about the boundaries (or lack of) established by the parent(s) and the parents' perception of their own roles. In some respects, you are using this theory when you cite the misplacement or laxness of parental boundaries when children go astray. The work in such cases is to restore clear and appropriate boundaries between children and parents that support parent caretaking and authority. This particular position is reflected in court decisions regarding the delinquency of adolescents and a judge's requirement, for example, that parents receive training on managing their children or that they supervise a child's curfew restriction.

Intergenerational Patterns   The identification of **intergenerational patterns** has likewise played an important role in social work practice with families. The term refers to the assertion that families transmit their patterns of relationship from one generation to the next (Papero, 2009). For example, if your adult client, Jane, is so closely connected to her mother that she experiences great anxiety when they are separated and therefore cannot work outside the home, Jane is likely to establish that kind of relationship with her daughter as well. The anxiety generated by any effort to be separate from her mother is contagious and makes it difficult for Jane to think clearly because her feelings are so intense. In this way she becomes dysfunctional, tends to be dominated by feelings, and passes that pattern on to the next generation. This emphasis on feeling in a family sometimes results in constant emotional uproar, frequent violence, major feuds, difficulties with the law, and generalized struggle in accomplishing the basic family functions considered earlier.

Although the whole of intergenerational theory is complex, it has influenced attitudes about families. The use of the phrases "welfare families" and "incestuous families" reflects the use of intergenerational theory. These terms reflect the assumption that problematic, emotional patterns and the resulting behavioral consequences (such as violence, inability to focus on work, and substance abuse) appear to be transmitted from generation to generation. Social work then involves breaking such thinking and cycles, bolstering the strengths, and supporting an appropriate level of autonomy in individual family members. These principles are reflected in many social and educational programs that are designed to break patterns of economic dependence, addictions, lack of educational focus, and build up healthy bonds between family members.

Professionals incorporate a systems orientation when considering crime, addiction, or school violence among youth, and assume the causes to be related to the families involved, regardless of evidence. Sometimes children behave illegally or violently even when they have caring, hardworking parents who are doing the best they can. Therefore, the applicability of family systems theory, like any other theory, can be questioned, and does not fit in all situations. The desire to find a rational cause for human behavior sometimes sets in motion the use of methods that have been used before. People are also often eager to blame a child's problems on the family's behavioral shortcomings or background while not addressing the broader (also systems) aspects of poverty, disenfranchisement, challenging school situation (e.g., bullying), or racism.

Systems perspectives can be helpful and support logical approaches in assessment, especially of complex arrangements, like the family. These perspectives have a general cultural appeal, and they do not constitute a magic, one-stop answer for conceptualizing about, assessing, or working with families. While systems views have strong currency in today's analyses of social issues, other ways of thinking about them may be relevant. You must be careful not to blame or scapegoat any particular person simply because it seems logical or fits with a possible systemic interpretation of a family situation. As you continue with your social work education and develop your approach to practicing social work with families, you will be exposed to a wide array of philosophical and theoretical frameworks. Your professional obligation is to consider all the available options and determine the approach(es) that is(are) most appropriate for the families you serve.

THE CONTEMPORARY CONTEXT FOR FAMILY SOCIAL WORK

The real-world, real live family of today is only rarely the idealized outdated television version with a stay-at-home mother, fully employed father, and two bright, talented (and usually white) children. Social workers often work with families who were once seen as "other"; that is, they did not fit dominant fantasies of family life. The following sections briefly identify several types of family constellations that have not traditionally been considered mainstream but are a vital part of the contemporary family landscape—grandparents rearing grandchildren; gay, lesbian, bisexual, transgender, and questioning parents; single-parent families; families of multiple racial and ethnic heritage; families that include persons with disabilities; blended families, international families, and families with multiple problems—and suggest some specific implications for working with them.

Beyond these types of families, other current configurations appearing in the literature (and in practice) include adoptive families, foster families, step families, dual wage earning families, multi-generational families, LGBTQ families, and, of course, many combinations of these types. In the coming generations, the social work profession will need to expect and remain open to ever-evolving forms of the family. This kind of sociocultural change provides social workers with the opportunity to contribute to a sustained and meaningful impact that will benefit clients across all levels of society. Exhibit 6.3 provides additional insights into this growing and changing population with whom social workers are working.

Grandparents Rearing Grandchildren

In many cultures of the past, grandparents had a significant and ongoing role in the nurturing and socialization of children. Some cultural groups today, typically those who are less mobile or those of strong ethnic identification(s), have maintained those patterns, as consistent with their cultural and instrumental needs. The extended family is an age-old pattern of organization that has been obscured by the mainstream societal changes of the industrialized and "informationalized" 20th and 21st centuries. These changes reflect a break with the traditional cultural patterns of their parents and their parents' parents.

According to the 2010 Census, there were 131,729 same-sex married couple households and 514,735 same-sex unmarried partner households in the United States (U. S. Census Bureau, 2011a). This information does not include LGBTQ couples who do not live in the same households. As of 2013, nine states and Washington, D.C. have passed legislation allowing same-sex marriage, but 31 states continue to constitutionally prohibit same-sex marriage.

Social workers need to stay abreast of public policies that impact LGBTQ couples:

The Defense of Marriage Act (DOMA) "amends the Federal judicial code to provide that no state, territory, or possession of the United States or Indian tribe shall be required to give effect to any marriage between persons of the same sex under the laws of any other such jurisdiction or to any right or claim arising from such relationship" (Library of Congress, 1996). DOMA establishes that the Federal definition of marriage includes legal unions only between one man and one woman. It also defines "spouse" as only a person of the opposite sex (Library of Congress, 1996).

As of the beginning of 2013, there are 37 state laws and/or constitutional provisions, which limited marriages to relationships between a man and a woman. There are nine states, along with the District of Columbia, which issued marriage licenses to same-sex couples. In California, a federal appeals court found that the state constitution's restriction on same-sex marriage was invalid, but has postponed enforcement pending appeal.

Five states allow civil unions, providing state-level spousal rights to same-sex couples. Same-sex marriage has recently replaced civil unions in three other states, Connecticut, Vermont, and New Hampshire. In six states, domestic partnerships are provided by states, which grant nearly all or some state-level spousal rights to unmarried couples (National Conference of State Legislatures (NCSL), 2012).

Upcoming Supreme Court Cases—Two same-sex marriage cases were heard by the U.S. Supreme Court in 2013. The Supreme Court reviewed California's ban on same-sex marriage along with New York's previous ruling eliminating a benefit of DOMA which addresses same-sex couples' access to the same benefits as heterosexual couples.

Sources: Library of Congress, 1996; National Conference of State Legislatures, 2012; U.S. Census Bureau, 2011b; Stempel, 2013.

In contemporary society, there has been a reemergence of grandparents assuming primary (rather than supportive) parenting roles (Hayslip & Kaminski, 2005), many as a result of family violence, drug addiction, and/or incarceration of their adult children. In fact, over 1.8 million children currently reside with a grandparent and have no parent living in the home (Kreider & Ellis, 2008). The growing pressures on many child protection agencies have contributed to the increase in parenting grandparents because child protection workers often see biological relatives as preferable to, and more available than, unrelated foster parents. Many grandparents are healthy, active, and potentially able to take on the responsibility of raising their children's children.

Much more is involved, however, than simply being "able." Many grandparents have reached a point in their lives when they can pursue their own interests and dreams that have been put on hold while they worked and reared families or they may still be engaged in the workforce on a full or part-time basis. Others may find it exhausting to keep up with young children, who have come from dysfunctional situations and have multiple needs, demands, and activities. Some grandparents take on the unexpected role joyfully and fully, and others are enormously burdened, and sometimes guilt ridden because of their own children's inabilities to parent. They may also be struggling with aging, illness, and their own continued need for employment. In any event, many parenting grandparents, even if eager to care for grandchildren, are likely to want and need significant support from social agencies.

Social workers working with grandparents need to use the skills and perspectives of generalist practice. Generalist practitioners are trained to recognize the need for and offer several types of support as they sensitize themselves to the complexities of the emotional and instrumental stresses that grandparents experience. Grandparents may need financial support (Fuller-Thomson & Minkler, 2005), empowerment, self-esteem building communication skills, resource navigation, advocacy, policy development (Cox, 2008), and frequent reassurance that they can and do offer their grandchildren a secure and stable home (Bullock, 2005). In some situations, birth parents recovering from substance abuse or other challenges have visiting privileges or partial child caretaking responsibilities on a preliminary or trial basis. In such cases, there may be considerable tension between grandparents and parents. These and other conflicts may indicate the need for additional ongoing assistance from social workers. Despite the multiple challenges present in such situations, the focus of assessment and intervention should remain on the child(ren) and can include the school system and other involved community resources (Shakya, Usita, Eisenberg, Weston, & Liles, 2012).

Lesbian, Gay, Bisexual, Transgender, and Questioning Couples and Families

Social workers work with LGBTQ clients in a variety of ways, as individuals, as couples, as families, and as groups. Social workers can play an important role when working with same sex couples as families, at all levels of social work practice. One of the most difficult and distinctive issues that LGBTQ couples face, compared to heterosexual couples, is a lack of marriage equality. At the micro level, sexual and gender minority therapy (SGMT), previously referred to as "gay affirmative therapy" or "sexual affirmative therapy", is integrated by practitioners within existing therapy models (Butler, 2009). SGMT is based on the premise that practitioners should first educate themselves, understand and challenge the context of heterosexism, self-reflect, and locate her or his own position and transparency in order to ensure he or she can provide competent services to this population (Butler, 2009; Rostoky & Riggle, 2011).

LGBTQ couples may be considered unique in that they struggle for recognition of their commitment, both culturally and legally. They may have to overtly psychologically support one another (more than a comparable heterosexual couple). They also have unique challenges regarding gender roles; that is, traditional gender roles may not be applicable, and they must negotiate them.

In the context of couples and family interventions, social workers need culturally specific knowledge, skills, and values. Practitioners can convey support and validation of the same-sex relationship in the context of promoting psychological health and wellness by supporting self-determination and human intimacy needs (Rostoky & Riggle, 2011). In working with SGMT couples, social workers should have specific cultural competence in the area of gender roles as they have been found to have a greater impact on the relationship than sexual orientation (Butler, 2009). Using a narrative approach, social workers can work with LGBTQ couples to deconstruct gender role expectations (Butler, 2009).

Social workers can also support same-sex couples by collaborating with the couple to learn strategies for coping with the stress that accompanies discrimination in the form of marriage inequality. Incorporating a strengths-based approach and intervention is also helpful as such an approach can enable the same-sex couples to identify and appreciate the stresses they have faced and overcome together (Rostoky & Riggle, 2011). Taking into consideration the marriage inequality faced by these clients in most states in the U.S., social workers need skills to support and encourage the couple to obtain legal documentation to protect their relationship (Rostoky & Riggle, 2011).

At the group practice level, social workers again have the opportunity to address the discrimination couples face in the form of marriage inequality by providing psychoeducational support and consultation within the community (Rostoky & Riggle, 2011). SGMT promotes connecting LGBTQ couples with wider systems and valuing multiple perspectives (Butler, 2009). Social workers can work with local community organizations, school, religious groups, and other agencies to reduce the prejudice and discrimination directed toward LGBTQ couples and to find support for marriage equality (Rostoky & Riggle, 2011).

In working with organizations and communities, social workers' knowledge and research skills position us well to facilitate marriage equality, thus filling in the gaps in societal awareness of LGBTQ couples (Rostoky & Riggle, 2011). Currently, most of the research that has been conducted with this population has focused on LGBTQ family issues, specifically children or heterosexual family members. Social workers can also engage in political advocacy efforts to show their support for marriage equality among all sexes and genders, as well as educate themselves about local and state laws that affect their clients (Rostoky & Riggle, 2011).

Parenthood may come differently to lesbian, gay, bisexual, transgender, and questioning (LGBTQ) individuals and couples who are married or in civil unions. The person may be the custodial parent of children from an earlier relationship. Some seek artificial insemination and give birth to children, while others become adoptive parents. Also, many informal arrangements for parenting still exist, particularly in some cultural communities.

Recently, states have begun to support the adoption or foster care placement of children in state's custody with LGBTQ parents. The ever-increasing pool of children needing a home and the increasing number and type of adoptions being granted has led, just as with grandparents, to less traditional, more creative efforts in placement planning (Barth, 2008). These types of arrangements have been a highly controversial strategy for dealing with child custody arrangements within the child welfare community because it strikes at the core of the idealized version of the family. Concerns about identity issues for the child, parental adequacy, and the overall mental health of the parents and children have been raised and researched. More than two decades of research on the impact of parental sexual orientation on children's well-being, however, demonstrates no detrimental effect on children's emotional, psychosocial, or behavioral well-being as a result of being reared by LGBTQ parents (Pawelski et al., 2006).

As prospective parents, lesbian, gay, bisexual, transgender, and questioning persons (LGBTQ) still face obstacles in their pursuit of foster care or adoption and experience institutionalized stigma even at the hands of social workers. Lacking any evidence to the contrary, social workers in both the practice and policy components of the profession should support the efforts of all persons seeking parenthood who are deemed eligible through the assessment process (i.e., able to provide a loving, supportive, and stable environment for a child). Social workers can de-emphasize the search for dysfunction and pathology as they give expression to the strengths and resilience of the parents (see Van Den Bergh & Crisp, 2004). Social workers can also recognize the effects of lingering cultural discrimination directed against the LGBTQ community and draw upon a critical awareness of their own biases regarding the strengths and viability of such people as parents.

Issues that the social work practitioner can be aware of to work effectively with gay, lesbian, bisexual, transgender, and questioning parents revolve around sensitivity to the strengths and challenges they face. The strengths perspective may be particularly helpful in working with LGBTQ parents. Helping the parents identify not only their own strengths, but the strengths of the system in which they live, can be an informative, and even transformative, strategy for your work together.

Competent practitioners must also engage in reflection regarding their own attitudes, values, and expectations about LGBTQ parents (Hull & Mather, 2006, p. 218). You must be aware of the challenges they face that are similar to those encountered by all parents (e.g., parental roles, disciplines, etc.) and those that are different (e.g., lack of legal protections, community supports, etc.). Consider the family in which one of the partners of a lesbian couple gave birth to a child conceived through a sperm donation. Given that gay marriage is currently legal in only fourteen states and Washington DC, the two mothers cannot be married in their state. Should the couple end the relationship, the non-biological mother may

have no legal rights to share custody of the child. These family arrangements are strengthened by strong social worker emotional and logistical support.

Single Parent Families

While competence in the language that you use is critical in all social work encounters, speaking with and about client systems in a linguistically competent manner is particularly important when working with families. Social workers are ethically bound to develop awareness of appropriate language (oral and written) to be used with the diverse communities with whom they work (NASW, 2012–2014a). Single-parent families are a group that is often referred to in ways that are not strengths-based or empowering and can be, in fact, derogatory. A term like "single parent," without the corresponding "double parent," implies that one is normal and does not require description, while the other is "other." As you notice the implications of such terms as "broken family" or "split family," consider how deprecating labels influence initial perceptions and may affect the work that follows. It is easy to lose sight of the strengths and commitment of women or men managing families on their own if the work is prefaced with a sense of deficiency or deviance.

Society and, at times, some social service providers, have historically viewed single parenthood as a blight that necessarily leads to insecure, delinquent, and otherwise unhappy and dysfunctional households. At any point, over one quarter of children live in a household headed by a single parent; particularly if the household head is female, these families report lower levels of income than two-parent families or single male-headed households (Kreider & Ellis, 2011). A review of research on single fathers yields findings that indicate that single fathers, who tend to come to single parenting later than single mothers and often do not experience the financial disadvantages that single mothers do, and may approach parenting differently than their female counterparts, are shown to be caring and effective parents to their children (Biblarz & Stacey, 2010).

While research has shown that children reared in single parent families can face more economic, educational, and well-being challenges than their counterparts in two-parent families, having two parents in the home does not ensure the absence of negative outcomes (Musick & Meier, 2009). Growing up in a family in which conflict is handled in a healthy manner also has a strong correlation to the children's later well-being (Musick & Meier, 2009). On the other hand, there is some support in both the scholarly literature and practice community for recognizing the unique challenges of single parenting, and the way that such parenting impacts both the social work relationship and the parenting functions. Four major issues that frequently arise from divorce or separation are: (1) a lack of resources to cope with stress, finances, or other responsibility; (2) unresolved family-of-origin (family in which you grew up) issues often brought on by the single parent's need for assistance from her or his parents, at least temporarily; (3) unresolved divorce or relationship issues, such as anger, grief, or loneliness; and (4) an overburdened older child. Known as a **parentified child**, an older child who is not yet an adult may be pressed into providing excessive household chores or care for another family member. This, in turn, creates concern that the parentified child's own physical and emotional health and well-being is compromised due to the developmentally inappropriate life experiences (Earley & Cushway, 2002).

With the focus of engagement, assessment, and intervention being on the family itself, social work practice with single parent families can use the family's strengths to create and stabilize coping skills. Drawing from the work of several family scholars, skills for social work practice with single parent families include (Atwood & Genovese, 2006; Jung, 1996):

- *Joining*, similar to engagement, reflects the social worker's effort to show clients that they are cared about and that the social worker understands them and their struggles.

- *Empowering clients* supports their activities and capacity to address their own issues; and values their uniqueness and skills. In particular, the social worker can aid the parent in clarifying and reinforcing the parental role, while serving in a nurturing and supportive role to the other family members.

- While maintaining a focus on the family, the social worker can *aid the individual members in identifying strengths and resources within the family unit* (e.g., the parent is fully employed with a flexible work schedule to allow for involvement at the children's school), the extended family (e.g., grand-parents are committed to helping with childcare), and the community (e.g., the community has active, well-organized after school programming).

- *Involving significant family members* emphasizes collaboration, reduction of stress, and pooled resources.

- *Allocating agency resources* focuses on agency planning, outreach, and networking.

- *Highlighting small changes* emphasizes the strategy of making small shifts that ease overextended schedules and increase energy; such changes can also highlight success and autonomy.

- *Articulating self-efficacy* emphasizes competence, accomplishments, and empowerment for greater control over management of family issues, ideally for all family members.

These knowledge and values are consistent with a strengths-based, empowering approach that recognizes both internal and external factors and supports single parents in their ongoing efforts to provide security and nurturance for their children. Further, these knowledge and values can enhance the social worker's efforts to engage and assess the family system by conveying a sense of care and concern for the individual members, identifying and building on the strengths of each member and the unit as a whole, and emphasizing the self-efficacy of the family system.

Families of Multiple Racial and Ethnic Heritages

The growth of families with multiple racial and ethnic backgrounds is notable in most U.S. cities and towns. Interracial and interethnic marriages, civil unions, and partnerships have been gaining in acceptability since the 1960s and are certainly increasing in real numbers (Amato, Booth, Johnson, & Rogers, 2007; U.S. Census Bureau, 2011a; 2012a). Shifting immigration patterns in the United States, global-ization, and the breakdown of ethnic barriers all appear to have an effect on the incidence of racially and ethnically mixed families.

Perhaps few other developments in the everyday life of our communities offer a greater opportunity to view people differently than the growth of families with multiple racial and ethnic heritages. While some members of society will persist in grieving for the purity of "race" (a social and cultural construction by most accounts), others value the contributions of other cultures and challenge the notions associ-ated with racial privilege. It is important, however, not to minimize the negative power of the persistent oppression met by many ethnically diverse families in our culture. In this arena, professionals also need to be educated in this multicultural society regarding our national and cultural history. Gaining awareness of our own cultural and ethnic heritages and values and oppressions we have encountered is a critical step of becoming a culturally competent practitioner (Kohli, Huber, & Faul, 2010). Flexibility, shared goals, and a willingness to explore and address challenges are critical in working across culturally and ethnically diverse communities. As with all other aspects of individual and family assessment and intervention, race and ethnicity should not solely define the family (Logan et al., 2008). The social work assessment should encompass the many and varied facets of the family's life and the environment.

There are a number of models that can guide your intervention with a multiracial family. Two are highlighted briefly here. "**Posture of cultural reciprocity**," proposes an approach for working with diverse families (Kalyanpur & Harry, 1999). This process requires that social workers recognize the cultural aspect of their own personal values as well as those of the social work profession. As depicted in Exhibit 6.4, this posture occurs in four steps. These principles imply a constructionist understanding of cultural difference and value the distinctions without the value of the social worker's orientation. These principles also provide a useful framework for working with people of other cultures and are consistent with social justice and human rights as they enhance inclusion and reflect a basic assumption of cultural strengths.

Cultural attunement embodies self-awareness as a strategy to inform practice. The concept of cultural attunement requires the social worker to go beyond just raising her or his own self-awareness of their own and others' cultural heritages. Being culturally attuned to multiracial families means that you must gain new information about "racial legacies" and the way in which they influence racial self-identity (Jackson & Samuels, 2011, p. 239). Social work skills that can be particularly helpful in assessing and planning with a culturally attuned frame include: asking open-ended questions regarding racial identity; connecting multiracial families to resources for multiracial families; being vigilant about racial/ethnic-focused issues; and developing practice wisdom regarding the unique experiences of the multiracial family (Jackson & Samuels, 2011).

Families Including Persons with Disabilities

Social workers work with families in which one or more members has a physical, cognitive, and/or mental health disability. Grounded in systems theory and currently used in developing health care-supported patient care programs, **family-centered care** is a ". . . philosophy of care that permeates all interactions between families and healthcare providers. This philosophy places a high value on the contributions made by the family members in relation to their healthcare needs" (Bowden & Greenberg, 2010, p. 5). Family-centered care has evolved into a concept of services as "family-driven." This shift expands the notion of family-centered services and is based on the assumption that the family determines what it needs (Seligman & Darling, 2007, p. 14). This strengths-based approach is a promising method for working with families in many arenas, especially with those who have

© Rob Hainer

disabilities. When children have comprehensive and severe health challenges, such as neuro-developmental delays, interdisciplinary teaming (group of professionals from different disciplines who work together toward the client's goals) is an appropriate response. Social workers can play an important role on such teams that address many needs of children with disabilities that go beyond medical and educational requirements across the life span. With our commitment to a strengths-based, person-in-environment perspective, we have the opportunity to empower families by recognizing that they are the experts on their lives (Tomasello, Manning, & Dulmus, 2010). As an example of a role for a family-centered social worker, many agencies employ social workers to help higher-functioning adults with developmental disabilities learn job skills. Thus, it is very valuable for social workers to be able to work with adults who have developmental, mental or physical health, or cognitive disabilities and their families and support networks.

As one example, when a child with profound disabilities is born, family members usually have to reorganize their everyday lives as well as their long-term dreams. One parent may have to stop working to facilitate the services and treatments the child needs. The time requirements for involvement with school teams, health care teams, and interprofessional teams, as well as the individual services of a speech therapist, audiologist, occupational therapist, pediatrician, psychologist—the list is sometimes quite long—can turn a family upside down. Siblings are affected, family interactions are affected, and parents often struggle with the

STEP	EXAMPLE	
"Step 1: Identify the cultural values that are embedded in the professional interpretation of a student's [or client's] difficulties or in the recommendation for service."	This would lead to asking why, for example, a culturally different client's behavior is bothersome to you. (Is she late for appointments? Does she interrupt you? Does she respond to you indirectly? How do you interpret her behavior?)	**EXHIBIT 6.4** *Working with Diverse Families: Racial and Ethnic Diversity*
"Step 2: Find out whether the family being served recognizes and values these assumptions and, if not, how their view differs from that of the professional."	For example, you may discover that your client has a different sense of time from yours and that punctuality has little meaning for her. Here you would want to explore how she approaches time, what it means to her, and whether she recognizes your approach to it.	
"Step 3: Acknowledge and give explicit respect to any cultural differences identified, and fully explain the cultural basis of the professional assumptions."	This requires you to enter into a dialogue regarding your assumptions and beliefs and how they are different from those of your client. For example, you might recognize and appreciate the less frantic approach to time and deadlines while you explain the need in your agency to abide by a schedule.	
"Step 4: Through discussion and collaboration, set about determining the most effective way of adapting professional interpretations or recommendations to the value system of this family."	Work out a solution that respects the nature of the family's values. You might settle on a more flexible appointment time at the end of the day, or agree on a time range, or make outreach visits if that is possible.	

Source: Kalyanpur & Harry, 1999, pp. 118–119

emotional ramifications as well as the physical consequences of exhaustion. Social workers can offer support, time management ideas, and help with expanding parents' ability to identify resources. In addition, many families struggle with gaining access to services they are entitled to receive and therefore may need social work advocacy to negotiate a complex system.

When working with families that have members with disabilities, social workers may be challenged by societal views of individuals and families that are not strengths-based, but emphasize the individual's deficits. In response, social workers and disability scholars have proposed the following set of beliefs as a foundation for working with such families (Mackelprang & Salsgiver, 2009):

- Persons with disabilities are capable, have potential, and are important members of society.

- Devaluation and a lack of resources, not individual pathology, are the primary obstacles facing persons with disabilities.

- Disability, like race and gender, is a social construct, and intervention with people with disabilities must be political in nature. There is a Disability culture and history that professionals should be aware of in order to facilitate the empowerment of persons with disabilities. There is a joy and vitality to be found in disability. Persons with disabilities have the right to self-determination and the right to guide professionals' involvement in their lives (pp. xvi–xvii).

Grounded in a strengths-based perspective, each of the previous statements is critical not only for the social worker to adopt, but equally as important for the person with a disability, the family, and the community in which the individual and family live. Social workers have the opportunity and ethical responsibility to empower clients systems to embrace such a belief system. Individuals and organizations within our society may not always embrace a strengths-based perspective. In such situations, the social worker may need to become an advocate for the person with a disability.

Disabilities should be viewed within a diversity (or social) model in which societal attitudes, structures, policies, and institutions are seen as responsible for imposing limitations on persons with disabilities. Person-first language is currently in use but "disability identity language" may more appropriately frame the disability as a characteristic of diversity. These ideas imply a social work presence based on advocacy, structural principles, and the skills to work for social justice.

There is a growing need for social workers who want to work with families in which a member has a disability. Social workers may engage in significant relationships that focus on empowering the family and the person with a disability to engage in self-determination, self-advocacy, and independence negotiating life transitions with family members, organizations, and themselves (Beaulaurier & Taylor, 2007). Working within a framework of promoting client needs and self-determination, the person with a disability and their family members can be empowered to: (1) expand their range of options and choices; (2) prepare them to be more effective in dealings with professionals, bureaucrats, and agencies that often do not understand nor appreciate their heightened need for self-determination; and (3) mobilize and help groups of people with disabilities to consider policy and program alternatives that can improve their situation (Bueaulaurier & Taylor, 2007, p. 65). It is important, however, to clarify the role the family members, including siblings, would like to have in the assessment and intervention process. While family-centered care is built on the notion of the professional partnering with the family members, not all families may want a high-level role (Lotze, Bellin, & Oswald, 2010).

Lastly, consider that the social worker often has a dual responsibility when working with the family that includes a member with a disability (Hull & Mather, 2006). In working with both the person with the disability and the other family members, the social worker may have to balance differing or conflicting needs and goals. For example, a child may resent the attention given to her or his sibling related to the sibling's disability, not understand the reasons the family cannot participate in a certain activity, or be embarrassed to have a sibling with a disability. The social worker's role may be to focus a part of the intervention on the needs of the sibling who does not experience a disability.

Blended Families

Families become blended in different ways. For U.S. Census purposes, a blended family is considered one in which a parent remarries and the children who reside in the home do not share a biological parent (Kreider & Ellis, 2011). Other blended families include domestic partner relationships, civil unions, and nonrelated families who co-reside in the same household. Approximately 16 percent of children are part of a blended family (Kreider & Ellis, 2008).

While most blended families come together without specifically seeking the services of a helping professional, working with families prior to or as they blend into the new family constellation can be a valuable experience for the family. An intervention with the "pre-blended" family can incorporate four stages of work: discovery, education, parental unification, and family unification (Gonzales, 2009). These stages of work entail working through the process of getting to know one another, helping the family anticipate upcoming events through education about child and family development, and aiding the parents and then family member to unify can serve to prevent challenges in the future.

Social workers working with a blended family should be aware of the family history and be sensitive to the dynamics that may occur when two families merge into one. Incorporating information about family blending is a critical component of the assessment and intervention process. Family members may not be aware of or able to articulate challenges they are experiencing regarding the "merger" of the two family units. The social worker who strives to stay attuned to the issues that can occur when families consolidate can identify the reason the family is struggling.

When working with a blended family, the social worker begins by identifying the strengths of the individual members and the family as a unit. Within the assessment process, the social worker can help the family to identify and discuss the roles of individual members along with boundaries between members and the multiple families coming together. It is important to remember that each member of the newly created family unit must be viewed within the context of both of the systems (i.e., original family and new family) in which they exist. There are, however, unique aspects of working with the blended family. Competence in working with blended families requires knowledge of family development and transitions, involvement of noncustodial parents, extended families, and helping families negotiate new and different family roles, boundaries, relationships, and traditions. The social worker can also engage with and assess blended families by helping them identify their expectations for the forming of this new family. Adapted from Shalay and Brownlee (2007, p. 24), the following questions for clients may be helpful to this process:

1. What do you perceive others think it means to be a family?
2. How do you think your views of what it means to be family have been shaped by what other people think it means to be a family?
3. How might ideas about families on TV have influenced how you expected things would be as a family?
4. If you were a nuclear family what might be different in how you relate to each other?
5. What do you think expectations about a perfect family encourage you to believe about each other?
6. How might expectations about what a family should be have influenced what you expect from each other?

International Families

Social work practice with families in contemporary society requires global competency. If you are practicing social work with families in the U.S., you will likely encounter families who have arrived in the U.S. as immigrants or refugees. If you are a social work practitioner outside the U.S., you must have extensive knowledge of international issues. While working with families in the U.S. or abroad may require a different knowledge base regarding immigration, legal and governmental issues, cultures, and customs, there is a practice skill set that is common to work to all international family social work practice.

To gain competencies in thinking and working internationally, you can learn as much as possible about the family or families with whom you will be working. As with social work practice with individuals who have relocated to the U.S., it is important to be prepared for working with families who are new to their country. Before you meet the client(s), expose yourself to information about their culture, heritage, relocation history and experience, language, customs and traditions, spiritual practices, and community. While reading about your client's country of origin and culture can be helpful, seek out others who can provide you with personal or professional experiences and guidance. Remember also that the client family can ultimately be your best source of information and insight. Allow yourself to learn from them, especially about them as a unique family. While it is important with all client systems to explore their views about working with a helping professional, it is particularly important to understand the perceptions and beliefs about receiving help from the family and those who share their cultural beliefs and traditions.

While there may be common characteristics to groups of people who share a country of origin, culture, or traditions, each person within the family and the family itself should be viewed as individual. You may find as many similarities between a family from the U.S. and a family from Ghana as between two families from Ghana. Learning about the lives of the families that you work with will be an ongoing process that can unfold as you build rapport and trust with the members.

While much of social work practice knowledge and skills you learn is applicable to all families, there are certain competencies that are unique to working with a family that has relocated from their country of origin. First, it is critical to understand the cultural norms of your client family related to the definition of family. Be certain that you have a clear understanding of who is considered to be a member of the family, the relationships of family members to one another, the meaning of those relationships, and any hierarchical traditions that may exist within the family unit. For example, is "family" considered to be the nuclear unit or the larger, extended family? Are persons who are not biologically or legally linked considered to be part of the family? What rules and tasks guide the family members in their daily lives and in making major life decisions such as marriage, parenting, residential arrangements, education, careers, religion/spirituality, and financial priorities?

Regardless of the family's origins, you can use a strengths-based approach in completing your assessment and intervention planning. Using the International Family Strengths Model, DeFrain and Asay (2007a, p. 452) suggest that family strengths can be assessed on the basis of: (1) appreciation and affection; (2) positive communication; (3) commitment to the family; (4) enjoyable time together; (5) sense of spiritual well-being; and (6) ability to manage stress and crisis effectively. While these attributes can be applied to families of any ethnic, cultural, or heritage background, they are particularly helpful when considered within the cultural context of the family with whom you are working, as these family dynamics can have different meanings when viewed within the cultural background of the client system.

Building on family strengths can serve as a particularly helpful strategy as families work to adjust to their new country and environment. Parents, for example, may struggle with their children adopting the customs, language, and dress of their culture or older adults may find it challenging to live in a world that is unfamiliar to them. Using the family's strengths can empower the family members to find their place within their new home while maintaining their connections to their heritage. You can help to make the global connections between the world from which the family has come and the one they have entered by pointing out and affirming a family's ability to enjoy being together despite the challenges of adjusting to life in their new country and home.

While the preceding discussion has focused on family situations and circumstances, the real world of social work practice means that individuals and families may present multiple concerns and dilemmas. Known as **multi-barrier families** or families with multiple problems, the challenges may encompass economic, health, behavioral, social, and psychological issues (Hull & Mather, 2006). For example, a grandparent who is rearing her adolescent grandson may also be faced with a custody battle with his biological parent; a couple with a child born with a disability may, at the same time, be grappling with the grandmother's cognitive impairment; a blended family may be coping with employment layoffs and foreclosure proceedings on their home.

Even with multi-barrier families, the social worker's role is to approach each family as a unique system with strengths and individualized needs. Listening to each member of a family unit enables the social worker to gain insight into the perceptions, relationship dynamics, and possibilities held by the individuals within the collective family system. To be a social worker who is competent in working with families, one needs to develop a repertoire of practice behaviors that encompass family-focused knowledge, skills, and values. Prioritizing problem-solving into short and longer-term goals and promoting a supportive and nurturing environment can be a focus for the social worker. The social worker may find that attention must be given to both the internal and external challenges that are confronting the family (Janzen, Harris, Jordan, & Franklin, 2006). For example, an internal challenge faced by a family may be the substance abuse by one of the members; an external challenge may be the family's inability to qualify for subsidized housing or financial assistance. While different practice behaviors may be required to address internal versus external issues, the social worker may find that she or he serves a number of roles (e.g., broker, advocate, counselor, or educator). The remainder of this chapter will highlight a sampling of those practice behaviors needed to work effectively with families.

CONTEMPORARY TRENDS AND SKILLS FOR ENGAGEMENT AND ASSESSMENT WITH FAMILIES

Theoretical perspectives are a reflection of the sociocultural context and climate. As with social work practice with individuals, there is a wide array of theoretical approaches for assessing and intervening with families. "Most practitioners, educators, and researchers tend to practice, teach, and do research based on multiple and interrelated theories" (Logan et al., 2008, p. 177). While three different theoretical perspectives are presented here, you will, through your career, develop the approach that is most consistent with your philosophical and practice perspectives. Each of the frameworks presented here has some components in common and others born in reaction to each other. All correspond in some ways to traditional perspectives and offer an evolving focus. Regardless of the theoretical approach(es) that you use, social work practice with families should encompass goals that are situational-focused, structured, realistic, concrete, and achievable (Logan et al., 2008).

Narrative Theory in Family Engagement and Assessment

Narrative theory is based on a postmodern, constructionist perspective that enables client systems to make sense of their lives through "stories" or the client system's perception of an individual or a situation. Family interpretations of ongoing events either tend to support the ongoing narrative or refute it. Those stories that are included in the interpretation serve to organize subsequent experience. When there are exceptions, they are often dismissed or forgotten as not representative of the real family. The language used to interpret and describe various family stories is significant and fits into the context of the ongoing experience. Exhibit 6.5 outlines the tenets on which a narrative family assessment and intervention is based. The following examples explore the main ideas of an approach based in narrative theory.

As opposed to seeking a diagnosis, conducting an assessment from the narrative perspective involves helping the family members to tell their stories which then be used to inform the intervention. In essence, this results in the intertwining of the assessment and intervention processes as the stories bring to light the family's strengths and provide direction for the deconstruction of the old stories (Williams, 2009).

The issue that brings the family to the social worker is daughter Liza, who is six years old, the last child, and the only girl in a single parent, male-headed household from an economically affluent neighborhood. Liza has been cast in the role of the family "misfit." Her behavior has been described as oppositional and she is clumsy, speaks disrespectfully, and is disruptive. Any incident involving Liza (e.g., forgetting her pencil or knocking over her milk) becomes just another piece of evidence

1) Language (i.e., word choices) helps to define the meaning given to life events and provides the context for change.
2) Related to language, stories help families give meaning to their life events.
3) The stories created by each family member shape subsequent life events and family members may recall life events differently. It is important to acknowledge all stories as multiple realities can and do exist simultaneously.
4) Social context, specifically culture, influences values, social roles, gender relationships, and concepts of justice which, in turn serve to define the stories family members create.
5) Stories are not necessarily based in facts, but may be the result of family members' perceptions of life experiences, causing strengths and positive alternatives to be lost.
6) Stories can be used to encompass possibilities for growth and healing.
7) Families are not the problem, families experience problems.

EXHIBIT 6.5

Tenets of a Narrative Family Intervention

Source: Adapted from Van Hook, 2008, p. 169–170.

for the family. Her family members often shake their heads at her behavior, and wonder what to do with someone who is (in their view) oppositional, clumsy, disrespectful, and disruptive. When Liza's first-grade teacher reports to her father that Liza is exceptionally well liked by both her peers and teachers and that she is bright and fun, Liza's father is incredulous. He suspects the teacher has her confused with another student. Or Liza must be faking at school. The *real* Liza, as everyone knows, is oppositional, clumsy, disrespectful, and disruptive, as misfits are inclined to be.

The story that Liza tells about herself is different from that which is perceived by her family. Each story carries the power of the context to perpetuate and expand it, which in turn will influence the way Liza, as the major character, plays her role. If her family persists in maintaining the original perception of Liza, she is likely to respond over time by becoming increasingly rude, failing, or developing truly disruptive conduct. On the other hand, if her family at any point re-authors their perceptions by recognizing the exceptions to their ideas about Liza, her story may unfold quite differently. Everyone has multiple stories, but some have more power, relevance, and a wider audience than others. Liza's alternative story (told by her teacher) has the potential to influence her future in positive and significant ways.

Thickening the Story   Although the narrative framework has many components, the exploration in this chapter will include the most relevant concepts for generalist social work practice with families. You may recall, **thickening the story** refers to the social worker's effort to expand "thin" (Morgan, 2000) or **problem-saturated stories** that are one-dimensional perspectives on a truth that client systems created about themselves that may or may not be based in fact (Kelley, 2009). This attempt to create a more complex story may achieve the larger goal of instilling hope that the client system can make positive changes. Liza's first story is a good example of a thin account. She has no redeeming virtues and is simply perceived as an oppositional, clumsy, disrespectful, disruptive misfit. A thickened version of Liza's story reveals her likable personality, talents, and ability to connect with people in spite of, or in addition to, any behaviors that are oppositional, clumsy, disrespectful, and disruptive.

The Smith family provides another example of the value of reframing the story. The Smiths are a family that has experienced considerable challenges in child rearing. One child has been taken into the custody of the state, and now child protection workers are investigating to determine if another child should be removed for reasons of safety. The mother disparagingly claims, in defeat and sarcastic resignation, that her family is "just one of those families." Child welfare workers may likewise view the family as "just one of those families" because various children have been in custody for three generations (as was Ms. Smith).

Rather than assessing the narrowly-defined dysfunction of this family, the narrative social worker would search for the exceptions to this story to enrich it and make it more complex. Rather than maintaining a focus on problem-solving, the narrative social worker collaborates with her or his clients to "enhance their awareness of how cultural forces have lulled them into accepting problem-saturated ways of living (Williams, 2009, p. 205). For example, the social worker can ask about Ms. Smith's ability to keep a family together for ten years in the face of poverty, or to overcome a major childhood health challenge, or survive homelessness. The effort is to expand the narrow failure story so that the family can see itself as having potential, which in turn can support re-authoring the story to reflect the way the family would like it to be. The family then can shape its future to fit the new story. Such an approach can be contrasted with the one taken in the section "Intergenerational Patterns," earlier in the chapter. Through a different lens, it offers the potential for hope through development of the family's resilience and positive attributes.

A family's ability to be resilient can be a powerful aspect of the social work intervention. In keeping with the practice approaches presented here, the social worker should perceive that resilience begins with the beliefs, socially constructed judgment and evaluations that each family member creates (Benard & Truebridge, 2013, p. 205). Some families need help identifying their areas of resiliency. Social workers can help families by incorporating the following resiliency-oriented beliefs about families (Benard & Truebridge, 2013:

- All people have the capacity for resilience.

- Most individuals do survive and even thrive despite exposure to severe risk.

- One person can make a difference in the life of another person.

- Coming from a risk environment does not determine individual or family outcomes.

- Challenging life experience and events can be opportunities for growth, development, and change.

- There is nothing wrong with you that what is right with you cannot fix.

- Bad behavior does not equate with being a bad person.

- As a practitioner, it is how you do what you do that counts.

- To help others you need to help yourself.

- Resilience begins with what one believes (p. 207).

Resiliency can be viewed as the family's ability to "absorb the shock of problems and discover strategies to solve them while finding ways to meet the needs of family members and the family unit" (Van Hook, 2008, p. 11). The social worker's role is to focus on empowering the family to operationalize their capacities for resilience, specifically by:

- Incorporating a sense of hopefulness and purpose into the meaning that families assign to situations (e.g., pointing out ways in which the family can show support for the family member who has just completed a substance abuse treatment program);

- Supporting organizational structures that provide effective leadership and a balance of flexibility and stability;

- Promoting clear, empathic and supportive communication patterns;

- Emphasizing existing positive family members' relationships;

- Promoting family members' problem-solving abilities; and

- To the extent possible, improving and enhancing the social support system and community and economic resources accessible to the family (Van Hook, 2008, p. 23).

Externalizing Problems   The notion that problems are external to the family is known as **externalization**. The problem is not the client system itself but is the result of an issue that is separate from the client, thus the focus of the intervention is also then external to the client system (Kelley, 2009). Narrative social workers try to identify and help the family to name the issue that is creating difficulties. By objectifying or personifying it, family members can develop a relationship with the challenge, rather than be consumed by it, and ultimately they may control the challenge.

For example, if a family feels overwhelmed by the demands of a child with disabilities, the resulting "worry" may be externalized. The social worker can then ask about the feelings of being overwhelmed, help family members label their feelings, and support all those times when the family takes control over "the Worry." By separating the issue (or "worry") from the family's identity, the worker and the family can explore ways to defeat their concerns or at least keep them at bay.

Unearthing the Broader Context   One of narrative theory's most relevant contributions to generalist social work practice is a consistent emphasis on the political context of the family. The social worker will be highly sensitized to the danger of reinforcing the oppressive dimensions of a dominant pattern (such as racism) in society. For example, consider six-year-old Damion who appears to be having a fearful reaction about going to school. The reaction seems to be extreme for the situation. The social worker will not want to externalize this prematurely as "the school creeps" or "school scares" if in fact Damion is being taunted and bullied because of his ethnicity. Using narrative theory, the social worker seeks to identify any political factors that impact the situation with the client and family, and through a partnership with the client and family, address those factors that are negatively shaping and impacting the challenge at hand. In the case of Damion, it will be important for the social worker to elicit the client and his family's perception of the climate at his school that may promote an environment in which Damion does not feel safe. The social worker can work with Damion and his family to develop an externalized version of the story and incorporate the school into the situation.

Solution-Focused Family Work

Like many contemporary family models, **solution-focused practice** deemphasizes history and underlying pathology by defining the family broadly and not limiting its conception to traditional forms or even requiring all the members to be present in the meeting with the practitioner (Nichols, 2011). With a focus on brief interventions that narrowly define the arena of specific problems within the context of particular environmental variables, solution-focused family work has been used with a range of life situations and groups.

Approaching family social work from a solution-focused perspective is grounded in a set of assumptions, that include (Koop, 2009):

1) The family is the expert.
2) Problems and solutions are not connected.
3) Make unsolvable problems solvable.
4) Change is constant and inevitable.
5) Only a small change is needed to make an impact.
6) Keep it brief.
7) Keep the focus on the future.
8) Focus on the family members' perceptions (pp. 147–148).

Solution-focused social workers usually emphasize a cognitive approach, support a collaborative stance with clients, and tend to reject notions that problems serve any unconscious or ulterior motive. Accordingly, solution-focused social workers believe that individuals want to change, and they believe that any attribution of resistant behavior to families is more about the interpretation of the practitioner than it is about families. The founder of solution-focused therapy, Steve deShazer (1984), early in his work declared resistance "dead" and in turn redefined clients' balking at practitioner directives as their way of educating the social worker about what is needed to help them. As depicted in Exhibit 6.6, solution-focused family interventions are based on seven tenets.

Solution-focused social workers emphasize the future, in which solutions can be used within the specification of clear, concrete, and achievable goals. The simplicity of this approach, along with its time-limited, specific emphasis, has enabled solution-focused work to become an important contemporary model as it generally aspires to short-term, specific, and direct results, thus avoiding costly protracted professional relationships. Long used in community-based programs, solution-focused interventions have shown promise in addressing family and relationship problems, particularly related youth and families (Kim, 2008b; Nowicki & Arbuckle, 2009). The strengths and client perspectives of the approach have made

EXHIBIT 6.6 *Tenets of Solution– Focused Family Interventions*	1) Emphasis is placed on future and ways in which the future will differ from the past.
	2) Solutions may be unrelated to the problem's history; therefore, understanding the past may not be helpful to developing future-focused solutions.
	3) Negativity and pessimism can overshadow family members' abilities to see positive alternatives to their ways of relating to one another.
	4) People do want to change. Resistance can be a trigger for the social worker to identify different strategies for intervening.
	5) Because family members can be influenced by the social worker, the practitioner's focus should remain on empowering the family to understand their problems as well as the possibilities for solutions.
	6) Family members can be encouraged by the social worker to change the language they use to discuss their issues from problem-oriented to solution-oriented.
	7) Family members determine those areas of focus that are important to them and, as a result, are most appropriate to formulate goals for the intervention.

Source: Adapted from Van Hook, 2008, p. 148–149.

solution-focused practice popular for use in schools settings along with the other components, including portability, adaptability, brief time frame, and the opportunity for small changes to matter and applicability for cultural competence (Kelly, Kim, & Franklin, 2008, p. 8).

In solution-focused work with more than one person, the emphasis is on the relationship, not the individual, and finding and maintaining a common goal (De Jong & Berg, 2013). Solution-oriented social workers need specific skills for working with families as families often have one or more of the following pre-conceived notions about their needs (Sebold, 2011):

- Families see problems stemming from the relationships among the members.

- Families often see one person as needing to change.

- Families often view problems as belonging to the child(ren) (p. 211).

With a focus on developing solutions and de-emphasizing ongoing descriptions of the problem, the solution-oriented social worker enables the family to "know" their problems *and* the solutions and work together as a group to build on one another's ideas and competencies to develop solutions (Sebold, 2011). This strengths-based, future-oriented perspective approach is established from the outset of the social worker-family relationship and continues on throughout the intervention.

The assessment process begins with a series of questions to elicit the perceptions of each of the members. The social worker then uses the family's perceptions to co-construct a plan for intervention (De Jong, 2009). With family groups, questions can focus on the relationships among the members, even the ones who are not present. Questions included in a solution-focused intervention are:

- *Joining:* Initially chatting informally with the family members can serve to build rapport (Koop, 2009).

- *Normalizing:* When possible, helping the family to view the current situation as normal behavior can help them to envision a future in which they do not feel in crisis (Koop, 2009).

- *Goal-formulation:* Questions aimed at goal-formulation prompt the client system to consider the way in which their situation will be different if the problem that brought them to the social worker is no longer a problem (e.g., "What will be different if the problem is resolved?"). The "miracle" questions are aimed at helping the client system envision life if a miracle occurred that eliminated the presenting problem. In the engagement and assessment phases of work, goal-formulation can serve several purposes: enable the members of the family to communicate their individual goals to one another; focus on the members of the family on a common direction for work; and enable the members to identify and build on individual strengths in pursuit of the agreed-upon goals.

- *Exception-finding:* Critical to the assessment process, questions developed to identify exceptions help family systems recall experiences in which they were successful and provide opportunities for identifying strengths and resources available to incorporate into the intervention.

- *Scaling:* Scaling questions invite the family system to quantify the past and the future within the context of the problem or crisis they are experiencing. The clients are asked to use a scale of 1–10 to rate their belief that a solution will be found for the issue that brought them to see you. During the engagement and assessment phases of the intervention process, scaling questions help to establish the point from which the work will begin and identify current and past successes and areas for future growth.

- *Coping:* Aimed at issues of coping, coping questions strive to connect the family members to coping strategies that have or could be used. Such questions can engage and invest the client system in the helping process as well as assess past successes and failures, which can then be used to develop the plan of work for the current intervention.

- *Circular questions:* A family member's perception about what other people (including other family members) think of her or him can influence actions;

therefore, asking questions about what the family members believe others think of them can serve to can deeper understanding of the clients' concerns (e.g., "What do you believe your wife thinks about you when she feels you are not listening to her?") (Koop, 2009).

Like narrative proponents, solution-focused social workers concentrate on identifying and bolstering the attempts made by families that have been successful. The goal for solution-focused social work with families is to increase the discussion about solutions and decrease the focus on problems. Client families are asked to remember when their efforts worked, even when they seem like very small incidents occurring rarely. Solution-focused social workers direct their attention to those exceptions and explore the contextual factors that made the exception possible. In this way social workers give families the message that they have the strengths to cope, that they have in fact done it successfully before, and that they can do it again (De Jong & Berg, 2013).

Solution-focused practitioners have been credited with promoting a greater emphasis on strengths through their "exception" question that encourages the identification of, and focus on, those strengths that are relevant to the current situation (Weick, Kreider, & Chamberlain, 2009). The "exception" questions allow the client to place strengths within the context of times and situations in which the client was successful.

Environmental Focus   With an ecological orientation, solution-based social work looks to the community as a resource and always seeks to understand the problem in terms of the relationship to the surrounding context.

For example, when the social worker views the client within the context of the environment in which the client has grown up and currently lives, the social worker may assume that a woman who abandoned her children is embedded within a culture in which she experiences gender discrimination, poverty, unmet mental health challenges, or perhaps racism. Such assumptions can then help to explain the client's current inability to care for her children. The intervention may then be focused on education, mobilizing resources, and developing a support system to support the client.

All of these considerations are part of the assessment, and a single diagnostic or strictly pathology-oriented label as a unitary explanation is viewed as inadequate. The overall understanding of the family's difficulty is rooted in their everyday, unique living experience to which they bring their own personalities and idiosyncrasies within the larger context, which also shapes that experience.

Constructionist and Social Justice Approaches to Family Social Work

The contemporary approaches described in this chapter are complementary and share some constructionist notions that are represented in the client-defined meanings of family, the lack of rigid ideas of so-called normal family development, and the collaborative partnerships built with client systems. Constructionist theories incorporate a critical perspective that reaffirms the long-standing tradition in social workers working with families. Critical social construction suggests the development of a perspective that focuses more directly on constructionist ideas and social justice principles. Narrative and solution-focused concepts also relate to social justice issues in their concerns for the contextual locations that clients experience on a daily basis. In that respect, the approaches are more alike than they are different, and each has a positive contribution to make to contemporary social work practice.

Approaching social work interventions with families from a constructionist perspective enables the social worker to help families to tell their stories and acknowledge the meaning of those stories. During the assessment and planning phase of the intervention, the social worker can use the family's stories to identify individual and family strengths and those times when the family was able to respond in a way that is different from their current situation, and explore the implications of those stories on their functioning and potential change (i.e., exceptions) (Holland & Kilpatrick, 2009). Principles of constructionist thought that are helpful in working with families include (Holland & Kilpatrick, 2009):

- Family stories transmit meaning, create coherent sequences, shape identity, organize values and explain choices, and involve alternative interpretations.

- To function as a family, the family members must have shared meanings.

- The meanings of stories cannot be changed by outside individuals (p. 26).

Critical Constructionist Emphasis   Critical constructionist social workers explore the meaning of family within a broad contextual framework. Constructionist descriptions of the family present the social worker with multiple perspectives that can be viewed critically; as such models have implications for social work practice. For example, if you assume a theoretical model in which the family is considered basic for human survival and absolutely sacrosanct, you might view the family, as many did for centuries, as immune from external interference in its internal dynamics, including family violence. If, however, you assume that the meanings (or realities) that client systems make of their lives occur within a larger community, you and the client system can view their situation within the context of the groups to which they belong (e.g., racial, ethnic, socioeconomic, religious, etc.) (De Jong & Berg, 2013). Using the critical constructionist emphasis, the solution-focused intervention then becomes a collaboration between the social worker and the family in which the members of the family explore their realities (i.e., problems, miracles, successes, strengths, and solutions) while incorporating the influence of the multiple groups within which they live their lives (e.g., neighborhood, extended family, schools, job settings, and church) (p. 369).

Social Justice Emphasis Constructionist theorists call for consideration of both external and internal dimensions of social justice. From an external perspective, social workers will direct their attention to ensuring that all families are granted the rights and privileges of society, not just the idealized families of dominant groups. Diverse families, by ethnicity, sexual orientation, socioeconomic class, or any other difference, should be guaranteed the same access to the benefits of the culture. When they are not, the social worker is called upon to intervene in whatever ways are applicable, including legal advocacy, legislative advocacy, public education, or other forms of social action.

The internal focus requires the social worker to look within the family itself for reflection of justice for all family members. Clearly the social worker needs to challenge overt and specific oppressive behaviors, such as intimate partner violence and child abuse, but also is encouraged to look at family structure, gender dynamics, and roles. Critical constructionist social workers will address concerns that are external and have clear internal ramifications through such activities as education and advocacy for more just family practices and policies. Such a perspective reflects the continuous and energetic efforts of the social work profession to develop practice models that both confront and support various dimensions of contemporary society.

Generalist Practice Skills Guidelines for Family Engagement and Assessment

While models may differ somewhat, the following list includes family-oriented engagement and assessment practice behaviors that are common to most models:

- Ensure the family is as physically comfortable as possible.

- Work to facilitate a respectful tone throughout the meeting.

- Transmit positive regard or warmth, support, and respect in verbal and nonverbal practice behaviors.

- Engage with and hear from each member of the family, inviting each to share their perception of the family's strengths, areas for concern, and reason for seeking services.

- Ask each family member her or his perception of the family's purpose and goals in coming to see you.

- Agree upon the expectations and focus of the work.

- Recognize your own biases around family forms and norms.

- Observe the family's communication and interrelationship patterns.

- Inquire about, observe and discuss the role and emotional function that each family member fulfills within the family, particularly within the context of intergenerational relationships.

The engagement and assessment process should be completed expediently and thoroughly. A key aspect of the engagement process is for the social worker to "join" with the client system. The concept of joining entails the development of an alliance between the members of the family and the social worker in order to build trust and rapport (Van Hook, 2008). Having established a trusting relationship is critical for moving forward into the assessment and planning phases of the social work intervention. Family systems are complex and encompass multiple perspectives, thereby creating the need for an assessment process that is unrushed and includes the perspective of each member of the family system (Logan et al., 2008). Family assessment processes are typically determined by the agency. Your agency may or may not use a standardized assessment process. If you are in a setting where you will use a formalized assessment protocol with standardized measures, your role is to clarify for the family the purpose and logistics related to the measures to allay potential anxiety and frustration. Specifically, you can clarify the timing, place, and format of the standardized assessment measure, the meaning of the score or outcomes, and the way in which the information will be shared and used (Corcoran, 2009). While your agency protocol may provide a structure for completing the assessment, content areas that a social worker can address include (Van Hook, 2008, p. 67):

- What are the sources of distress in the lives of family members?

- How do family members view these issues?

- What aspects within the family and their extended world contribute to these sources of distress?

- Are there additional factors that contribute to this distress?

- What are the resources for coping and support possessed by family members, the family as an organization, and their external world?

- How can family members use these resources?

- How can these resources be enhanced?

- What barriers are preventing family members from using these resources?

Family assessment encompasses an array of assessment tools and strategies. The following discussion highlights the use of mapping with families.

Mapping: A Family Assessment and Planning Tool Competency in assessing and planning for family-focused interventions includes gaining skills in mapping the family situation. Chapter 4 presented genograms and ecomaps as helpful mapping tools for assessment and planning with individuals. Typically included as part of the assessment phase of the social work intervention, these two tools are also widely used with families and offer many uses for social workers. Genograms and ecomaps are compatible with most models of social work practice with families. For example, everyone in the family may be asked to participate in the genogram, or each member could make her or his own map of the family relational patterns (see Exhibit 6.7). Whether it is a genogram or another mapping activity, the process of collecting the information can provide the social worker with insights into the way in which the family members define membership in the family, perceive the current situation, or

EXHIBIT 6.7

Graphic Representation of Different Views of the Family within the Family

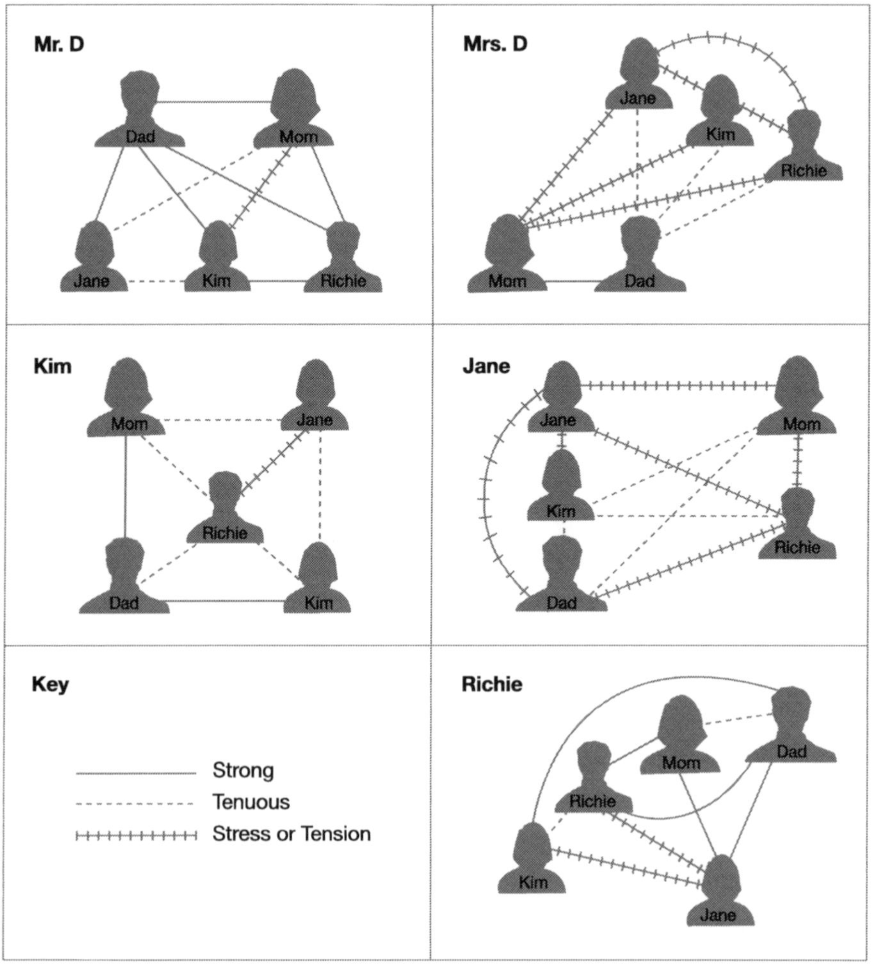

Key

——————— Strong
- - - - - - - Tenuous
+++++++++ Stress or Tension

Source: Van Treuren, 1993, p. 119

interact with one another within the interview and on paper (Minuchin, Colapinto, & Minuchin, 2007).

Genograms are particularly illuminating assessment tools for family social work because they provide a visual depiction of family structure and patterns. Beyond collecting factual information about multiple generations of family members, the genogram can serve as an "information net" in which data and insights can be all captured within the larger, intergenerational content. For example, the presenting problem may be viewed within the larger context of the family's issues, the immediate household may be seen within the context of the extended family and community, the current family situation is a component of the history of similar patterns, nonthreatening questions are perceived in light of painful inquiries, and facts are compared to judgments regarding family patterns and function (McGoldrick, 2009, p. 411).

The Cultural Genogram is a tool with multiple purposes—building rapport, family assessment, and supporting culturally competent practice (McCullough-Chavis & Waites, 2008). Building on the foundation of the genogram, a cultural genogram incorporates the perspective of the client system in areas of culture that impact the family's experience. Culture can encompass, but is not limited to, race, ethnicity, sexual orientation, social and political influences and oppression, socioeconomic status, and religious and spiritual influences. McCullough-Chavis and Waites (2008) outline the role of the social worker in completing a cultural genogram, which is to identify intergenerational patterns and focus on strengths within the context of the larger socio-cultural-political world in which they live.

First developed by Hardy and Laszloffy (1995) for use with family therapy students, the cultural genogram has been adapted for use with social work practice (Warde, 2012). Students are encouraged to complete their own cultural genogram to gain insight into the way in which the client family might experience this aspect of assessment. Modifying the original list of items to consider when developing a cultural genogram, Warde (2012) presents a list of eleven questions one should consider when completing a cultural genogram. For a list of the questions, see Quick Guide 18.

Ecomaps and other variations that demonstrate relationship patterns can liberate some families from what seems like endless talking, and they usually enjoy developing them and examining the final product. Ecomaps can be used in a visual service evaluation when the goal has been to expand community connections in general or specifically (for example, engaging in more recreational pursuits) or to alter them (such as improving the relationship between the school and the family of a child with disabilities).

Other mapping techniques can prove helpful in social work practice with families. Maps are limited only by imagination. They represent relationship complexities, the passing of time, interacting components, interpersonal interactions and patterns, levels of intimacy, specific types of connection (such as material or emotional support), and spirituality (Hodge, 2005b). One such map is the

QUICK GUIDE 18   QUESTIONS TO CONSIDER WHEN
COMPLETING A CULTURAL GENOGRAM

1. If other than Native American, under what conditions did your family come to the United States?
2. What were/are your family's experience with oppression?
3. What significance do race, skin color, and hair play in your family?
4. What role does religion play in your family?
5. How are gender roles defined in your family?
6. How does your family view people who are lesbian, gay, bisexual, transgender, or questioning?
7. What prejudice or stereotypes does your family have about your own racial group and other racial groups?
8. What principles shaped your family's values about education, work, and interaction with people outside the family?
9. What are the pride/shame issues of your family?
10. What impact do you think these pride/shame issues will have on your work with clients who are culturally similar and dissimilar?
11. As you reflect on the answers you gave to the previous questions, how do you think the values you got from your family of origin will influence your ability to work with clients whose values and beliefs are discernible different from yours?

Source: Warde, 2012, pp. 574–575.

culturagram which represents a family's experiences in relocating to a new culture (Congress, 2004; 2009). With the increase and diversity of families coming to this country as immigrant or refugees, social workers need culturally competent assessment skills. Targeted specifically for use in engaging and assessing families who have immigrated to this country, the culturagram enables the social worker and family to empower from the perspective of their culture. The resulting map illustrates content from inquiries relating to the specifics of the family's experience from immigration to their celebration of values in a new land. A culturagram and the areas for discussion are shown in Exhibit 6.8. This visual and interactive tool helps social workers and families understand the family's internal experiences, recognize differences between and within families, see ways in which the family has been successful, and, importantly, pinpoint areas for planning for potential intervention (Congress, 2009).

More literal maps of physical arrangements such as floor plans in housing situations illustrate concretely the challenges in daily living or the disparities in economic circumstances. For example, a map that shows five children's cots in a tiny bedroom or an older adult on the couch demonstrates a person-in-environment reality that may be difficult to comprehend fully through verbal means. A legend on the map that describes the meaning of all symbols and a general heading to orient the reader can be used and are especially helpful in any creative or unconventional mapping.

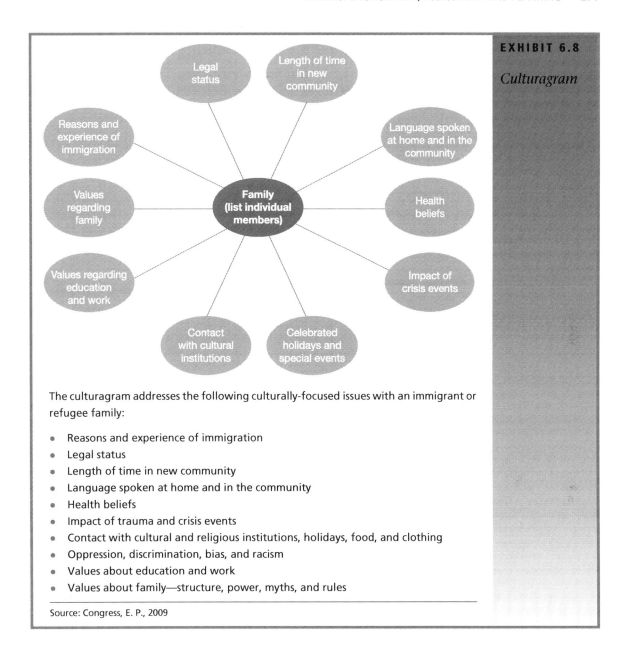

EXHIBIT 6.8

Culturagram

The culturagram addresses the following culturally-focused issues with an immigrant or refugee family:

- Reasons and experience of immigration
- Legal status
- Length of time in new community
- Language spoken at home and in the community
- Health beliefs
- Impact of trauma and crisis events
- Contact with cultural and religious institutions, holidays, food, and clothing
- Oppression, discrimination, bias, and racism
- Values about education and work
- Values about family—structure, power, myths, and rules

Source: Congress, E. P., 2009

STRAIGHT TALK ABOUT FAMILY SOCIAL WORK PRACTICE

Families are a powerful ingredient in our lives. Families have inspired fierce loyalties, lethal conflicts, abject miseries, and quiet pleasures throughout all of history, and continue to do so today. Whether you view your own family as supportive or toxic or any of the many positions in between, reaching a peace with your own feelings can enhance your work with other families. It is difficult to assess and intervene with the family situations of others if they trigger feelings because of their similarity to (or even difference from) your own. Your family concerns need not be perfect or even fully resolved, but your feelings and concerns about your own family situation should not intrude into or influence your work in ways you do not recognize. Such an issue falls into the arena of supervision, and you will benefit from sharing with your supervisor any current struggles you are engaged in with your own family, especially if you are also seeing families in your practice.

Granting that you enjoy a sense of comfort with your own family, you will likely experience situations, at some point, in which your feelings are difficult to manage. Egregious abuse exists in some families, and although contemporary theoretical perspectives can help you temper your responses and recognize that individuals and families do the best they can, the litany of injuries or aggressions emerging in court reports or police accounts or living room conversations can bring on powerful emotions in the most seasoned and balanced social worker. Fortunately, you can use supervision, agency supports, peer connections, and personal strategies for coping with such feelings and reactions. Many social workers see professional therapists to process their family challenges and avoid the influence of their family challenges on their professional practice. The most encouraging dimension for social workers today is that the majority of families inspire the greatest admiration for their resiliency, spirit, resourcefulness, and agency in the midst of potentially demoralizing circumstances.

Another important "straight talk" item for social work practice with families is the need for accurate and comprehensive documentation. Family-related interventions to be documented can include child welfare situations (i.e., child protective services and foster care), adoptions, and early interventions. Such cases may require the creation of documents for: intake assessments, progress/case notes, reports, case referrals or transfers, treatment planning, and evaluations (McGowan & Walsh, 2012). Social workers working with families of adults may have to initiate documents plans for members with addictions, disabilities, health concerns, relationship challenges, or residential placements. In all situations, the social worker's focus should focus on including only relevant information framed in a strengths-framework that represents the perspectives of all members of the family.

As in social work practice with individuals, documentation is a critical, although more complex, practice behavior. You will recall from Chapter 4 the components of basic documentation (see Chapters 4 and 5 for a review of the guidelines). While these guidelines are applicable to documenting the family interventions, there can be the "group" aspect of family work to consider. Recording the assessment and intervention phases of social work practice with families requires the social worker to encompass all members of the family who are participating in the intervention process and to give voice and perspective to the individual contributions. Quick Guides 19 and 20 provide guidelines for family-focused information to be included in the documentation of a family assessment.

QUICK GUIDE 19   DOCUMENTATION OF A FAMILY ASSESSMENT

Demographic Data (include all members participating in the assessment and intervention):

- Names, birthdates, and relationship to others
- Contact Information

Family Information:

- Presenting need(s) or concern(s)
- Living situation (e.g., members of household and level of stability)
- Family (composition—parents, siblings, spouse/significant other(s), children, and others (extended family and friends); level of support; and family history of mental illness, as applicable). A genogram and/or ecomap may be a helpful tool to gather and depict this information
- Timeline—significant life events experienced by the family
- Cultural environment (traditions and cultural view of help-seeking)
- Religion/spirituality (statement of beliefs and levels of activity and satisfaction)
- Family strengths and significant events, including trauma (e.g., physical, sexual, and/or emotional abuse or neglect and experience with perpetrator(s))

Individual Family Member Information:

- Individual family member information, including:
  - Educational history of each member (highest level achieved, performance, goals, and challenges)
  - Substance use/abuse (history of addictive behaviors—alcohol, drugs, gambling, sexual, or other)
  - Emotional/behavioral functioning and treatment history
  - Risk factors
  - Physical health
  - Legal status or concerns
  - Financial/employment circumstances (employment status, satisfaction, financial stability, areas of concern or change)

Social and Environmental Information:

- Strengths and concerns regarding physical environment, as applicable (e.g., structure, neighborhood, and community)
- Safety issues (e.g., risks or concerns of and for individual members and social worker)

Summary

- Current providers (including psychiatrist, primary care physician, therapist, caseworker, etc.)
- Community resources being used (including support groups, religious, spiritual, other)
- Family goal(s) for intervention
- Summary of social worker's observations and impressions

Adapted from St. Anthony's Medical Center, St. Louis, Missouri; Missouri Department of Social Services

QUICK GUIDE 20   DOCUMENTATION OF A FAMILY INTERVENTION PLAN

Intervention Plan:

- Preliminary assessment
- Preliminary plan for intervention and plan for change (to be developed at first visit), including:
  - What will each family member do differently?
  - How does each family member view themselves accomplishing changes?
  - What support and services are needed to accomplish plan for change?
  - Who will provide support and services?
  - Who will arrange for support and services?
- Interventions and plans for emergency/safety needs
- Other interventions needed
- Needs (include date, identified need, status (active, inactive, deferred, or referred), and reason for deferral or referral)
- Strengths
- Facilitating factors for intervention
- Limitations
- Barriers to intervention
- Other care providers/referrals and purpose (including plan for service coordination)
- Plan for involvement of individual family members, extended family members, significant others and friends
- Review and termination criteria/plan
- Planned frequency and duration of intervention

Adapted from St. Anthony's Medical Center, St. Louis, Missouri; Missouri Department of Social Services

CONCLUSION

The contemporary family both supports and challenges the social worker. Social workers engage with the family and its struggles in our culture, thus a goal for the profession is to develop additional and relevant models for working with them that recognize their strengths, agency, and resilience. Education and advocacy for shifts in the structural and political arrangements that exist for families are also required.

As a culture we still value the family, and social workers can be a part of the solution for creating environments in which families of all kinds are validated and supported.

As the structure and meaning of family itself continue to change, you can stay alert for your own capacities to honor those notions of others. As a form of "group," the family has particular resonance and serves as a grounding point for understanding human collectives. With that dimension in mind, this exploration will move to the intervention, termination, and evaluation of your work with families.

MAIN POINTS

- Historical antecedents for involvement with families, including family function and systems theories, shape the way in which social workers engage with and assess families.

- An idealized, or fantasy, notion of the American family still exists today, but social workers recognize and work with many forms, including grandparents raising grandchildren; lesbian, gay, bisexual, transgender, and questioning families; single parent families; families of multiple racial and ethnic heritages; families with members who have disabilities; blended families; and families with multiple challenges.

- Several contemporary theoretical perspectives have emerged that are consistent with critical social construction, the strengths perspective, and social justice orientations, including narrative, solution-focused, and constructionist approaches.

- Your practice setting will guide much of your work with families, but the skills and practice behaviors that you have learned for engaging and assessing individuals and groups will be applicable in working with families. Additionally, family-oriented skills and practice behaviors are needed, including engaging the whole family, reframing, and recognizing your own biases around family forms.

- Mapping tools can be helpful in assessing and evaluating the work with families; they can also help to empower families to change.

EXERCISES

a. Case Exercises

1. Go to www.routledgesw.com/cases and review the case file for Roberto Salazar. As the undocumented nephew of Hector and Celia Sanchez, Roberto has consistently earned an income but has also experienced several health challenges. He is currently living with the Sanchez family due to an injury that prevents him from working. He has a number of skills but his current injury and inability to work has him feeling defeated.

   You are the social worker charged with monitoring the status of Hector and Celia's Section 8 housing voucher. While Hector and Celia generally manage their rent payments, they are having difficulty meeting the schedule due to extra expenditures in support of Roberto. Your agency is responsible for controlling expenses and complying with federal regulations. Your supervisor is especially concerned with this aspect of the program.

   On your visit to the Sanchez home, Hector assures you that—even though he knows the landlord can evict him and his family for violating regulations regarding occupancy—Roberto is family and, of course, he and Celia will house and feed him. He remembers his own loneliness when he came to the U.S. and that his uncle helped him. He has no doubt that he can assist Roberto by providing temporary housing and support. Hector explains to you that it is important for immigrants to stick together and support one another, especially family. You are feeling some pressure from the agency to report and help resolve the issue of Roberto's unacceptable presence in the Sanchez home. You are concerned that your supervisor will look unfavorably on you if you allow Roberto to continue to live in the house.

   Respond to the following questions:

   a. How might a family focus differ from an individual focus in this situation?
   b. How will you respond to Hector? Your supervisor?
   c. How might diversity be a factor in this situation? Compare your responses to those of your peers. Identify and team up with another student whose approach seems similar to yours and develop a unified approach. Brainstorm in class regarding different or creative ways to approach this situation.

2. Go to www.routledgesw.com/cases and review the case for Carla Washburn. Create a genogram of her family. Explore the connections between Carla and her family members and the ways in which those connections impact her relationships within the family. Address the following:

   * What are the strengths of the family?
   * What are the issues that have impacted the family?
   * How have those issues impacted the various relationships?
   * Who has the "power" in the family?
   * If you were a social worker working with this family, what issues would take precedent?

3. Go to www.routledgesw.com/cases and review the case for Brickville, focusing on Virginia Stone and her family. Review the genogram for the Stone family and provide an analysis of the information provided by responding to the following questions:

   * What additional information do you believe would be helpful to include in the genogram?
   * What are the patterns that emerge as you review the Stone's genogram? In addition to general patterns, comment on potential themes in the areas of:
     ○ boundaries between family members
     ○ intergenerational family relationships and patterns
     ○ single parenting
     ○ grandparents rearing grandchildren
   * What strengths and areas of challenge are evident?
   * What information does the genogram yield that suggests priorities for planning a social work intervention?

4. Go to www.routledgesw.com/cases and review the case for Hudson City. The Patel family is one of the many families displaced by Hurricane Diane. The members of the Patel family include:

- Hemant and Sheetal—both in their late 40s, they immigrated to the U.S. from India fifteen years earlier. They own and operate a family restaurant in the neighborhood in which they live.
- Rakesh, Kamal, and Aarti are the Patel's three children. The oldest son, Rakesh, is 18 years old and is his first semester at the University of the Northeast. He lives at home and commutes to school each day. The younger son, Kamal, is a 16-year-old high school junior. The Patel's daughter, Aarti, is age twelve and in the 7th grade.
- Bharat and Asha are Mr. Patel's parents who came to live with their son and his family when the restaurant opened ten years ago. They are both in their early 70s and help part-time in the restaurant. Bharat had cardiac bypass surgery last year. Asha suffers from hypertension. Their medications were left behind when the family fled from the storm.

All the members of the Patel family work full- or part-time in the restaurant. The Patel's restaurant and home sustained major damage as a result of the storm. While the restaurant and house can be rehabilitated, the damage is extensive and repairs will likely take weeks to months to complete. The Patels are staying with friends in a nearby community, but feel they should make other arrangements and not impose on their friends' hospitality. As the entire family income is derived from the restaurant, money is a concern.

You are working as a volunteer mental health disaster responder and have been asked to work with the Patel family who has come to the Emergency Center. Develop a list of culturally competent engagement strategies that will be helpful as you begin your work with the Patel family, including additional information and resources you will need.

5. Go to www.routledgesw.com/cases and click on the case for Hudson City. Returning to the information provided regarding the Patel family, click on Assess the Situation and respond to My Assess Tasks. Using the Patel family information provided here, complete Tasks #1 and #2 as it relates to the Patels. Once you have assessed the issues and needs facing the Patels, develop a preliminary plan for your social work intervention.

b. Other exercises

6. You are a social worker on an interprofessional team that works with children who are on the autism spectrum, and their families. Three-year-old Jenny is referred to your team. She is the light of her father's life—she is lively, energetic, and bright-eyed. In the last year, she has become quiet, preferring to play by herself, and is less interested in the special outings her father loves to share with her.

After a series of anxious appointments with the pediatrician, Jenny was referred to a specialist in developmental pediatrics. Many observations and checklists later, Jenny was diagnosed on the autism spectrum. Her parents, Catherine and Jason, were devastated. Her two-year-old brother, Sammy, was oblivious.

Over a period of a month, Catherine began to adjust to the diagnosis. She connected with a supportive group of parents coping with children on the autism spectrum and read all she could about autism. She also spent considerable time with Jenny, playing and coaxing her to interact with her. Jason, however, was notably uninterested in Catherine's activities. He began to refuse to go to Jenny's doctor's appointments. During one argumentative dinner with Catherine, he stated that he did not believe the diagnosis; he thought Jenny was fine, just going through a stage, and accused Catherine of "selling out" her own daughter. Jenny was referred to the interprofessional team by her pediatrician. Catherine engaged in the process enthusiastically, if painfully. Jason attended the assessment and seemed sullen, participating very little. The team concurs that the family would benefit from your "support work" around the diagnosis. Catherine and Jason agree to meet with you and you speculate this might be your only chance to engage Jason.

Respond to the following questions to compare with your peers.

a. What is your assessment of this family? Identify a theoretical perspective that is most applicable to working with this family. How does your choice of perspective influence your approach to this family? Be specific.

b. Generate a list of three questions or issues that you think are important to address in your first meeting.

c. How might you attempt to engage the family, especially Jason? As you compare responses with your peers, what different (from your own) perspective was most useful to you?

7. In working with Jenny's family (from exercise #6), develop a solution-focused plan for the assessment and planning phase of the social work intervention.

8. In an alternative approach to working with Jenny's family (from exercise #6), develop a plan for assessment and planning using a narrative approach.

9. This chapter includes a range of contemporary family structures about which social workers must have knowledge and skills for competent practice. Select one of the groups discussed in this chapter and conduct a search of the evidence-based practice approaches currently utilized with the group you have selected. Prepare a brief summary of the knowledge and skills needed for effective practice.

10. Create a genogram of your family. Explore the connections within the family and the ways in which those connections impact the relationships within the family, particularly your relationships. Address the following:

• What are the strengths of your family?

• What are the issues that your family has faced?

• How have those issues impacted the various relationships?

• Who has the "power" in the family?

• If you were the social worker working with your family, what issues would take precedence?

• What have you learned about your family from this exercise?

Social Work Practice with Families: Intervention, Termination, and Evaluation

> . . . to think larger than one to think larger than two or three or four this is me this is
> my partner these are my children if we say, these are my people who do we mean?
> how to declare our bond how to keep each of us warm we are in danger how to face
> it and not crack
>
> Melanie Kaye/Kantrowitz, in *We Speak in Code: Poems & Other Writings*, 1980

Key Questions for Chapter 7

(1) What competencies do I need to intervene with families? (EPAS 2.1.10(c))

(2) What are the social work practice behaviors that enable me to effectively intervene with families? (EPAS 2.1.10(c))

(3) How can I engage in research-informed practice and practice-informed research to guide the processes of intervention, termination, and evaluation with families? (EPAS 1.2.6)

(4) What potential ethical dilemmas might I expect to occur in intervening with families? (EPAS 2.1.2)

SOCIAL WORKERS HAVE A LONGSTANDING HISTORY OF intervening in family situations and crises. Dating to the era of Mary Richmond and the Charity Organization Society, and Jane Addams and the Settlement House movements, social workers have focused on intervening with families (Logan et al., 2008). Just as social work practitioners respond to societal changes, social workers have also adapted their practice behaviors, including knowledge, skills, and values, to the developmental stages of families or changing structure of families. While families are generally self-sufficient in meeting their ongoing financial, emotional, and caregiving needs, when they seek help outside the family, they require a response that is developed for that family's needs (Briar-Lawson & Naccarato, 2008). Family social work interventions require competencies to address the complexities of the contemporary family, which may include culture, racial and ethnic diversity, financial and legal challenges, and intergenerational relationships and dynamics. Different from family therapy, family social work is an approach based on generalist social work skills for intervening with families who are at-risk. Family social work assumes the intervention is family-centered, and support can be provided in the family's home or in the social worker's office and in times of crisis (Collins, Jordan, & Coleman, 2013). Family social work practice interventions may be focused on: (1) reinforcing family strengths to prepare families for long-term change, such as a member arriving, leaving, needing care, or dying; (2) creating concrete changes in family functioning to sustain effective and satisfying daily routines independent of formal helpers; (3) providing additional support to family therapy so families will maintain effective family functioning; and/or (4) addressing crises in a timely way to enable the family to focus on longer-term concerns (Collins et al., 2013, p. 3).

Essential to an effective intervention with families is the engagement and assessment. Building on the assessment that focused on the family's strengths and self-determined needs, the intervention process is an opportunity to collaborate with the family to facilitate growth and change. With its emphasis on brief, efficacious interventions, managed care has influenced contemporary social work practice with families by focusing the social worker clearly, systematically, and succinctly on identifying and assessing the problem or concerns, developing and implementing an intervention plan, and terminating the working relationship (Jordan & Franklin, 2009, p. 429). This chapter will highlight theoretical frameworks and practice behaviors that will be helpful to your work with families.

THEORETICAL APPROACHES TO INTERVENING WITH FAMILIES

Just as with individuals, family intervention is a planned change process in which the social worker and client system work together to implement the steps to reach the goals established in the assessment and planning process. Research has shown that families, even those who endure intense or chronic stressors, can be resilient (Benard & Truebridge, 2013). An array of theories provide the underpinning for the approaches to social work practice with families, including systems, ecosystems, family life cycle, cultural and social diversity, strengths-based, and empowerment (Logan et al., 2008, p. 184). The social worker who is well grounded in theoretical approaches to working with families can select the approach(es) and techniques that is (are) best suited for the social worker's practice philosophy and the needs of the client family. In an effort to best serve the families with whom they work, practitioners "often use a combination of family techniques from different models rather than adhering to one particular approach. Integrationism [i.e., blending models and techniques], technical eclecticism [i.e., using different techniques] and the use of common factors are the preferred ways that most practitioners work" (Franklin, Jordan, & Hopson, 2009, p. 434). As a practitioner, you will recognize that theories each have their own limitations within the context of the client family's ethnic, cultural, familial traditions and your scope of practice as a social worker (Hull & Mather, 2006). However, the family intervention models that are most effective typically share certain elements, including education, opportunities to practice and model new behaviors and skills, and multi-faceted intervention plans (Franklin et al., 2009). As an ethical and culturally competent social work practitioner, you are responsible for gaining the training necessary to use the evidence on available family models and select the approach or combination of approaches that you believe will be most effective for your client.

Created by Hull and Mather (2006), Exhibit 7.1 depicts a framework for approaching family intervention from a multidimensional perspective. As shown in the exhibit, the process of developing a family intervention begins with viewing the family within their environment, followed by the selection of a relevant theoretical approach, and concludes with the creation of an intervention that uses appropriate techniques.

Following is a discussion that explores theoretical approaches using the strengths and empowerment, narrative, and solution-focused perspectives. In keeping with the overall approach of this book, the theoretical perspectives presented here will be within the postmodern grouping of frameworks. We will also learn to help families grow and change by aiding them in identifying and building on strengths, reconstructing their life experiences, and developing new realities. While postmodern approaches may be perceived as counter to traditional systemic approaches, Logan and colleagues (2008) posit that, in fact, the two complement one another. Systems theories help the practitioner to view and frame the family within the context of environment, while the postmodern constructs help the social worker to view the family within the context of the meaning of the presenting issues that are provided by the family.

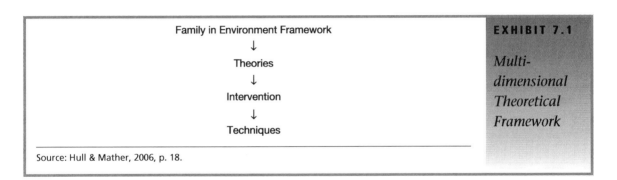

Family in Environment Framework
↓
Theories
↓
Intervention
↓
Techniques

EXHIBIT 7.1

Multi-dimensional Theoretical Framework

Source: Hull & Mather, 2006, p. 18.

Strengths and Empowerment Perspectives and Family Interventions

Having completed an assessment and planning process that identifies the strengths on which the family can build, an intervention in the strengths tradition strives to not only enhance the family's assets but to empower the family to develop new coping and resiliency strategies. From a strengths perspective, challenges are viewed as opportunities and possibilities (Saleebey, 2009). An intervention that is grounded in a strengths perspective is one that builds capacity and assets and focuses on solutions (Briar-Lawson & Naccarato, 2008). For example, an intervention that emanates from the traditional deficit-based perspective will view the family as the source of its problems (e.g., poor parenting, dysfunctional relationships, or irreparable problems). A strengths-based intervention identifies the family's assets (e.g., the parents are committed to placing value on being together as a family, productive children and the family has remained together in the face of adversity) and capacities and focus on solutions (e.g., the family is willing to work on the challenges that brought them to a social worker).

In the face of the complexities of "being" a family in contemporary society, practitioners may find it easier (although not ultimately as effective) when developing an intervention plan with a family to focus on the problems that exist within the family, rather than the strengths. Instead, a strengths-based approach could entail asking the family members, for instance, to describe the characteristics of a healthy, strong family can lead to a discussion of those characteristics that are shared by their own family. To address the family's current situation, it is important to understand their views on strengths and to incorporate those strengths into the planning and intervention process (DeFrain & Asay, 2007b). Engaging in an exploration of those actions that the family members can take individually and collectively can result in an altered perspective for the family (and possibly the social worker, as well). Gaining insight into interacting in a new way with one another and the environment can be an empowering experience for the family. For example, consider the case of the resident of Brickville (www.routledgesw.com/cases), Virginia Stone. You will recall from previous chapters that Virginia is currently struggling with an array of challenges. In your initial intervention, you might lean toward focusing on the most compelling issues (e.g., her caregiving stressors or home ownership dilemma). It may be most helpful to Virginia in the longer term to help her to identify the strengths and previous coping experiences that her family and she possess so that she may use those strengths-based experiences to help resolve her current challenges. For example, strengths possessed by this family include their commitment to caring for older members and remaining connected to one another even through times of adversity.

Grounded in a commitment to build on family strengths, empowerment-oriented practice is applicable to family interventions. Having been developed over the past several decades from a concept to practice principles and methods, empowerment-oriented interventions extend beyond intentions to encapsulate the principles and actions (Parsons, 2008, p. 124). As an example, Dunst and Trivette (2009), leading scholars in this arena, have continued to evolve their family-systems model for early childhood and family support interventions. Moving away from the traditional paradigm that emphasizes an intervention based on the family's deficits and the professional's expertise to a contemporary capacity-building paradigm, Dunst and Trivette propose that effective interventions should focus on models that embrace: promotion, empowerment, strengths- and resource-based, family-centered models (2009, p. 128). This paradigm shift is intended to aid professionals in developing help-giving practices that encompass a capacity-oriented approach to identifying and mobilizing family concerns and priorities, abilities and interests, and supports and resources. In a capacity-building approach, the role of the social worker in providing services becomes more relational and participatory. In addition to demonstrating traditional social work practice skills of active listening, compassion, empathy, and respect, the capacity-focused family social worker emphasizes possibilities for change in an individualized, flexible, and responsive manner (Dunst & Trivette, 2009, p. 131).

Empowerment-driven interventions are helpful for families in crisis—especially those who have experienced a history of crises—and can aid the social worker in helping the family to create solutions. An empowerment perspective is grounded in a belief that the stressors and trauma a family experiences can be buffered by a repertoire of protective factors available in their environment (i.e., family provides caring relationships, maintains high expectations, and provides opportunities for meaningful participation and contributions) (Benard & Truebridge, 2013, p. 208). In essence, the family has the skills and resources they need to be resilient and adaptive in the face of adversity. For example, consider the family who has survived 2012 Hurricane Sandy but lost their home. They are a large family and could not find temporary housing in one place. As a result, they are staying in different locations with family, friends, and in shelters, but they come together once each week to work on rehabilitating their home so they can return there as a family.

An empowerment approach uses seven principles of practice (Wise, 2005):

1. Build on strengths and resources and diminish oppressive factors. As noted, the strengths that can be used in addressing the challenges must first be identified by the family. The family then reviews existing and potential resources and begins the mobilization of those resources. Oppressive factors or barriers to growth and change may lessen as family members perceive options and possibilities. Strategizing with the family about ways in which oppressive factors may be confronted, ameliorated, or minimized can also be empowering. A first step, however, may be for family members to confront the oppressive factors that may be perceived to exist *within* the family. For example, family members may be stifling anger at another member for having a disability. Until this anger is acknowledged and addressed by all the members of the family, the family is

unlikely to be able to collaboratively work toward resolution of the presenting concern.

2. Multicultural respect. Multicultural respect requires attention to a wide and growing array of phenomena, including race, ethnicity, gender, age, socio-economic status, religious/spiritual beliefs, sexual orientation, differing ability, language, and developmental phases. The family may be impacted in multiple areas. The role of the social worker in helping the family create an intervention is to ensure awareness by all members of their perceptions and experiences in these areas and to help the family understand the meaning and impact and confront stereotypes and barriers.

3. Recognize needs at the personal, interpersonal, and community levels of empowerment. While family members may well know their needs, they may have difficulty, particularly during a crisis, articulating those needs to one another or the social worker. A successful empowerment-focused intervention relies on the social worker to help the family create solutions that are directly linked to their needs. Regular individual and group check-ins are necessary to ensure that the needs have been accurately and thoroughly voiced and are being addressed through the plan that was developed for the intervention. Needs can and do change and the social worker can help the family to recognize that and maintain a realistic approach to success.

4. With sufficient resources, family can empower themselves. Upon identifying and mobilizing resources, the social worker can facilitate an intervention plan. The social worker does not have the ability to complete the work for the family, but can, however, monitor and interpret the family's use (or lack) of the resources. For example, consider the value of helping the family to mobilize resources from their religious or spiritual community. The religious community can not only provide tangible and emotional resources but can serve as a recognized authority that may be of help in engaging and intervening with family members (Nakhaima & Dicks, 2012).

5. Support is needed from each other, from other families, and from the community. Receiving support from within the family and outside the family can be the impetus that the family needs to reach their agreed-upon goals and solutions. The role of the social worker may be to normalize experiences, provide information, and connect the family to one another and others.

6. Establish and maintain a "power WITH" relationship. Power can serve as an asset and a barrier in a family intervention. Being able to convey to the family that each member has power, the family as a group has power and the social worker has power. Most importantly, the social worker and the family can share the power for the purposes of achieving the goals of the intervention. Interventions should not rely on the "power" of any one or sub-group of the family-social worker partnership, but should be shared in a collaboration using the strengths, assets, and resources that each person or sub-group brings to the intervention.

7. Use cooperative roles that support and assist family members. Implementing the intervention requires that each member assume a variety of roles over the course of the relationship. Such roles may include co-consultant, co-collaborator, guide, co-teachers/learner, co-investigator, and co-creator (pp. 86–88). The social worker is in a position to point out ways in which the family members can use their knowledge and skills.

To bring these principles to life, consider the situation being faced by the Murray family, a three generation family living together in the same house. William (55-year-old high school teacher) and Genevieve (50-year-old occupational therapist) Murray have been married 27 years and have three children: Elle, a 25-year-old unemployed licensed practical nurse, recently returned to her parents' home with her two children ages four and two years, following a divorce; Stephen, 21, who lives at home, works part time, and attends a local university; and Samantha, 16, who is a high school junior. Recently, William's mother, Edna, 76, moved into the house. Edna suffers from Alzheimer's disease. After a recent car accident, the family determined that Edna is no longer able to safely live in an independent living situation. The arrival of Elle and her children and Edna resulted in Stephen and Samantha having to give up their bedrooms. A makeshift bedroom has been created for Samantha in the basement and Stephen is sleeping on the fold-out couch in the den. While the crisis that brings the Murray family to your agency is Samantha's arrest for driving under the influence of alcohol and subsequent suspension from school, it is immediately evident that this is a family in crisis in several additional areas: Edna's illness and increasing need for care; Elle's adjustment to divorce and single parenting; displacement and lack of privacy for Stephen and Samantha; and the stress experienced by William and Genevieve in supporting the family.

Using strengths and empowerment-based perspectives, how can this family be supported through this challenging period in their lives? Consider first the strengths and resources that exist. William and Genevieve have a longstanding marriage; are employed; have opened their home to their daughter, her children, and William's mother; and are willing to provide care for these family members. The family can be a resource for itself but an important intervention strategy is to ascertain from each member their perception of the issues and any factors that are barriers to resolution of the issues. Samantha, for example, may view her grandmother as the problem as Edna has taken her room and her parents' time and resources, leading her to argue constantly with her parents and spend as much time away from home as possible. Helping the family to articulate their needs within a multiculturally respectful way is the next step in creating alternatives with the family. For example, providing information about Alzheimer's disease and its course may help the family better understand and accept Edna's behavior and needs. The social worker can enlist ideas from each family member about ways in which each member of the family can help and offer suggestions for accessing resources outside the family.

Collaborating with the family to access and mobilize resources can not only provide a model for them, but can also engage them in an alternative to their present incapacitation. Examples of collaborating with the family include: (1) Capitalizing on Elle's professional expertise as an LPN, the family can apply for a family caregiver program in which a family member can be paid to care for an older adult. Elle can contribute financially to the family, care for her grandmother and her children, and work toward rebuilding her life; (2) Co-investigating with Stephen options for using his experience as a camp counselor to apply for a live-in resident assistant position on campus can provide him with space and privacy; and (3) Samantha's substance use and arrest has effectively gotten her parents' attention. Guiding the family to consider the various responses and treatment options can enable them to make choices together and learn from one another to co-create a new way of being a family. While the social worker may guide the family members toward resources, the members would be encouraged to handle as many of the logistics of accessing resources as possible.

Narrative Theory and Family Interventions

Like strengths and empowerment approaches, a narrative approach to intervening with families also incorporates strengths, viewing the family as experts on the family unit, and collaboration between the social worker and the family. In hearing each family member's perceptions of the family and the problems that brought them to a social worker, the family members are able to identify the meaning of the problem and discover alternatives to those meanings that will aid in changing the family's interactions (Kelley, 2009). As with the narrative approach to working with individuals, the problems confronting the family are assessed through respectful listening. The family's perceptions are reflected upon and deconstructed, then reconstructed by challenging perceived truths. Through the reconstruction process, the family members in collaboration with the social worker are able to create an intervention plan that enables them to arrive at unique outcomes that have meaning and viability within their family unit.

Implementation of an intervention based in a narrative approach is the culmination of the family-social worker partnership. The family members' story is the intervention and the social worker's role is to empower the clients by supporting their strengths (Williams, 2009). A narrative approach provides the social worker with a variety of strategies that will optimize the family's strengths to expand their perceptions of themselves and their problems and to create a new vision. Within the discovery process, the family has the opportunity to envision a future in which the current problem persists or a future in which the problem is altered or resolved through their actions. Through collaboration with the social worker, clients can become empowered when their stories are heard, resulting in their capacity to construct new stories (and realities) (Williams, 2009).

Narrative social workers find that a variety of strategies and questioning formats are needed to empower clients for change. Interventive techniques can include (Van Hook, 2008, pp. 171–175; Williams, 2009):

- *Listen to the family tell their problem.* Ask each member of the family to share their concerns.

- *Normalizing.* Listening and empathizing can serve to build rapport and trust between the family and the social worker.

- *Externalizing the problem.* Collaborating with the family, the social worker can help them to separate the problem from the person. The partners can then create a team to tackle the problem and not the individuals who make up the family.

- *Mapping the problem.* Looking for patterns from the past can help the family to understand the ways in which the problems were sustained and the impact the problems had on the family. Mapping strategies can include:

  - Searching for a unique outcome—identify a time when the family experienced success in overcoming a problem.

  - Asking spectator questions can help the family to consider how others view them.

  - Reauthorizing the family's story to emphasize a perception in which the members have been able to overcome adversity (also known as significance questions).

  - Identifying cultural messages that support problem-saturated stories—examining the influences of previously received cultural messages on the family's ability to interact with one another and handle life's responsibilities.

- *Findings news of a difference:* Identifying evidence of change, no matter how small, can serve to move the family beyond the problem behaviors and into a new, alternative reality.

- *Asking therapeutic questions:* Ongoing use of questions can help the family to continue to tell their stories and re-author new stories that create a healthier environment. Therapeutically-focused questions can focus on: opening space for possibilities; effecting change to amplify news of differences; preference questions (i.e., comparing past and the present times); developing stories that highlight differences; meaning questions (e.g., getting to the perceived meaning of family's actions); and future-oriented questions.

- *Scaffolding:* Once the old story begins to be deconstructed, a new story (i.e., competence) can be constructed to replace it. Scaffold questions can help to move the story focus from exceptions (e.g., a time when the family was happy) to significance questions (e.g., acknowledging the importance of an action/event) to spectator questions (e.g., understanding ways in which family members experience one another).

- *Collapsing time and raising dilemmas:* The past and present are both important aspects of evolving the problem to a newly constructed story.

- *Enhancing change:* The social worker may challenge the story to motivate clients to examine the old stories to abandon their reliance on their problem-saturated stories.

- *Predicting setbacks:* The social worker can help the family to accept that they will find it difficult to give up on problem-saturated stories and setbacks are likely to occur. Anticipating such an eventuality may disempower the potential impact of the setback.

- *Creating ways to reinforce the new narrative:* Encourage the family members to identify strategies and individuals who can help them maintain the changes they have made.

Returning to the Murray family, their crisis could be framed using a narrative approach by the social worker listening to each member sharing her or his views on the family situation. As you can imagine, the perceptions of the Murray family are likely to be quite different. William and Genevieve may share that they are doing their best to provide for all the members of the family and they feel betrayed by Samantha's arrest and suspension. Samantha (as noted earlier) may believe her parents have given more to other members than they have to her, particularly her grandmother. Struggling with cognitive impairment, Edna may feel she is a burden to her family but feels powerless to change the situation. Elle likely also feels guilt for being unable to support her children and herself. Stephen is feeling pressured to hold down a job and maintain his grades and scholarship so that he can move out of the house. After reaching a consensus with the family regarding the desired outcomes, the social worker can begin deconstructing and reconstructing the family's perceptions by externalizing the problems (i.e., focusing the family on the issue not the person). Should the family, for example, choose to focus on stabilizing the situation with Edna's care; the social worker can externalize Edna's behaviors as, because of her cognitive impairment, outside her control. The social worker can then help the family to envision life if they take no steps to improve their perceptions of Edna's situation, as well as a life in which they understand the disease, coping strategies, care and respite options, and ways to enjoy their remaining time with Edna. While reconstruction of Alzheimer's disease will not alter the course of the disease, the quality of life for Edna and her family can be enhanced through challenging the family's problem-saturated perceptions. Edna will be viewed as an honored member of the family, not as a burden.

Solution-Focused Family Interventions

Like other postmodern family-focused interventions, solution-focused family interventions also emphasize strengths and empowerment, client self-determination, and collaborating with the social workers to construct new realities by mobilizing assets and resources. Solution-focused interventions differ from other similar approaches in the use of questions that move the client from crisis to solution through the co-construction of solutions (De Jong, 2009).

With an emphasis on the relationships and competence, family solution-focused interventions incorporate explorations of the skills, strengths, and competence of clients in a way that is consistent with many postmodern approaches. This focal point solidifies the social worker-client relationship as a collaboration focused on building on past successes (De Jong & Berg, 2013). The assumptions inherent in their ecological orientation encourage social workers to look to environmental, structural supports for solutions rather than to internal dynamics for pathology. Social workers do not disregard individual responsibility for behaviors such as those that occur in child abuse or intimate partner violence, but these are viewed as evidence that the client's external resources and skills are underused (Christiensen, Todahl, & Barrett, 1999). For instance, family violence may occur when a family is experiencing stress but not using resources outside the family (e.g., social, health, mental health, or financial aid services).

Employing a solution-focused intervention with a family shifts the family's focus to a hopeful, future-oriented view of their lives. The social worker's role in creating interventions is to help the family mobilize their energies to achieve solutions using existing and expanded coping strategies in a concrete behavioral approach (Van Hook, 2008).

You will recall from Chapter 6 that a series of questions are used for assessment and planning of the solution-focused intervention. Upon completion of the assessment, the social worker and the client develop a plan for change. While the intervention process should be driven by the family's identified needs, goals, strengths, and resources, the social worker can be most helpful by developing a repertoire of skills and strategies for aiding the family in achieving their mutually-determined goals. Exhibit 7.2 provides a listing of six tasks for implementing a solution-focused approach.

Once the plan is underway, the social worker checks in with the members to monitor progress through the use of "what's better?" questions. The scaling questions that were included in the assessment phase can become a part of the intervention as well. Scaling questions can help review previously discussed solutions and exceptions, and highlight changes as they are made (Nichols, 2011). For example, the social worker might ask the family members to rate on a scale from 1–10 their feeling when they first came to see the social worker and compare those responses with a current rating of feelings on the same issue. Scaling questions can also be used to anticipate future feelings and behaviors (e.g., "on a scale from 1–10, how confident are you that you will be able to sustain this change?").

EXHIBIT 7.2

Solution-Focused Social Worker Tasks

- Create interactional balance and balance between the problem and solution-focused talk. Maintaining a balance between the persons who speak ensure that each voice is heard. Maintaining a balance of content ensures that the emphasis remains on talk about solutions and not about the problems.
- Use effective listening and summarizing skills. Staying tuned in to the contributions of each member of the family and regularly summarizing their input can serve to re-energize the clients and the social worker to remain focused on the goal and ensure that each person's voice is heard.
- Introduce transitions that will move the conversation from problem-focused to solution-focused. To maintain the focus on solutions, the social worker can regularly infuse affirmations or the family's strengths that include statements that convey support of the family's efforts.
- In order to sustain the solution emphasis, the social worker must focus on the family's current realities, that is, key in on those issues being raised by the members. When issues are not addressed, there is a tendency for them to be forgotten. The social worker can help to redefine such issues from problem- to solution-focused, but can promote the process by staying focused.
- Facilitate a "family reflecting pool." As issues are discussed and solutions initiated, each member must be given the opportunity to reflect on the issue or change from her or his vantage point, as each is likely to view the item or issue in a different way from other family members.
- Establish goals and negotiate tasks. While "homework" is typical in any social work intervention, solution-focused tasks should emphasize the desired goals and solutions versus the problems. For example, one of the stated goals is for the family to spend more time together. Before the next session, the family agrees to have dinner together three times in the upcoming week.

Source: Sebold, 2011, p. 217–228.

Additional techniques for completing the solution-focused intervention include (Koop, 2009, pp. 158–160; Nichols, 2011, pp. 257–258; Van Hook, 2008, p. 155):

1) Providing compliments as often as possible to emphasize strategies that have been successful. Compliments may be direct, indirect, or self-compliments.

2) Focusing attention on the family members' relationships with one another. Questions such as "how is your relationship different when you actively listen to her when she speaks?" can help the family keep the emphasis on changing their relationships.

3) Maintaining throughout the intervention phase a positive, future-oriented emphasis on "who, what, when, where, and how" questions.

4) Once the family has identified goals, the social worker can shift the focus to a range of behavioral tasks in which the family can engage, including:

    • Doing more of what works—if the family has identified interactions and strategies that work, encourage them to continue them.

    • Doing something different—introducing the idea of trying new strategies for relating to one another.

    • Going slowly—promoting a slow, incremental approach to change.

    • Doing the opposite—encouraging the family members to engage in behaviors and interactions that are the opposite of what they are currently doing.

    • Predicting tasks—helping the family to predict outcomes and to identify patterns that occur when changes are experienced.

5) Finding, amplifying, and measuring progress for the purposes of monitoring signs of positive movement toward desired goals.

6) Taking a break within an interaction for the social worker and family to provide feedback to one another.

7) Recapping at the end of the meeting the work of the family and social worker and providing suggestions for future work (i.e., "homework" that focuses on observing successes, engaging in new tasks, and predicting desired changes). Tasks can be considered as three different types: formula—general tasks in which family is asked what they might do differently; perception tasks—observational tasks in which family is asked to pay attention to and note differences in one another's behaviors; and behavioral tasks—tasks in which the family members take action and interact different with one another.

Returning to the Murray family once again, consider the intervention from a solution-focused perspective. During the assessment and planning phase, you questioned each of the members regarding their perceptions of life in their household. Imagine William and Genevieve responses to goal-formulation or miracle questions. They will likely talk about having imagined a near "empty-nest" household with their two older children living on their own and Samantha about to head off to college. Samantha's response to the "miracle" question might likely involve her grandmother not living with the family, and not facing legal issues related to her driving under the influence arrest and her school suspension. Elle's "miracle" might include employment, a supportive partner and a home of her own. Stephen's miracle may involve a room of his own. Edna may wish desperately to have her memories back and to return to independent living.

Given the diverse array of goals that may be expressed by each of the family members, helping the Murray family to connect with a realistic set of goals can be a complicated process. Highlighting the fact that the family members care for one another is a technique to foster goodwill and find common ground on which the members can agree (De Jong & Berg, 2013). In working with the Murray family, reminding them of their commitment to and concern for one another can be a regular part of the intervention. Imagine that the agreed-upon goal is to find a solution to the overcrowded housing situation. Your role can be to work with the family to develop concrete and achievable short- and long-term solutions, check in regularly with "what's better?" questions, and terminate when you and the family agree the goals have been achieved.

Regardless of the theoretical approach that guides your work with families, your social work values and ethical standards will provide the foundation on which you will develop interventions to be implemented with families. Ensuring that the client system's rights to self-determination, strengths, and diversity are honored is the priority for your intervention with families. Emphasizing the practice behaviors to enable you to become a practitioner who is competent in social work practice with families will be the focus of the following discussion.

CONTEMPORARY TRENDS AND SKILLS FOR INTERVENING WITH FAMILIES

Families are made up of individuals and are a form of a group, and as such, benefit from the careful use of the same practice behaviors that assist individuals and groups. Interventions with families are likely to vary according to your practice setting and the constraints of your agency. For example, if you are a member of the intake unit of a child protection team, your intervention with the family will probably differ from that of your colleague who works in a community mental health agency. The theoretical lens through which you are working will also influence the way you intervene with family members. You may develop an intervention plan from a systems focus, or you may work with family members to build an intervention plan based on their perceptions of ways in which you might help them, as in solution-focused work. In any situation, your intervention begins with an invitation to the family to tell their story, but your agency mission and purpose and your own theoretical biases will influence the intervention approaches you take.

Social work practice interventions with families shares many similarities with individually-focused interventions. Recall from Chapter 5 the discussion on roles that a social worker may have in working with individuals (e.g., case manager, counselor, broker, mediator, educator, client advocate, and collaborator). Each of these roles is applicable for working with families, particularly in light of the setting in which the intervention may occur. Family-focused social work practice can take place in an array of settings, including child welfare, mental health centers, schools, health care facilities, and community centers, to name a few. For example, the social worker working with a family in a child welfare setting may engage in all the roles, but emphasize case management and brokering activities in particular in order to reunify the family. In a health care setting, the social worker's emphasis may be on education and advocacy, for instance. With families, it is important to consider all the members' perspectives, recognize relationship dynamics, and the strengths-based intervention goals that will optimize family functioning.

As with individuals, the setting in which you practice and your philosophical and theoretical approach will frame your intervention activities. While model-specific practice behaviors have been previously discussed, there are additional general practice skills and behaviors that transcend the continuum of practice approaches. Building on the practice behaviors used in the phases of family engagement and assessment, the following strengths-based skills for intervening with families can be helpful (Benard & Truebridge, 2013, p. 207; Hull & Mather, 2006):

- Identify the issues and concerns, use active listening to enable the family members to tell their story and reflect on the information shared by the family members.

- Acknowledge the pain.

- Look for and point out strengths.

- Ask questions about survival, support, periods of time that were positive for the family, interests, dreams, goals, and pride.

- Resilience begins with what one believes and all people have the capacity for resilience.

- Link strengths to the goals and dreams of the family members (both group and individual).

- Find opportunities for family/members to contribute to the intervention by helping to educate other members and serve as helping agents in achieving the family's agreed-upon goals.

- Use brainstorming for solutions as a strategy to help the family to view the situation and themselves differently.

Written homework assignments, task designation, and teaching are strategies that can be helpful but must be appropriate to the family's situation, their investment in the process, and the framework you are using in the intervention. Return for a moment to the Murray family scenario and consider the above list of practice behaviors. In order to mobilize the family into working toward crisis resolution, you can begin by asking each member her or his priorities for change. From those verbal-izations, it is likely that you will glean the pain, strengths, goals, and dreams felt by each of the family members. You may choose to engage the family in brainstorming strategies they can use to address each of the areas of concern or assign the family homework in which they develop ideas to address their concerns. An alternative may be to ask the family to have a family conference and bring their ideas back to the next meeting with you. Once the family has developed a range of ways to address their prioritized concerns, consider asking them to have a discussion in which specific tasks are identified and assigned. Be sure to explore the possibility that the expertise for problem-solving resides within the family, and individual members can function as teachers and guides.

In addition to the individual and group skills, reframing, perspectival (or circular) questions, family group conferencing, motivational interviewing, and reenactments (i.e., role-playing or rehearsals) are a sampling of practice strategies with good applicability in many family situations when carefully used. Discussed in Chapter 6 as an assessment tool, mapping is an important strategy for the intervention process.

Reframing

An approach used frequently in social work with families, as well as with individuals, groups, communities, and organizations, reframing is a practice skill in which the social worker conceives of and describes a situation in different terms. Reframing can be particularly helpful in family conversations in which one member makes an incendiary statement to or about another family member. Carefully used, reframing can assist both recipient and "sender" to view the situation with diminished uproar so they can begin to listen to each other. Focused on strengths and positive alternatives, reframing must be appropriately timed to have a meaningful impact. To have a significant effect, the social worker must stay carefully attuned to the family members' dialogues to identify opportunities for reframing as they occur (Minuchin et al., 2007).

For example, a 15-year-old boy, who sees his mother as an autocratic barrier to his enjoyment because she will not allow him to go out with friends who drive, says, "There is no person on the face of this earth who is more controlling and over-protective than my mother. She is just like Hitler! She keeps me locked up in the prisoners' camp." You may suggest that the teen's mother cares so much for him that she fears he will be hurt in an automobile accident or in some other way if he goes out with his friends.

When reframing, offer a plausible alternative that does not resonate as a "gimmick" or "Pollyanna" type of effort to diffuse strong feelings and, accordingly, will be heard by the parties involved. The danger lies in interpreting the thoughts or feelings of another person without directly having been told. In the example of the 15-year-old teen and his mother, it is quite likely that the mother is not intentionally attempting to torture her son (and that she truly worries about his going out with friends who drive), but he may or may not be able to "hear" her sentiment as reframed. Another reframing effort may be more effective depending on the nature of the relationship and the people involved. Developing the content of such interpretations requires judgment and skill; use reframing cautiously and only when conditions are relatively straightforward. How can reframing be used with the Murray family? Instead of focusing on the upheaval created by Edna, Elle, and Elle's children moving into the house, consider emphasizing the strong family commitments and caring environment for members who are in need of support.

Perspectival Questions

Mentioned in connection with individuals in Chapter 5 and with group work practice in Chapter 9, perspectival questions can be effective in family social work. By seeking the perspective of another family member, you can help clarify the feelings and meanings of one member's view of another. If the family is experiencing stress because the eldest son is leaving home, you may ask the teenage daughter, "What do you think your mother will do to prepare for Johnny's leaving?" Or you may ask the mother, "What will your daughter miss most about Johnny?"

The responses to these questions can communicate ideas and feelings that no one in the family has openly or previously recognized. Such assistance in communication is relevant when family members assume they know all they need to about the responses of other family members as a result of long-term, "stuck" patterns of argument or difference or "saving face." As in the use of reframing, perspectival questioning is a strategy to be used carefully and only when you are confident that you can respond appropriately to any statement. The daughter in the example just provided may respond with, "Mother will sew name tags in Johnny's underwear so he won't lose it in the dorm laundry room at college," or, alternatively, she may say, "Mother will no doubt start to drink again." The same element of the unexpected that can create new ways of thinking for families can also throw a curve ball to the unwary or unprepared social worker. Utilizing perspectival questions with the Murray family could potentially yield some illuminating insights. Consider, for example, the new perspective that could be uncovered if Edna were asked about the support that her son and daughter-in-law have provided to Elle and her children and her response was that they should not have invited Elle and the children to move into their house. By expecting the unexpected and maintaining flexibility, the social worker who incorporates perspectival questions can be prepared for the unexpected.

Family Group Conferencing

A strategy for use with families, family group conferencing (FGC) is an empowerment-focused intervention aimed at creating or strengthening a network of support for families as they are experiencing a crisis or transition. Originally developed for work with families in which children were at risk for abuse or neglect, this practice strategy has been extended to other family situations, including families with older adults experiencing life changes. The family conference usually occurs after the assessment and planning phases, and is a collaborative effort that includes the social worker, family (including extended family members), and members of the family's community who are existing or potential resources for the family (Wise, 2005).

The conference goal is to gather the family members with people who are connected to the family in order to make decisions regarding a response to the presenting challenge. The social worker confers individually with each potential participant prior to the conference to ensure that each agrees to be actively involved in decision-making and action steps. During the conference itself, the desired outcomes are determined by the participants themselves with the strengths and areas for concern being included in the planning process (Brody & Gadling-Cole, 2008). Once a plan is established, the group adjourns and may reconvene after a period of time has elapsed in which the plan is implemented to discuss progress or re-negotiate the plan.

Return for a moment to the Murray family. If you were to convene a family group conference with the Murrays, consider those people you would invite to participate and the reasons for inviting them. What goals could provide the Murrays

© Lisa F. Young

with a much-needed support network and stronger coping skills? What are their strengths? How might they benefit individually and collectively from participation in a family group conference? What is your role? While answers to these questions can only be speculative, you can use this exercise to begin to see yourself in the role of a family social work practitioner.

Motivational Interviewing

As you recall from Chapter 5, motivational interviewing (MI) has been introduced for use with a variety of clients, including those who are non-voluntary, experiencing substance abuse, or intimate partner violence (Wahab, 2005). Using the four processes of MI—engaging, focusing, evoking, and planning—to promote behavior change, MI is well-suited for situations in which the client is uncertain about making the change and/or the time is limited (Miller & Rollnick, 2013; Wagner, 2008).

Motivational interviewing is also applicable to social work with families. Miller and Rollnick (2013) offer strategies for engaging in motivational interviewing with families with adolescents. Using the FRAMES strategy, the social worker can conduct a Family Check-up that provides the social worker and the family with the opportunity to: (1) **F**eedback of personal status relative to norms; (2) **R**esponsibility for personal change; (3) **A**dvise to change; (4) **M**enu of change options from which to choose pursuing change; (5) **E**mpathetic counselor style; and (6) support for **S**elf-efficacy (Miller & Rollnick, 2013, p. 375). For example, using the FRAMES strategy in the case of the Murray family, the social worker may opt to check in with the family in this way:

1) Provide Feedback to each family member regarding their proposed solutions for the identified stressors currently affecting the family.
2) Designating Responsibility for change—clarifying roles and tasks for each member of the family.
3) Advise on change—provide information to the family on the impact of ongoing stress, Alzheimer's Disease, and potential positive outcomes of collaborative change.
4) Provide a Menu of options—presenting family members with an array of options for behavior change, healthier interactions, services and resources that may be mobilized within and outside the family.
5) Empathetically validate the concerns expressed by each member of the family and acknowledge the pain they are experiencing.
6) Self-efficacy of each member of the family can be regularly reinforced by the social worker identifying their strengths, commitment to change, and progress toward goals.

Motivational interviewing provides another opportunity for you, as a social worker, to engage in a collaborative partnership with the client family aimed at providing the opportunity for change. If you opted to employ motivational interviewing with the Murray family, you may begin by providing feedback to them based on the perceptions they have shared with you regarding the various crises that are occurring within the family. They also have the opportunity to provide feedback to one another. After they share feedback, you can empathetically reiterate that the family members are the experts about themselves and it is within their power and responsibility to implement change. Try to create an environment in which the family is empowered to view themselves as having the capacity to respond to their crises with resilience and efficacy.

Incorporating motivational interviewing into social work practice with families can present challenges that do not exist in working with individuals. Given that families come to social workers often times as the result of their inability to resolve relationship challenges on their own, ensuring that each member of the family is given adequate opportunity to speak is critical (Miller & Rollnick, 2013). Moreover, the social worker will need to be able to balance the interactions to maintain a focus on positive change as opposed to continuing with arguments and negative discussions.

Re-enactments

Participation in experiential activities can provide insights and alternatives for families who are experiencing a crisis or challenging transition. Re-enactments can be completed in the form of role-plays or rehearsals. Re-enacting a particularly challenging interaction and then role-playing or rehearsing the scenario with alternative behaviors can be a powerful experience mechanism for the family to "try on" new ways of being a family. Viewed as a safe way to share feelings and rehearse, role-plays can be carried out in a variety of settings, for a range of situations, and revisited as the work progresses. Considerations for developing role-played activities include (Hull & Mather, 2006, pp. 163–164): (1) purpose and parameters are to be discussed; (2) members can play themselves or other members of the family; (3) members should play the roles accurately and consider their feelings as they move through the rehearsal; (4) the role-play can be stopped so members can discuss, reflect, and change interactions; and (5) the role-play should be de-briefed so alternatives can be explored. A re-enactment may be an ideal activity in which to engage the Murray family. Once the family has identified the issues that are their highest priority to address, you can help them to "rehearse" the change strategies they have brainstormed through an experiential exercise. With the multiple generations, issues, and priorities that exist within the Murray family, role-playing can enable the family to work on individual issues and relationships. Imagine a role-play in which William and Genevieve share with Samantha their feelings and concerns regarding her life choices and decision-making. More importantly, envision a dialogue between Samantha and her parents that any one of the three may stop so they may regroup, change course, or ask for input. Such a rehearsal may enable the family to change a pattern of interactions.

Mapping as an Intervention

Mapping strategies have been examined primarily within the context of assessment. They do, however, have a place within the intervention process itself. If not completed during the assessment phase, mapping can be incorporated into the intervention phase of work. During the intervention, mapping in the form of genograms, in particular, can be used for clarifying family patterns, framing and detoxifying family issues, and in developing the intervention plans (McGoldrick, Gerson, & Petry, 2008). Using the patterns and unhealthy family issues to identify and facilitate change plans can be a liberating experience for the family members. McGoldrick and colleagues (2008) promote the use of genograms as an intervention strategy to empower clients through changing existing relationships. Being able to see the historical patterns of loss, relationships (healthy and unhealthy), physical and mental health issues, substance use, responses to stress and crisis, and cultural traditions can illuminate for family members the options they have for change. Creating and discussing genograms can also provide family members with an opportunity to engage in intergenerational dialogue. Consider the Murray family, for instance. Providing the family members with the opportunity to engage in dialogue with Edna could provide them with family history they had not previously known, as well as have meaningful time with her before her memory fades away. The social worker can incorporate the genogram into the development of the intervention by asking members to identify strengths on which they can build in relationships and cultural traditions (McCullough-Chavis & Waites, 2008). They may also be able to identify patterns of substance abuse, trouble with the law, or other troubling patterns that can inform their present collective and individual work.

Ecomaps and culturagrams are also assessment tools that can be integrated into the intervention. Using the baseline ecomap or culturagram as a strategy for monitoring change throughout the intervention provides the family and the social worker with a visual depiction of their work. Updating the ecomap or culturagram can indicate those areas in which progress is being made or not made and the barriers preventing success. New maps can be constructed as a means for ritualizing a successful outcome. As with social work practice with individuals, documentation is a critical component of the family intervention. Along with maintaining copies of the assessment tools mentioned here, the client portfolio also includes a record of the intervention plans. Exhibit 7.3 offers a sample family intervention plan template followed by Exhibit 7.4 which provides an example of documenting the intervention plan developed with the Murray family.

As with social work practice with individuals, intervening with families requires the social worker to complete comprehensive and ongoing assessments from which flexible, individualized interventions can be created through collaboration with the family. The outcome of a successful intervention is, of course, the termination.

EXHIBIT 7.3

*Documenta-
tion of a
Family
Intervention
Plan*

Intervention Plan:

- Preliminary assessment
- Preliminary plan for intervention and plan for change (to be developed at first visit), including:
  - What will each family member do differently?
  - How does each family member view themselves accomplishing changes?
  - What support and services are needed to accomplish plan for change?
  - Who will provide support and services?
  - Who will arrange for support and services?
- Interventions and plans for emergency/safety needs
- Other interventions needed
- Needs (include date, identified need, status (active, inactive, deferred, or referred), and reason for deferral or referral)
- Strengths
- Facilitating factors for intervention
- Limitations
- Barriers to intervention
- Other care providers/referrals and purpose (including plan for service coordination)
- Plan for involvement of individual family members, extended family members, significant others and friends
- Review and termination criteria/plan
- Planned frequency and duration of intervention

Adapted from St. Anthony's Medical Center, St. Louis, Missouri; Missouri Department of Social Services

Our focus will now turn to the phases of terminating and evaluating the family intervention.

ENDING WORK WITH FAMILY CONSTELLATIONS

The general principles for ending interventions apply to all levels of practice. The need for culturally sensitive practice plays out in individuals, families, groups, communities, and organizations. Just as you need to explore the meaning of endings with individual client systems, so you do for families. This discussion assumes a cumulative recognition of the important areas for ending the work, based on considerations covered so far, and a flexible application with greater emphasis on some principles than others according to context. With those principles in mind, we will look to some specific variations as additional perspectives.

In voluntary family work, endings tend to occur when the family is satisfied that they achieved their goals. In some circumstances , the restrictions of third party

Preliminary assessment

The Murray family has requested services from this agency in order to address a number of crises and concerns within the family. The family is comprised of William (55 year-old-high school teacher) and Genevieve (50-year-old occupational therapist) and their three children (Elle, 25-year-old divorced single mother of two- and four-year-old children; Stephen, 21-year-old college student; and Samantha, 16-year-old high school junior). Along with William's mother, 76-year-old Edna, all members of the family reside in the couple's now overcrowded home. Stephen and Samantha were displaced when their bedrooms were given to Edna and Elle and her children. Edna can no longer live alone as she is experiencing cognitive impairment (Alzheimer's Disease) and presents safety concerns at her assisted living facility.

The Murrays sought help because Samantha was recently arrested for driving under the influence and suspended from school. During the assessment, information was shared that suggests the family has been in crisis for some time and that Samantha's arrest and suspension brought the crisis to a climax.

Preliminary plan for intervention and plan for change

During the first meeting of the entire family, each member was asked to share their concerns, needs, and potential solutions. After each person had the opportunity to articulate each of these areas, the social worker provided a summary of the information shared and the family and social worker collaborated on a list of highest priorities, resulting in the development of the following preliminary plan:

1) Genevieve agreed to contact the local chapter of the Alzheimer's Association to obtain information on services available for families experiencing dementia. She will specifically inquire about programs that provide information on Alzheimer's Disease and provide financial support for care needs (e.g., Family Caregiver Support Program).

2) All family members agreed they would attend a presentation for families on Alzheimer's Disease provided by the Alzheimer's Association.

3) Stephen will contact the campus housing department at his university to learn about applying for a resident advisor position which would provide him with tuition support and free housing in exchange for living in one of the student residential facilities. In the interim until this goal may be achieved, William and Genevieve agreed to work with Stephen to fix up the basement so he may have a private bedroom and workspace.

4) Genevieve, William, and Samantha all agreed to attend the court-mandated program for teens arrested for driving under the influence.

5) Samantha agreed to attend the alternative school program for the duration of her school suspension.

Interventions and plans for emergency/safety needs

Two areas of immediate concern were raised regarding safety needs. The following plan was agreed on by all members of the family:

EXHIBIT 7.4

Documenting the Intervention Plan: The Murray Family

EXHIBIT 7.4

Continued

1) Elle agreed to provide care for Edna during the day when Genevieve and William are at work. This will allow Genevieve and William to feel that Edna is safe and that Elle can provide supervision and transportation. Elle will be able to remain home with her children and not bear the expense of child care.

2) Samantha agreed not to drink and to be subject to a periodic alcohol test if her parents are uncertain about her sobriety.

Other interventions needed
Longer term interventions may include:

1) Exploration of all family members' feelings regarding the overcrowded living conditions in the home and stressful relationships.

2) Discussion regarding Stephen's living arrangement if he is not accepted for a resident advisor position.

3) Decision-making regarding Edna's ongoing care needs as her disease progresses.

4) Discussions regarding Elle's permanent employment and living situations.

5) Reestablishing a trusting and healthy relationship between Samantha and her parents.

Needs
At this preliminary phase, the primary needs are:

1) Establish a safe environment for Edna

2) Address Samantha's legal, school, and alcohol issues

3) Provide adequate space for Stephen and Samantha

4) Address family stressors

Strengths
The Murray family has several important strengths on which to build, including:

1) Couples' longstanding marital and employment history and commitment to each other and their family members as evidenced by their willingness to open their home to Edna and Elle and her children.

2) Families' commitment to care for one another

Facilitating factors for intervention
The family members' willingness to care for one another is the primary facilitating factor in the intervention. Additionally, having resources within the family (e.g., Elle's availability to care for Edna and her expertise in nursing care) and outside the family (e.g., Alzheimer's Association, alternative school, etc.) enable the family to access needed services.

Limitations and barriers to intervention

1) While plans are underway to address the overcrowding situation, change may take some time. Coping with the stress of the cramped living quarters in the interim presents a particular challenge.

2) While she agreed to attend the alternative school and participate in family therapy, Samantha appears angry and may become reluctant to actively engage, particularly if the home continues to be a stressful environment and she feels she has no attention or privacy.
3) The family may be feeling so overwhelmed by the multitude of issues and tasks to be addressed, they may be unable to mobilize for change.

Other care providers/referrals

1) School personnel at the alternative school and Samantha's regular school
2) Alzheimer's Association
3) Family Caregiver Support Program
4) Substance Abuse Treatment Program

Plan for involvement of individual family members, extended family members, significant others and friends
At this time, there is no plan to include other family members. However, the family mentioned that William has two sisters that live out of town and may be willing to help with Edna's care at some point.

Review and termination criteria/plan
All agreed that the goals will be achieved when the family members feel they are in better control of their lives, specifically:

1) Overcrowded housing issue has been resolved
2) Plans for Edna's long term care needs are determined
3) Elle's employment and housing plans are clarified
4) Samantha has successfully completed the court-mandated program and has returned to a student in good standing at her school (one-year minimum of no school violations)
5) Stephen has a permanent solution for housing.

Planned frequency and duration of intervention
Initially, the plan is for the social worker and family members to meet weekly. Social workers will be available by telephone in the interim. After the first four meetings, social worker and family will discuss the plan for ongoing contact. As issues resolve, meeting frequency will decrease with the plan being for termination to occur within three months of the intake.

Adapted from St. Anthony's Medical Center, St. Louis, Missouri; Missouri Department of Social Services

insurers or managed care companies may mandate an earlier end point. With a lessened focus on the relationship with the social worker than exists in individual work, the emphasis often falls on examining the ways the family wanted the dynamics of their relationship or their relationship with outside entities to be different, and the extent to which they have been successful. There is also likely to be some focus on translating the gains into future situations that the family can anticipate so that responses can be predicted. For example, if a family is struggling with the decision to allow an adolescent son freedom to develop a unique identity when he has a history of legal altercations, it will be useful for the family to consider ways in which they will manage that issue when he leaves home for college or when the next sibling reaches an age to declare herself or himself a separate person. These positions are all consistent with the principles of review and exploration highlighted earlier in Chapter 5 regarding terminating with individuals.

To take a different perspective, the following discussion will identify brief responses to ending work with families from the perspectives of the previously discussed theoretical frameworks, strengths and empowerment, narrative, and solution-focused approaches. These approaches strive to minimize the difficulty of endings. In general, they propose a naturalized and comfortable process that is flexible and controlled by clients whenever possible.

Endings with Strength and Empowerment

Viewing each family as individuals and as a whole means that the social worker's role is to help each person articulate her or his feelings about the ending (Wise, 2005). The family members, individually and as a group, can benefit from the opportunity to talk about feelings and insights about the strengths that each individual and the group brought to the intervention. These insights can reinforce the successes that have been accomplished through the intervention and enable the members to acknowledge the ending. Keeping in mind the original goal, the social worker and the family can focus on the future and the ways in which the changes can be sustained. If the goals they hoped for were not achieved, but the relationship is terminating nonetheless, the termination phase can focus on lessons learned that the family can use in the future.

Just as assessment and intervention with families is approached from a strengths perspective, so too is the termination process. Building on the strengths that were identified in the assessment process and those identified or created during the intervention phase, the strengths- and empowerment-oriented social worker can focus the termination process on strengths as well. The existing and new strengths can become the basis for the family to sustain the changes they have made. Together, the social worker and the family can review the family's strengths. The social worker can then ask the family to consider the way in which they can apply these strengths to future situations. The family can also use these strengths as coping skills when and if they encounter new challenges. For example, the social worker may ask the family members, "How can ending our work together help you to achieve your goals?" (Wise, 2005, p. 215). To further probe, you can ask the family members to speculate on their motivation and ability to continue working on their goals even after the formal intervention has ended.

Endings in Narrative-Focused Work

In narrative work, as with other approaches, there is an emphasis on normalizing the point at which the family decides to end. Narrative social workers often punctuate the ending of their work by working with families to develop rituals or ceremonies in which the family invites an audience to witness the changes they have made and to rejoice in their achievements. For example, asking siblings, other professional who have worked with the family, and/or extended family to attend a meeting can be a validating experience for all. Public acknowledgment of the family's successes not only celebrates them but also provides a structure for their supportive maintenance when the work is over (Morgan, 2000). This focus, like solution-focused work, represents a departure from traditional views of endings while acknowledging the same concerns about maintaining gains. The reduced emphasis on stages with specific boundaries in both these approaches emphasizes the view of the client as the expert.

Endings in Solution-Focused Work

Solution-focused work emphasizes ending almost from the beginning. As a short-term intervention approach, a solution-focused approach stresses that the clients have abilities to manage their lives competently. Because this approach is built on the premise that change can occur within a brief, time-limited period, using scaling,

© Lisa F. Young

an early question the social worker might ask is, "What [number] do you need to be in order not to come and talk to me anymore?" (De Jong, 2009). This question refers to the number from 1 to 10 that reflects the degree of well-being that the client reports. In this approach, a family's concerns about needing further work are honored, and they determine the number and content of further sessions. There is very little emphasis on the relationship between the social worker and the family because "not coming to talk to me anymore" is seen as the preferred reality and a natural and comfortable conclusion to a problem for which the family is already likely to have a solution (which the social worker helped to bring to light). In this sense, then, ending is seen as success almost by definition. Termination, as well as follow-up (e.g., checking in with the family, inviting the family for a return of follow-up session, or making referrals) when possible, is as equally important to the planned change process as any other stage of the relationship. Bringing the intervention to a close can serve as an opportunity for the social worker and family to engage in: (1) a recital (i.e., a review of the work); (2) creating an awareness of the changes made; (3) consolidating gains (i.e., celebrating changes and successes), and; (4) providing feedback to the social worker; and (5) preparing the family for handling challenges that arise in the future (Collins et al., 2013, p. 447).

Evaluation of Social Work Practice with Families

Evaluation of family interventions helps you as a practitioner and your organization determine if the intervention has been complete and is effective. By gathering information from the family members at the beginning of the working relationship, evaluation of family interventions also enables the social worker to identify the changes that were or were not made and the reasons that the intervention was or was not effective (Hull & Mather, 2006). If you have used evidence-based practice approaches, your evaluation can provide insights and contributions to your practice or your agency's practice. While evaluation of your interventions with individuals can yield similar information about your practice, it is critical that you do not assume that evaluation of family interventions can be completed with the same evaluative strategies. Just as families are unique, so, too, are evaluations of family interventions.

The ongoing evaluation of the family work that social workers do is often largely contingent on, and defined by, the context and goals of the original contact. For example, if you are working with a family in child or adult protective services, the first goal may be the continued safety of a child(ren) or adult. There may be other goals, such as the parents' improved skills in managing a family, meeting the health needs of a particular child or adult, or providing appropriate care for an older adult. Goals in cases such as these, in most cases, are documented in written goals, and you will want to pay attention to them along the way.

QUICK GUIDE 21   STRENGTHS-BASED MEASURES FOR FAMILIES

Caregiver Well-Being Scale

I. ACTIVITIES

Below are listed a number of activities that each of us do or someone does for us. Thinking over the past three months, indicate to what extent you think each activity has been met by circling the appropriate number on the scale provided below. You do not have to be the one doing the activity. You are being asked to rate the extent to which each activity has been taken care of in a timely way.

| 1. Rarely | 2. Occasionally | 3. Sometimes | 4. Frequently | 5. Usually |

	1	2	3	4	5
1. Buying food	1	2	3	4	5
2. Taking care of personal daily activities (meals, hygiene, laundry)	1	2	3	4	5
3. Attending to medical needs	1	2	3	4	5
4. Keeping up with home maintenance activities (lawn, cleaning, house repairs, etc.)	1	2	3	4	5
5. Participating in events at church and/or in the community	1	2	3	4	5
6. Taking time to have fun with friends and/or family	1	2	3	4	5
7. Treating or reward yourself	1	2	3	4	5
8. Making plans for your financial future	1	2	3	4	5

II. NEEDS

Below are listed a number of needs we all have. For each need listed, think about your life over the past three months. During this period of time, indicate to what extent you think each need has been met by circling the appropriate number on the scale provided below.

| 1. Rarely | 2. Occasionally | 3. Sometimes | 4. Frequently | 5. Usually |

	1	2	3	4	5
1. Eating a well-balanced diet	1	2	3	4	5
2. Getting enough sleep	1	2	3	4	5
3. Receiving appropriate health care	1	2	3	4	5
4. Having adequate shelter	1	2	3	4	5
5. Expressing love	1	2	3	4	5
6. Expressing anger	1	2	3	4	5
7. Feeling good about yourself	1	2	3	4	5
8. Feeling secure about your financial future	1	2	3	4	5

Source: Berg-Weger, Rubio, & Tebb, 2000; Tebb, Berg-Weger, & Rubio, 2013.

QUICK GUIDE 22   STRENGTHS-BASED MEASURES FOR FAMILIES

Family Support Scale

Name _____   Date _____

Listed below are people and groups that oftentimes are helpful to members of a family raising a young child. This questionnaire asks you to indicate how helpful each source is to your family.
Please circle the response that best describes how helpful the sources have been to your family during the past three to six months. If a source of help has not been available to your family during this period of time, circle the NA (Not Available)

How helpful has each of the following been to you in terms of raising your child(ren):	Not Available	Not at All Helpful	Sometimes Helpful	Generally Helpful	Very Helpful	Extremely Helpful
1. My parents	NA	1	2	3	4	5
2. My spouse or partner's parents	NA	1	2	3	4	5
3. My relatives/kin	NA	1	2	3	4	5
4. My spouse or partner's relatives/kin	NA	1	2	3	4	5
5. Spouse or partner	NA	1	2	3	4	5
6. My friends	NA	1	2	3	4	5
7. My spouse or partner's friends	NA	1	2	3	4	5
8. My own children	NA	1	2	3	4	5
9. Other parents	NA	1	2	3	4	5
10. Co-workers	NA	1	2	3	4	5
11. Parent groups	NA	1	2	3	4	5
12. Social groups/clubs	NA	1	2	3	4	5
13. Church members/minister	NA	1	2	3	4	5
14. My family or child's physician	NA	1	2	3	4	5
15. Early childhood intervention program	NA	1	2	3	4	5
16. School/day-care center	NA	1	2	3	4	5
17. Professional helpers (social workers, therapists, teachers, etc.)	NA	1	2	3	4	5
18. Professional agencies (public health, social services, mental health, etc.)	NA	1	2	3	4	5
19. _____	NA	1	2	3	4	5
20. _____	NA	1	2	3	4	5

Source: Dunst, Trivette, & Deal, 2003, pp. 155–157

QUICK GUIDE 23   FAMILY STRENGTHS PROFILE

Recording Form

Family Name _____   Interviewer _____

INSTRUCTIONS

The Family Strengths Profile provides a way of recording family behaviors and noting the particular strengths and resources that the behaviors reflect. Space is provided down the left-hand column of the recording form for listing behavior exemplars. For each behavior listed, the interviewer simply checks which particular qualities are characterized by the family behavior. (Space is also provided to record other qualities not listed.) The interviewer also notes whether the behavior is viewed as a way of mobilizing intrafamily or extrafamily resources, or both. A completed matrix provides a graphic display of a family's unique functioning style.

FAMILY MEMBER	DATE OF BIRTH	AGE	RELATIONSHIP

FAMILY BEHAVIOR	Commitment	Appreciation	Time	Sense of Purpose	Congruence	Communication	Role Expectations	Coping Strategies	Problem Solving	Positivism	Flexibility	Balance			TYPE OF RESOURCE Intrafamily	Extrafamily

NOTES

Source: Dunst, Trivette, & Deal, 1988

The focus of evaluation in interventions with families is on the family unit itself and not the individuals within the family. An examination of the family's ability to have new behaviors and coping skills, realistic attitudes, and new information and learning will promote enhanced well-being for the entire family (Wise, 2005). For example, if you and the family are able to determine that the power has shifted among and between the family members, this could be indicative of an effective family intervention. Alternatively, if family members agree that the stress level within the family has decreased or the quality of the interactions has improved, the intervention may be deemed successful. Family evaluations may focus not only on the outcomes of the goals established during the assessment and planning phases, but on the relationship with the social worker and the agency as well.

Strengths-Based Measures for Families   While family-focused intervention evaluations differ from evaluations of individual and group practice, the evaluative strategies described in Chapter 5 provide a basis for developing plans for evaluation of family interventions. Ensuring that the focus of the evaluation is on the family and not the individual members, strategies such as single-system design, goal attainment scaling, and case studies, can be effective evaluation tools. There has been an array of evaluation measurements developed specifically for use with families. While the scope of this book cannot address the vast number of selections that are available for evaluating your practice with families, the following discussion will briefly explore the selection of measures that are grounded in a strengths-based perspective.

Several instruments are designed to be used in strengths-based practice with families and also to allow social workers to document their service effectiveness (see Early & Newsome (2005) for detailed review of strengths-based family assessment tools). Standardized evaluative tools are increasingly important as agencies and practitioners are held accountable for measurement of outcomes by funders, boards of directors, client advocacy organizations, and the social work profession itself. Additionally, practice evaluation instruments can be helpful in maintaining the social worker's focus. Some of the instruments emerged as strengths-based emphases were introduced in the 1980s and remain useful tools today because they measure family perceptions and assets. With the advent of evidence-based practice, there has been an increase in the number of standardized family assessment measures from which to select. Early and Newsome (2005, pp. 390–391) offer the following guidelines to consider when incorporating standardized assessment measures in family-focused social work practice:

1)   Select a measure with an emphasis on consistency and appropriateness to client situation.
2)   Explain to the family the reasons for using the measure (e.g., method for efficiently collecting information to guide the helping process) and specific details about the measure's contents and outcomes.

3) Allow for adequate and appropriate time, space, and materials for completing the measures.
4) Ensure that the family members understand the items and feel comfortable asking questions about the assessment tool.
5) When at all possible, score the measure in the family's presence.
6) Share the scores and interpretations with the family.
7) Maintain the assessment in agency records for review/comparison in the future.
8) Repeat the measure over time to assess progress toward goals.

While your agency or you will select the evaluative strategy that is most appropriate to your setting and the families that you serve, the following is a small representative list of reliable strengths and empowerment-focused evaluation measures that may be of help to you as you consider evaluating your practice:

- *The Caregiver Well-Being Scale* (Berg-Weger, Rubio, & Tebb, 2000; Tebb, 1995; Tebb, Berg-Weger, & Rubio, 2013): A strengths-based clinical measure to help family caregivers or adults or children identify the strengths and areas for change in their caregiving experience, this scale is applicable for families caring for adults and/or children. See Quick Guide 21 for an example.

- *The Parent Empowerment Survey* (see Dunst, Trivette, & Deal, 2003): Designed to measure parental perceptions of control over life event (see Herbert, Gagnon, Rennick, & O'Loughlin, 2009 for review of empowerment measures).

- *The Family Support Scale* (see Dunst et al., 2003): Measures what is helpful to families. See Quick Guide 22 for an example.

- *The Family Strengths Profile* (see Dunst et al., 2003): Designed to chronicle family functioning, the profile provides a qualitative format for identifying and assessing family strengths and type of resources needed. Quick Guide 23 provides an example of this measure.

- *The Family Resource Scale* (see Dunst et al., 2003): Measures the adequacy of resources in households with young children and emphasizes success in meeting needs, while it also identifies needs.

- *The Family Functioning Style Scale* (see Dunst et al., 2003): Measures family values, coping strategies, family commitments, and resource mobilization. Families indicate to what degree various statements are "like my family."

- *The Family Empowerment Scale* (Koren, DeChillo, & Friesen, 1992): Measures family empowerment on three levels: family, service system, and community/political.

- *The Behavioral and Emotional Rating Scale: A Strengths-Based Approach to Assessment* (Epstein, 2004) and *The Behavioral and Emotional Rating Scale (2nd edition): Youth Rating Scale* (Epstein, Mooney, Ryser, & Pierce, 2004). These scales focus on children and youth to determine the presence of behavioral or emotional conditions.

In strengths- and empowerment-oriented measurements, self-reporting is seen as an asset. Self-reporting can complement the traditionally-oriented, scientific measurements in which the goal of objectivity is thought to conflict with the biases in self-reporting. Bias is inherent within self-reported information because it is difficult to be objective about yourself. The strengths perspective supports the expertise of individuals and families about their own lives, experience, and aspiration, thereby making self-report a natural and theoretically consistent method of data collection.

The empirical procedures in these scales are just a few among many. Some of these are flexible and, with creativity, they can apply to a variety of situations. Using both quantitative and qualitative evaluative strategies can provide the social worker and the profession with a comprehensive picture of the intervention. Remember, as well, that all evaluative measures have their limitations. Drawing conclusions regarding the impact of the change may not be possible because change may have occurred separately from the intervention (Hull & Mather, 2006). Further, just because the goals of the intervention were not achieved does not mean that positive or meaningful change did not occur. In those situations in which the identified goals are not met by the time the intervention must end (i.e., as in the case of managed care, court- or school-mandated treatment, etc.) or the family terminates prior to the agreed upon ending point, the social worker must process this experience. Talking with a supervisor or colleagues regarding the possible reasons for this unanticipated outcome can be an opportunity to professional development for the social worker. While practice evaluations can be immensely helpful tools, they must be viewed within a context for family, yourself as a practitioner, and your agency.

Consider also your own role with the family and reflect on the viability of your relationship with them. Reflection is typically a more introspective and interactive process. Some questions you can ask yourself and members of the family are: Does each member feel valued as if she or he can contribute to the work? Are there issues regarding the family's culture? Does the family still agree with the direction of the work? How is the work changing their experience? Checking in with families, through a dialogic process, to make sure they feel heard, understood, and are invested in the work you are doing with them is just as important as it is with other levels of practice. Be certain as well to remain attuned to non-articulated feedback from the family members. Lack of follow through with assignments or commitments and nonverbal gestures can be indicators of the family members' feelings about the intervention (Hull & Mather, 2006).

STRAIGHT TALK ABOUT FAMILY INTERVENTION, TERMINATION, AND EVALUATION

Practice with families is a complex enterprise, and the intervention, termination and evaluation processes can include the unexpected. Family members have individual relationships, networks, and influences outside the family; therefore, the work that is accomplished within the intervention may be positively or negatively impacted by those external persons or groups. Within the family unit, the members may establish alliances that can also serve to strengthen or, in some cases, undermine the work within the intervention. Staying attuned to the family members' descriptions of their activities, relationships, and pressures may aid you in identifying those potential unanticipated occurrences within the intervention.

Just as with terminations with individuals, ending work with families can be emotional, particularly if the family members have developed a positive relationship with the social worker. The social worker may even be viewed as a member of the family; therefore, termination can elicit powerful reactions from the family. Sensitivity to the family's cultural norms and feelings is important for the social worker (Logan et al., 2008). Terminations can also elicit negative responses from some family members. As a result, members may refuse to participate or may display anger, denial, anxiety, or even regression as the termination approaches (Fortune, 2009). As the social worker, you may find yourself juggling a variety of different responses from family members to the ending of the family intervention. Addressing the individual and collective reactions to termination, while building on the strengths and gains of the intervention, can serve as an intervention in and of itself. Empowering the family to handle a change (perceived possibly as another loss) can be a meaningful new experience for the family as they can provide support to one another, model new behaviors, and mobilize strengths and resources developed during the intervention.

Evaluations of family interventions may also yield unexpected results. As you complete the evaluative process, you may have anticipated a particular outcome. If, for instance, you completed a pre- and post-intervention evaluation and the members of the family provide responses different from those you expected, you may be surprised at the family members' perceptions. Such occurrences can provide you with the opportunity to explore with the family their responses so you may gain insight into differing interpretations.

CONCLUSION

Facilitating an intervention with a family from engagement through termination and evaluation can be an immensely rewarding professional accomplishment for you and transformative for the family. Working with families requires the social worker to develop a repertoire of practice behaviors that include theoretical frameworks and skills to optimize family strengths and create and mobilize needed resources. This chapter further explored the integration of several theoretical approaches into social work practice with families and provided examples of ways in which the approaches can be applied to family situations. While refining your theoretically-driven social work practice is a lifelong process, identifying the theoretical approaches that are most consistent with your professional and personal value systems is an important early commitment for your social work development. Clarifying your own views on families and your role as a family social worker are exploratory exercises that can be helpful along your journey. Along with the provision of theoretical underpinnings for developing family interventions, this chapter highlights strategies for working with families that can be used in a range of settings and with diverse types of families.

MAIN POINTS

- Social workers have an array of theoretical perspectives to choose from to guide interventions with families. The social worker's training, philosophical and value system, and agency orientation will provide the primary influence for selection.

- Approaches for developing intervention plans with family groups highlighted in this chapter include strengths, empowerment, solution-focused, and narrative perspectives. While each shares similarities with the others, each has characteristics that make it unique.

- While specific practice behaviors are included within the various models of family intervention, there are basic skills for working with families that are found in most of the models: collaboration, using strengths, and supporting each member of the family's voice.

- Both your own and your clients' families can impact your work with families. Ongoing evaluation includes not only documenting achievement of externally imposed goals (e.g., school or court system) but also determining if your role and relationship with the family are working.

- Because the social work intervention with a family is multi-faceted and vulnerable to influences in and outside of the relationships, the evaluation process should incorporate candid discussion of those potentially influential factors. When ending work with families, the social worker must consider the potential impact of the professional-client relationships that formed during the work, the theoretical perspectives they used, and the practical, contextual dimensions of the work.

• The evaluation of families may emphasize an empirical process and/or a qualitative one. Standardized tools may be helpful in the evaluation process of family social work. In some family models, the emphasis is on the family's qualitative satisfaction with the outcome of the work; postmodern views of evaluation question the emphasis on standardized, scientific, and quantitative measures and remind social workers of their susceptibility to bias even when their work is supported by numbers.

EXERCISES

a. Case Exercises

1. Go to www.routledgesw.com/cases and review the case files for each member of the Sanchez family. A number of potential ethical issues may emerge as you work with this family. Using the NASW *Code of Ethics* (available at naswdc.org), identify the ethical issues or dilemmas that you anticipate could arise, citing the core social work and ethical principle that is relevant to the issue you identify. Upon completing this task, write a brief reflection on your findings.

2. Go to www.routledgesw.com/cases and review the case file for Carmen Sanchez. Address Critical Thinking Questions 1, 2, and 3. For Critical Thinking Question 2, identify at least one article in each of the two areas that concern Carmen: the impact on families of children with special health needs and outcomes of children in different types of families.

   Gather into groups with four to five of your classmates and develop a potential work plan for the family, based on your answers to the Critical Thinking Questions, focusing on the following areas:
   a. Identify the areas of potential challenge.
   b. Develop strategies for working with the entire Sanchez family around these challenges.
   c. Develop a plan to insure Carmen's maximum participation in the process.

3. Go to www.routledgesw.com/cases and review the case file for Carla Washburn. While Carla does not have the traditional family network, she does have a support system of persons to whom she is connected. Strategize about ways in which you might integrate each of the members of her support network into your intervention with Carla, identifying the strengths and potential contributions each can make. You may wish to review the case files and ecomap to develop your plan.

4. Go to wwww.routledgesw.com/cases and review the case file for Riverton. While the Riverton case initially appears to be a case focused on a neighborhood and a community, each community is comprised of individuals and families. In your role as the social worker who has just moved into the Riverton community, consider the Williams family (not described in the case file). Joyce

is a 48-year-old single mother who lives with her two children, 18-year-old Amanda and 17-year-old Jason, and her mother, 77-year-old Nina. Joyce divorced her husband as a result of his chronic alcoholism and she is worried about Jason as she knows he regularly drinks and uses marijuana. She has come to your agency and asked for your help with Jason. In light of the alcohol and drug issues that are occurring in the neighborhood, she feels powerless to handle the situation alone. She cannot afford to move out of the neighborhood as the house is owned by her mother and Joyce is unable to work full-time due to the caregiving responsibilities she has for her mother. Utilizing your knowledge of the Riverton community, its resources and current culture, develop a strategy for engaging, assessing, and intervening with the Williams family.

5. Go to www.routledgesw.com/cases and review the case for Brickville, focusing on Virginia Stone and her family. Based on the initial assessment and planning process you conducted in collaboration with Virginia (you may want to review Exercise #3 in Chapter 6), you and she have determined that a family conference will help to address the multiple concerns related to her mother's care, home ownership, and response to the proposed plans for neighborhood development. Using the information available to you (including the eco-map and genogram), develop two separate written plans for a family conference from two perspectives (narrative and solution-focused), including your responses to the following questions:

   ● Who should be invited to participate in the family conference?
   ● What is an optimal location for holding the conference?
   ● Based on discussions with Virginia, develop a list of:
     ○ Potential agenda items
     ○ Individual and family strengths and areas of concern
     ○ Available and needed resources (within the family and community)
   ● What is your anticipated role?
   ● How might the family genogram and/or eco-map be incorporated into the family conference to develop a collaborative intervention, particularly as it relates to providing care for family members.

   Upon completing your plans for a family conference, reflect in writing on three areas:

   ● Differences and similarities of a narrative or solution-focused approach;
   ● Ways in which strengths-based perspective can be integrated into the conference;
   ● Possible motivational interviewing strategies you can employ during the family conference.

6. Go to www.routledgesw.com/cases and review the case for Hudson City and the information provided in Exercise #4 in Chapter 6 regarding the Patel family. Using a strengths-based, solution-focused approach, develop a summary of the four-phase planned change model intervention (engagement, assessment/planning, intervention, termination/evaluation) you would facilitate with the

family. Be sure to include your theoretical approach(es) and incorporate the available resources in Hudson City.

b. Other exercises

7. As a social work practitioner at a community mental health center, you serve primarily individual and family client systems. You have recently been called by the James family and will conduct an intake appointment later on today. You have the following information about the family:

   * The father, self-identified as African American, made the appointment.
   * The family includes the mother, father, their two adolescent sons, and the father's parents who share the home with the family.
   * The elder son, age 18, is of most concern to the family, having expressed suicidal thoughts and recent but increasing withdrawal from school, family, and community life. Last year this son was a well-known school athlete and this year is not active in any school or athletic activities.
   * The parents suspect that alcohol or other drug use is involved in the family.
   * Both sons are reluctant to attend the appointment but will because their father has indicated they will.
   * Mother will "go along."

   In your preparation for this appointment, you consider several dimensions of the work that appear below. In small groups, discuss these and explore the questions. Report back to the entire class.

   a. You are not African American but are of Jewish heritage, which is relatively rare in the town. You know there are cultural differences between this family and you but believe you can bridge those to some extent because you consider yourself different culturally as well. What might you need to consider in your own assumptions?

   b. What model of family social work (of those in the chapter) do you believe will provide the most useful base? Discuss the reasons for this selection.

   c. What specific information will be important to first clarify?

   d. What specific approaches will be most important here with this particular family?

   e. How would you begin your intervention with this family? What practice behaviors will you use? What might you actually say? (Give an example)

7. Using the strengths-based strategies highlighted in this chapter, review the following list and describe in detail the way in which you would incorporate each into an intervention with the James family (from exercise #6):

   * Identify the issues and concerns, use active listening to enable the family members to tell their story and reflect on the information shared by the family members.
   * Acknowledge the pain.
   * Look for and point out strengths.

- Ask questions about survival, support, periods of time that were positive for the family, interests, dreams, goals, and pride.
- Resilience begins with what one believes and all people have the capacity for resilience
- Link strengths to the goals and dreams of the family members (both group and individual).
- Find opportunities for family/members to contribute to the intervention by helping to educate other members and serve as helping agents in achieving the family's agreed-upon goals.
- Use brainstorming for solutions as a strategy to help the family to view the situation and themselves differently.

8. Using a solution-focused approach, identify the techniques reviewed in this chapter that you believe will be appropriate for use with the James family described in exercise #6. Be specific in describing the way in which you would implement the strategies.

9. Termination and evaluation are critical aspects of the social work intervention. Conduct a review of the research to identify evidence-based practice skills and practices that are applicable for facilitating an effective termination and evaluation with a family. Share your findings in class and compare the results of your review.

CHAPTER 8

Social Work Practice with Groups: Engagement, Assessment, and Planning

Alone we can do so little. Together we can do so much.

Helen Keller

Key Questions for Chapter 8

(1) What competencies do I need to engage with and assess client systems at the group level of social work practice? (EPAS 2.1.10(a & b))

(2) How can I use evidence to practice research-informed practice and practice-informed research to guide the engagement and assessment practice behaviors with groups? (EPAS 2.1.6)

(3) What are the potential ethical issues that may occur in social work practice with groups, particularly in the early phases of the group's development? (EPAS 2.1.2)

(4) What knowledge and skills do I need for culturally competent group-level engagement and assessment practice? (EPAS 2.1.4)

NONE OF US LIVES WITHOUT SOCIAL CONNECTIONS. Many of us spend much of our lives negotiating our closeness to family, neighbors, friends, associates, and colleagues. Regardless of the ways in which the connections are experienced, virtually everyone has relationships to small collectives of other people or groups. In this context, group refers to the natural or planned associations that evolve through common interest (e.g., supporting the local Little League), state of being (e.g., having a child with a disability), or task (e.g., working together at a place of employment). Connectedness to groups depends not only on an individual's needs for affiliation but also on cultural norms, social arrangements, and social location (e.g., faith traditions, children's school, or neighborhood of residence). Within social work, **group work** is a "goal-directed activity that brings together people for a common purpose or goal" (Toseland & Horton, 2008, p. 298).

This chapter addresses the nature of groups, briefly reviews the history of group work in social work practice, and explores the dimensions of group work that relate to types and purposes of groups. Along with Chapter 9, in this chapter you will explore the purpose of groups and the relationship of groups to other areas of social work practice and practice behaviors for approaching the various aspects of the process of group work from engagement and assessment through intervention, termination, and evaluation.

GROUPS: THE SOURCE OF COMMUNITY

The social dimension of social work implies that people need and want to relate to others within the context of a "community." Yet the ways to meet this need are not always clear to social work professionals or the clients they serve. In contemporary U.S. culture, there is a pervasive emphasis on independence, mobility, and pursuit of success. Employment opportunities far away, upward mobility, and pressures to achieve professionally, socially, and economically influence most people and have developed new definitions and parameters for community. Such influences are not necessarily negative, but they can take a heavy toll on one's sense of connection and linkages (i.e., community) to stable, consistent groups on which they can depend over time.

A brief on-line search using the term "support groups" or a review of the advertisement section of any major newspaper provides evidence for the need we have to be connected with others. The number of announcements for therapy groups, support groups, community groups, and educational groups suggests that, as a culture, people are looking for a way to relate to others that is outside of themselves. In other words, people seek out groups in order to form a community. What do artificially created group experiences (i.e., those group experiences developed as a service) offer to people? Such groups provide a sense of belonging or community, a chance for reality testing, a source of mutual aid, and a means of empowerment (Reid, 2009, p. 433). By implication, social group work affords people the means to participate in significant experiences that may be lacking in the natural contexts of their everyday lives. While family, friends, and co-workers may be empathetic and supportive of our challenges, we may find a stronger connection with others who share our lived experiences.

Group as a Natural Orientation

Beyond individual idiosyncrasy, culture has an important impact on the amount and type of connections people seek. "People relations" (Diller, 2011, p. 73) is one of the cultural paradigms that distinguish one cultural group from another. For example, European-Americans are more apt to be individual in their social relationships in contrast with the collateral focus of many other cultures, Latino/a Americans, in particular. The degree to which a culture embraces individualism over collective demands varies greatly. Cultural paradigms within some groups that place more emphasis on group or familial connection than on independence can create conflicts among group members and between members and the group leader or facilitator (Ringel, 2005). The social worker facilitating the group must be culturally astute and aware of the cultural backgrounds of the group participants, and the cultural influences that affect group dynamics. Brown (2013) offers strategies for culturally competent group facilitation:

- Be open to learning about cultures different from your own.

- Do not overwhelm group members with too much information at one time.

- Regularly check-in with group members to ensure clarity of understanding.

- Attend to your communication skills, including the use of open-ended questions and avoidance of technical words and jargon.

- Ask group members to share traditions related to respectful interactions, culturally sensitive issues, and taboos (p. 52).

Exhibit 8.1 provides additional suggestions for developing culturally competent group practice skills.

Implications of Cultural and Global Connections for Social Work Practice   Because our society focuses more on self-determination than on cooperation, the social work professional may observe and perhaps question the impact of social connections through group interventions. As a social worker, you can make a commitment to self-determination (a hallmark of social work practice) and still know that it is not understood the same way in all cultures. The postmodern, reflective thinker will notice that in some circumstances, these concepts are empowering but they can also be oppressive due, in part, to the fact that the primary focus is on the individual as opposed to the larger, more inclusive group.

An increasingly global perspective on social work practice adds support for increasing sensitivity in this area. In 1996, the NASW *Code of Ethics* was amended to include an international perspective in the statement "social workers should promote conditions that encourage respect for cultural and social diversity within the United States and globally" (Standard 6.04). This addition to the *Code of Ethics* indicated an increasing global consciousness, a perspective that has become well integrated into social work practice in the 21st century.

Most practicing helping professionals benefit from exploring the degree to which their own orientation to achievement, independence, and competition as

EXHIBIT 8.1

Cultural Competence in Group Work

Building on cultural competence practice with individuals and families, social workers practicing with groups can benefit from incorporating culture-specific strategies as outlined here. While these practice guidelines are intended to enhance your cultural competence in social work with groups, they are not intended to suggest that these strategies apply to all members of these populations or to detract from the need for you to gain person-centered skills that focus on the individual members.

Latino/a Americans—With a commitment to collectivism, family traditions, harmonious interpersonal relationships, and respect, consider the following as you develop a group:

- Ensure that written materials are available in Spanish.
- Assess level of acculturation within various contexts, including physical and mental health, school, family, and work.
- Make no assumptions about group members and be open to learning about individual members' language, origins, and history.
- Be flexible and fluid with the timing and flow of the group meeting.
- Allow adequate time for engagement and trust and relationship building, including facilitators sharing personal information about themselves and their family.
- Use story circles/storytelling to enhance relationship building, collaborations, and social action.
- Integrate use of activities to encourage artistic expression (e.g., painting, acting, theater).
- For curriculum-oriented groups, ensure content and materials are culturally specific and appropriate.

African Americans—Consider the use of an Afrocentric approach which brings together experiences of Western and African cultures by:

- Emphasizing the interconnections among the individual, family, and community to enable the individual to see her or himself within those contexts.
- Maintaining a focus on African American culture and use of its strengths.
- Presenting yourself as respectful and genuine.
- Upon gaining acceptance by the group, maintaining a consistent and active role in the group process.

Asian-Americans—Understanding that Asian-American cultures differ from that of Western culture in a number of different areas can be helpful in incorporating such strategies as:

- Recognizing the importance that the family (versus the individual), harmony, independence, privacy, expression of feelings, and respect for authority plays can make a group intervention complex.
- Given the diverse groups within the Asian culture, gaining insight into your own assumptions, biases, and lack of information and the implications of each of these for the intervention.

- Understanding potential differences in communication styles (i.e., emphasis on non-verbal communication) can enable you to be comfortable with silence, for instance.
- Acknowledging group members' strengths, particularly in terms of bicultural skills.
- Considering impact of similarities and differences in areas of: length of time in the U.S., cultural origins, migration and loss issues, acculturation to Western culture, intergenerational and gender roles/conflicts, and experiences in the U.S. (particularly related to discrimination and oppression).
- Consider such techniques as: normalizing feelings and experiences, psychoeducational activities, non-confrontational approaches, and self-disclosure.

Native Americans—While few group work approaches have been developed with specific emphasis on the Native American culture, strategies to consider including are:

- Strive for each member's voice to be heard, specifically in terms of sharing individual stories and making decisions for the group.
- Acknowledge and gather information on tribal-specific traditions, ceremonies, spiritual implications, and context.
- Incorporate positive and honest humor.
- Maintain consistency in being "present" and genuine with group members.

Undocumented Immigrants—With a diverse array of personal and family histories and a potentially high level of anxiety regarding legal status and possible deportation, group work with immigrants who are undocumented can benefit from a specialized skill set, including:

- Acknowledge and celebrate the members' resilience to face challenges and the strengths they have developed as a result of their lived experiences.
- Be knowledgeable about the legal issues associated with having an undocumented status.
- Ensure support of agency administration to provide services to this population.
- Active outreach may be needed to enable this population to feel comfortable in joining a group.
- Clarify for yourself the information that you need to know and that which you do not need to know—group members may be reluctant to share specific information regarding their living situations.
- Promote relationship building and trust by inviting members to share their stories and later, addressing such issues as marginalization, isolation, and discrimination.

Sources: Chen, Budianto, & Wong, 2011, pp. 90–93; Furman, Rowan, & Bender, 2009; Greif & Morris-Compton, 2011; Harvey, 2011, p. 268; López and Vargas, 2011, pp. 144–145; McWhirter et al., 2011, pp. 79–80; and Ringel, 2005.

cultural variants is not compatible with the cooperation and collaboration that clients from other cultures may value more highly. Regardless of your own cultural heritage, take care not to privilege your position as normal just because it is the one with which you are most familiar. You may be well served in some instances, but impeded in your effectiveness in others. For instance, independence, as an ideal, can create obstacles in working cross-culturally with clients who do not share an understanding or enthusiasm for its relevance in their lives. As an example, if you encounter a child, Jared, in a school setting, who appears to lack an eager, competitive spirit, who seldom raises his hand when a teacher asks a question, and who always defers to others, you may attribute a deficit of one kind or another to him. You may find him slow, shy, or lethargic, and you may see him as dependent, or even as depressed or developmentally delayed. Jared may simply be reflecting the cultural imperative to cooperate, to prioritize the communications of others, and to behave demurely in the company of people who are older and who have authority.

The nature of "groupness" is complex and variable according to social location. While all people need and seek social connections, this phenomenon is tempered and shaped by cultural expectations related to family and community, customs, propriety, loyalty, authority, individualism, and the way in which these factors fit together. Although Western values of competitiveness and individualism have been responsible for much of the accomplishments and power of U.S. culture, these values have the potential to create disconnection, isolation, and detachment as well as a fertile environment for the design of constructed groups, particularly in the human services. The social work profession has responded to and continues to be vigilant about this need throughout a long history of social work group practice.

Historical and Contemporary Contexts for Group Work

Like other legacies in social work, social work practice with groups has roots in England and the Industrial Revolution. The political and economic context of this time period resulted in disrupted lives and broken social connections of countless children and families. Such a sense of isolation led groups to come together around common interests and needs. With a sense of mission, volunteers of this era brought groups together for social, recreational, advocacy, and social action. The time was ripe for the development of group social work (Alissi, 2009; Furman, Rowan, & Bender, 2009; Reid, 1997).

Group work developed in the United States in the 19th century in the midst of professional and political tensions regarding the perceived need (or lack thereof) for public, religious, or philanthropic organizations to involve themselves in the lives of U.S. citizens. Inspired by religious and philanthropic organizations, the concept of bringing people together in small groups became a popular strategy for helping clients within community-based settings (e.g., YMCA/ YWCA, Boy/Girl Scouts, and faith-based community centers). The early approach focused on individuals and their need for change. In contrast, another group of helping professionals of the time used group efforts focused instead on social reform with a humanitarian impulse, and believed that social change was the critical ingredient in making a positive difference in people's lives. These reformers were more likely to see the group (rather than the individual) as the medium for that form of intervention. You will notice here some reverberations from the social control/social change tension discussed in Chapter 1. In addition, group work was not yet firmly a part of social work practice. This segment of the group movement were often partisan Socialists, concerned with political action and identified with not just social work, but also elected officials, clergy, and public health officials, to name a few.

By the end of the 19th century, the Progressive Era added fuel to the growth of group work. Settlement houses, community organizations, and self-help groups sprang up in response to the influx of immigrants and the dramatic needs of the teeming urban environment. These organizations stressed group methods (e.g., language classes, cooking groups, recreation, the arts, and youth services) and were aimed at the social justice issues of inclusion and acculturation. They were designed to maximize the ability of newly arrived residents to achieve their desired quality of life through access to society's assets. Still, group work was not clearly identified with social work.

Throughout the 1930s, group work continued to have less status than social casework in the minds of many professionals. This perception was due, in part, to the fact that recently-developed curricula in schools of social work were aimed at individual casework, a result of the pervasiveness of Freud's influence. Group work had by then a strong association with recreational activities (e.g., sponsoring dances or creating arts and crafts with children). Such activities were not held in as great esteem as the more clinically focused casework. When group work had developed a greater affinity to social work, practitioners proposed their own association, which emphatically declared itself a part of social work, but as a discrete unit, using distinctive methods within the practice of social work with groups.

In the 1950s, group work expanded from the community into hospitals and psychiatric facilities and introduced **therapeutic group work** or **treatment groups**. These therapeutically focused groups were designed to heal or help people change. This shift altered the nature of the formerly community-based model by adopting a more professional stance. Through the process, group work began to impede on the boundaries of casework, and the distinctions between the two started to blur.

Three classic models for group practice—the **social goals model**, the **reciprocal model**, and the **remedial model**—emerged between the late 1950s and the 1970s. They reflect much of the work that came before them, as well as after, because theory is often embedded in earlier theory. Social workers still use these perspectives in contemporary social work practice with groups in various current contexts and will be discussed in detail later in this chapter and in Chapter 9. See Exhibit 8.2 for a brief description of the origin and aim of these three classic models.

By the 1970s, the **Council on Social Work Education (CSWE)** the accrediting body for social work education in the United States, required all schools of social work to adopt a generalist focus throughout undergraduate programs and for the

EXHIBIT 8.2	MODEL TYPE	MAJOR FOCUS	SOCIAL WORKER ROLE	EXAMPLE	ORIGINAL AUTHORS
Classic Models for Social Group Work, 1950s to 1970s	Social Goals	Democratic values, social conscience, responsibility, and action; uses strengths of members.	Fosters social consciousness and serves as model for democratic values.	School groups that promote student affiliation and contributions to student governance.	Pappel and Rothman, 1962
	Reciprocal	Interaction in an attempt to fulfill mutual affiliation goals; mutual aid.	Serves as mediator between each member and the group as a whole; finds common ground.	Adolescent children of incarcerated parents developing coping skills.	Schwartz, 1961
	Remedial	Prevention and rehabilitation aimed at behavior change and reinforcing individual behaviors.	Works both in the group and outside of it to ameliorate conditions in environments; acts as motivator.	Discharge group in mental health settings to increase patient capacity to negotiate community.	Vinter, 1974

first half of master's programs. With an aim toward integrating all practice methods across levels, the generalist focus requirement served to de-emphasize the distinctive role of group work as a method and, many believe, to forsake its soul. Most school curricula already emphasized casework, and with the CSWE mandate, there was little incentive to develop more group work courses. The result was that many social work students did not complete coursework that focused on social work practice with groups. Nevertheless, a strong core of social workers committed to the power of social work with groups remained, and the International Association for Social Work with Groups (IASWG) was founded in 1979. First issued in 1999 and revised in 2006, the IASWG provides *Standards for Social Work Practice with Groups*, a guide for effective practice with groups that is widely used in contemporary social work practice. The second edition of the *Standards* provides practitioners with guidelines and practice perspectives for gaining knowledge, tasks, and skills for use in group work that include: core values and knowledge; phases of the group process (pre-group planning, beginning, middle, and ending); and ethical considerations.

The climate of social work practice today offers practitioners a unique opportunity to work with groups in ways that will help to meet the needs individuals have for genuine connection and social action. A group-focused orientation is one of the characteristics that distinguish social work group practice from psychology or mental health counseling groups. In group work, the social worker's effort is on the development of the group, and while individual well-being is one goal, it is achieved through the interactions and structures of the group.

DIMENSIONS OF SOCIAL WORK PRACTICE WITH GROUPS

For this discussion, a social work group intervention refers to a small, face-to-face gathering of people who come together for a particular purpose. The major dimension of a group experience is the interdependence among person, group, and social environment. Like many aspects of social work practice, the concept of group work can be delineated in several ways to represent distinctions. As we begin this exploration into social work practice with groups, the first issue to consider is the purpose that a group intervention can serve. To place the following discussion into a practice and organizational context, consider that groups provide avenues for socialization or re-socialization while occurring within an agency or community environment—which can, at times, result in a peace co-existence or conflict (Ephross, 2011).

Types, Forms, and Functions of Groups

The major division at the most basic level in social work groups is between formed or constructed groups and unconstituted, **natural groups**. Natural groups occur in the context of socialization and are not organized from the outside. These may be based on spontaneous friendships, common interests, or common social location, such as living in the sophomore wing of a college dormitory. Families are the original natural group. Natural groups usually do not have formal sponsorship or agency affiliation, but social workers may have occasion to work with them (particularly families). Social workers and their agencies can also provide support to these naturally formed groups in a variety of ways (e.g., offer meeting space, access to office equipment, or staff consultation).

Social workers are more likely to facilitate **formed groups**, which are organized by an institution or organization, such as a school or hospital, agency, or community center. Formed groups can be divided between three models: **task groups**, designed to accomplish a specific purpose; **social action** or **goals groups** (previously described), focused on advocating for social justice; and **client groups**, geared toward personal change. These models can be further delineated as follows:

1. Task groups include task forces, committees and commissions, legislative bodies, staff meetings, interprofessional teams, case conferences and staffing, and social action groups. The task group is aimed at facilitating a change that is external to the group with a focus on a specified purpose, policy development, completing a product or a plan, or creating a mechanism for collaborative

decision-making (Strand et al., 2009, p. 42). The social worker can function as a convener, member, chair/leader, facilitator, or a combination of these roles. The social worker in the leadership role is responsible for initiating and monitoring the meeting and progress toward the stated goals and objectives, managing the group interactions and maintaining focus (Furman et al., 2009). Task groups are explored in more detail in Chapter 10. You may also visit http://www.routledgesw.com/ to learn about a task group that functions in the community of Riverton to oversee the activities and growth of the community.

2. Social action or goals groups are a form of a task group created to address a social issue to empower individuals or a community (Toseland & Horton, 2008). The social action approach has a number of strengths, including (a) the collective effort of a group of people can be more powerful than that of the individual; (b) the social worker is not the expert leader, but a facilitator for the group; (c) groups can help to harness the individual capacity to create social change; (d) professionals and group members work in partnership; (e) the agenda is determined by the group members; and (f) groups can create a safe environment for the individual and collective exploration of issues of oppression, discrimination, and disadvantage (Fleming, 2009, pp. 275–276). As with task groups overall, the social worker can function in a variety of roles. As an example, the parents of the Riverton community come together to address their growing concerns about alcohol abuse among the youth in their neighborhoods.

© Blaj Gabriel

3. Client treatment groups may be aimed at support, education, growth, therapy, socialization, empowerment, and remediation. Client groups can be formed for two purposes:

    (a) **Reciprocal groups**, also referred to as support, mutual aid and mutual sharing groups, form to enable members who share a common experience to provide support and mutual aid to one another. With an emphasis on self-help and not specifically on therapeutic intervention, reciprocal groups can range from informal to highly structured to psychoeducational (blending of mutual support and educational focus). Reciprocal groups provide members with an opportunity to experience "shared empathy," which is the experience that brings members together and provides the potential for cohesion and mutual problem-solving (Furman et al., 2009, p. 63). Finding others who share similar life experiences can be validating and affirming for group members as well as provide opportunities to share valuable insights and coping strategies.

    This model for group work intervention has wide applicability, particularly among adults who face a new or unanticipated struggle and can benefit from education as well as group support. **Psychoeducational groups** focus on the education of group members regarding a psychological condition. One approach has been especially helpful to parents of young adult children experiencing mental illness. Frequently, the individual develops new symptoms in their early 20s; their parents may not have been touched by mental illness before. Local community mental health agencies often offer group sessions to the families to help them learn more about mental illnesses, what to expect in terms of their children's behavior and symptoms, how they can best provide support, and how they can cope with their own grief. These groups, which were started in the mental health arena by the National Alliance for the Mentally Ill (NAMI), have been particularly effective. Psychoeducational groups usually incorporate considerable factual information, but also rely on a supportive and accepting attitude both by worker/facilitators and other group members. Groups can be structured, with a curriculum and lessons in sequence, or freer in form. In some locations, parents who originally attended these groups have become group facilitators themselves, generally with training and technical support from the local agency.

    Social work involvement in reciprocal groups can range from initiator to facilitator to "silent" support person. The social worker role will be related primarily to the origins of the group (i.e., a larger role if social worker-initiated and a lesser role if member-initiated). In the case of a psychoeducationally focused group, the social worker may have a more formalized role based on possessing a particular knowledge or skill expertise. An example of a psychoeducational group is a grief support group for children living in the Riverton community who have lost a family member to alcohol or drug abuse.

An example of a **support group** in contemporary life is the support group for persons who are in the early stages of dementia, most often of the Alzheimer's disease type. Social workers are frequently in the position of working with persons who either have dementia, live with someone who has dementia, or love someone who has dementia. The associated stigma and isolation for some of the men and women living with dementia can be as devastating as the disease. This makes support a critical component, and the support group can offer a chance to share feelings, combat loneliness, gain information, exchange resources, and normalize the overall experience. Similar issues arise for families and other loved ones of someone with dementia and social workers may facilitate groups for them as well. Social workers need to understand the effects, symptoms, and issues that people with or touched by dementia experience. Alzheimer's disease and other dementia can invoke volatile emotions, therefore it is particularly important for facilitators to acknowledge and understand their own reactions and biases regarding the disease and those living with it.

(b) **Remedial groups** are for changing behavior, restoring functioning, or promoting coping strategies of the individual members who join the group voluntarily or involuntarily (Toseland & Horton, 2008). The social worker's role is typically that of facilitator or leader, because clinical knowledge and skills are necessary for direction. Returning to the Riverton community as an example, a remedial group may be formed at a mental health center or hospital to provide psychotherapy for substance-abusing clients.

In most cases, the group's major purpose and form is evident in its title. Many groups have multiple purposes. Groups may also be distinguished by the role of the social worker. In treatment or psychotherapy groups, the social worker may use methods consistent with counseling and interpretation, while in educational groups the focus may be on teaching and processing. Task groups are likely to direct the social worker's focus on facilitation, as she or he assists the group in taking action to address an undertaking. See Exhibits 8.3–8.5 which depict phases of group interventions, including social worker and member roles. Utilizing the descriptions of groups developed by and with residents of Riverton, these exhibits contain examples of the beginning phases—pre-group planning, engagement, and assessment—of group processes implementing the social goals/action, reciprocal, and remedial models.

The first decision that you must make is to determine if a group experience will meet the needs you have identified. While group interventions can be powerful and have the potential to address a number of individual, community, or societal needs, you must assess the situation at hand to discern if a group approach will be most

PHASE I: BEGINNING

EXHIBIT 8.3

Riverton Against Youth Drinking ("RAYD"): An Example of Social Goals/ Action Group

Background: Concerned about the use and abuse of alcohol among their adolescent children, a group of parents in the Riverton community approach a local community service agency to ask for help in addressing this problem. Later phases of the group's work will be highlighted in Chapter 9.

Note: While the stages of group interventions are not linear and may, in fact, overlap, the following depicts a possible approach to responding to the identified need.

PRE-GROUP PLANNING AND ENGAGEMENT	ASSESSMENT
Meet with parent groups to gather information	Determine individual and group members' "agendas"
Identify current and potential stakeholders who are/may be invested in the issue	Conduct community assessment, including needs, assets, and resources (see Chapter 10 for further information on community assessment)
Identify interests of group members	
Research evidence for approaches for facilitating social goals group on this topic	Gather and analyze data from assessment; identify and prioritize options for intervention
Determine general focus/goal of launching an intervention	Re-determine/confirm focus of Intervention
Identify role for agency and social worker	Finalize plan for intervention, including objectives, tasks, activities, persons/groups responsible, time frame, and plans for evaluation and sustainability
Arrange first meeting and logistics, including time, location, refreshments, etc.	Re-clarify agency and social worker roles and responsibilities
Develop agenda for first meeting	Revisit needs
	Make plans for continued assessment

effective. In addition to bringing people together who have a common life experience, concern, or need, a group effort can promote an environment for creativity and problem-solving, influence individual thoughts and behaviors, and provide a convenient strategy for delivery of services to a large group of clients with similar issues (Garvin & Galinsky, 2008). While all of these can be valid reasons for launching a group intervention, consider if the potential gains to be achieved for the group as individuals and a collective are optimally efficacious and efficient.

EXHIBIT 8.4

Riverton Children's Grief Support Group: An Example of Reciprocal Group

PHASE I: BEGINNING

Background: A social worker in a local community service agency has become aware of a number of children of Riverton who have lost a parent to alcohol and substance-related deaths. The social worker takes steps toward offering a support group to the community that includes to an educational focus. Later phases of the group's work will be highlighted in Chapter 9.

Note: While the stages of group interventions are not linear and may, in fact, overlap, the following depicts a possible approach to responding to the identified need.

PRE-GROUP PLANNING AND ENGAGEMENT

Gather information to support the need and appropriateness of this group intervention

Analyze data and confirm plans to move forward with forming group

Research evidence for approaches for facilitating reciprocal group with children

Determine group components:

* Composition of group (number, age, range, and gender)
* Recruitment strategies
* Format (open or closed)
* Time frame (time-limited or ongoing)

Determine and implement appropriate recruitment strategies

Conduct screening interview with potential members (see note in Assessment regarding group membership)

Invite group members (including obtaining written permission from legal guardians)

Determine roles of agency, social work facilitator, children, and legal guardians

ENGAGEMENT AND ASSESSMENT

Pre-Group

Prior to first meeting, meet individually with parents/guardians and separately with children to assess interest in and appropriateness (i.e., "fit") for psychoeducational support group

First Session

Introduce self and ask members to introduce themselves

Orient members to group, including review of purpose, goals, rules, norms, format, time frame, intervention plan, termination, evaluation, and confidentiality

Assess individual member goals, function, and interaction with other members

Assess group cohesiveness

Continue to assess individual and group needs (for support and education), interests, strengths, and "agendas"

Monitor and assess social worker role

Administer pre-group measurements to be utilized in the evaluation process

PHASE I: BEGINNING

EXHIBIT 8.5

Riverton Mental Health Center Group for Persons with Dual Diagnosis: An Example of Remedial Group

Background: A new social worker at the Riverton Mental Health Center has recently assumed leadership for a clinical intervention group for persons with dual diagnoses (i.e., substance abuse and mental illness) who receive outpatient services at the agency. The group is diverse in membership, including mixed genders, range of ages, and mandated and voluntary members. Membership turnover is dependent on members' "graduation" from the treatment program; therefore, the group often has entering and exiting members. Two new members have been referred to the group. This will be the first time new members have been referred since the social worker took over responsibility for the group. Later phases of the group's work will be highlighted in Chapter 9.

Note: While the stages of group interventions are not linear and may, in fact, overlap, the following depicts a possible approach to responding to the identified need.

PRE-GROUP PLANNING AND ENGAGEMENT	ENGAGEMENT AND ASSESSMENT
Obtain information on potential new members from referral sources and agency records, as appropriate	First Session
	Facilitate introduction of new members to group and review group expectations, norms, and rules
Research evidence on incorporating new members into an existing group	
	Assess individual member goals, interests, and "fit" with group
Determine structure for admission, including criteria and process	
	Assess member reactions to new group members
Meet with potential new members to screen for potential "fit" with group purpose, goals, and other members	
	Assess group cohesion
	Monitor/assess progress of other members
Invite new members to first session, introduce self, and provide orientation (e.g., composition, goals, expectations, norms, and rules)	

Recognizing that the individual's work is completed within the context of the group's fluid and interactive (and sometimes conflictual) dynamic, ask yourself if your desire to establish a group is meeting the client system's needs or your needs to efficiently serve a larger group of clients, meet your agency's revenue goals, mount an advocacy effort, or a combination of reasons. Quick Guide 24 provides a set of questions to consider as you are weighing the pros and cons of forming a group.

QUICK GUIDE 24   THE PROS AND CONS OF CREATING A GROUP: QUESTIONS TO CONSIDER

As you weigh options for intervening with client, organization, and community systems, your first task is to determine if a group intervention is the most effective approach. To clarify your goals, consider the following questions:

- What are my reasons for choosing a group intervention over an individual or family intervention? Specifically, what are the needs that I have identified within my clients, my agency, or the community?
- What type of group intervention am I considering—social action, task, reciprocal, or remedial? What are my reasons for selecting this format for the intervention?
- What would the goal(s) of the group be? For the group? For me? For the agency or community?
- Will the group be an open or closed group (i.e., continuous group of members or open to members entering and leaving as needed)?
- Will the needs of the group members be best met by the group's duration being time-limited or open-ended?
- What will be the eligibility criteria for membership in the group and who will determine that?
- Do I have the requisite competence to facilitate a group intervention?
- Is the best approach to be the sole facilitator or would have a co-facilitator better serve the group?
- Do I have the support of my supervisor and agency administration? If not, am I aware of the process for gaining approval?
- What resources do I need to offer the group—possibilities include: meeting space, supplies, and funds for recruitment, refreshments, transportation, and child or adult care.
- What options exist for gaining the resources needed for the group?
- If this is a client group, will there be a charge for participation?
- What is the optimal number of members needed to participate in the group?
- Is there an adequate pool of potential group members within my agency or community?
- If I am uncertain about the pool of candidates for the group, how would I recruit members? What marketing strategies would be appropriate?
- What are the appropriate meeting dates, times, frequency, and longevity for the group?
- When *will* the group meetings begin?
- How much time do I need to prepare for leading the group?
- How will the group activities be recorded and evaluated?

Group Work Logistics

Social work groups may occur in community agencies, schools, community mental health centers, medical practices, public assistance offices, job training centers, residential care settings, church or faith facilities, or any other setting in which participants come together. The physical location may be a setting that group members already use (such as a school), or it may be a local community facility that makes itself available to such activities (a community hospital housing a grief and loss group, for example). Many residential settings such as prisons or mental health facilities also host social work groups, and these may be restricted to residents, their significant others, or may include a mix, such as a group for about-to-be-released prisoners and their partners.

Social work groups may differ on other variables such as the number of group meetings or the way in which they are organized. A group may meet for a fixed number of sessions or it may be ongoing, with changing membership over time. Some groups are structured as **closed groups** in which the membership and number of sessions are fixed. Many others are **open groups**, which allow new members to join at any time (or occasionally only at fixed times, such as after the third and sixth sessions). In developing plans for a group intervention, consider which of these formats will best meet the needs of the target population for the group. Open groups may offer flexibility for the facilitator and group members and economic advantages for the organization, but this format may lack the cohesiveness and continuity which prevail in a closed group format. Consider also the similarities and differences in the skill set required for facilitating each type of group. To effectively lead an open group, the social worker must be able to quickly develop an empathetic connection to the group members, promote cohesion in each meeting, and know the appropriate times to use more active and less active facilitative skills (Turner, 2011).

Being a voluntary or mandated group is another important distinction. In mandated situations, the social worker may have different expectations (not always realized) of member investment, and the influence of the mandating institution (such as the court) is likely to be greater relative to voluntary groups. Many scenarios in involuntary treatment employ groups as the method of choice. For example, recall the innovative practice in the family group decision-making model in Chapter 7, which involved a child protection violation and used a large group of community and extended family members. More traditional models also use groups for working with clients challenged by intimate partner violence, parenting issues, and substance abuse. Group work focuses particularly on interrelatedness and extension to the "outside" world, thus creating opportunities to engage involuntary clients in a process from which they can benefit long after the treatment period.

Three important areas for social work group practice include process (how people do what they do), linking (making connections with other people and situations), and inclusion (involving everyone present) (Thomas & Caplan, 1999). These areas are especially applicable for mandated groups as they focus on connecting members through the group process. Some of the skills necessary for successful group work are validating experience, clarifying, paraphrasing, linking one member's response to another's, collaborating, developing group rituals, roleplaying, setting tasks, and processing body language (Thomas & Caplan, 1999). These skills draw upon a combination of individual and extended group work skills that can facilitate the work of connection.

THEORETICAL APPROACHES TO ENGAGEMENT AND ASSESSMENT WITH GROUPS

Just as with social work practice with individuals and families, developing competencies for engaging and assessing in group practice begins with identifying a theoretical stance from which you will work. In keeping with the commitment of this text to the strengths-based perspective, the following discussion will be grounded in the premise that social work practice with groups is approached from the concept that all members have strengths on which the goals and objectives can be built. As Kurland (2007) notes, "the very act of forming a group is a statement of our belief that every member of the group has something to offer the others, something to give to others, not just to get from them" (p. 12).

Since all groups create and function as a system, most theoretical frameworks for group practice derive from the systemic perspective (Garvin & Galinsky, 2008). Thus, you can apply the knowledge you have gained about systems theory with individuals and families to your work with groups. You may begin by viewing groups as fluid, dynamic interactions between a set of individuals who develop interdependence on one another. When the group composition is altered (e.g., a member joins or exits), the dynamics and interpersonal interactions of the group subsequently change as well. A systemic perspective suggests that the work of each phase of the group process "coalesces into a meaningful whole" (Manor, 2008, p. 101). Group work can be highly effective when approached from a strengths-based perspective. For example, consider the powerful impact to be made when you focus on the group members' strengths and abilities as opposed to their limitations (Ephross, 2011). Building on the conceptualization that social work group practice is guided by both systemic and strengths-based frame works, the following discussion will look at narrative and solution-focused perspectives and group work.

Narrative Approach in Group Engagement and Assessment

Incorporating a narrative approach with groups begins with viewing the client system as a collaborator. With a group, the number of potential collaborations is significantly increased. Having a group of individuals who share common experiences can further aid in the process of engaging the client to elicit her or his story, then challenging the client's perspective, and partnering to reconstruct a new story/ reality. Members can benefit from not only sharing and reconstructing their own narrative, but listening and contributing to other group members as they reconstruct their own, individual stories.

The narrative framework places an emphasis on the client as the expert on her or his life (Kelley, 2008). Within the context of assessment in group practice, group members can work together with one another and the social worker to identify members' strengths. The assessment process can also help members externalize or separate themselves from their problems for the purpose of planning for change. As with social work practice with individuals and families, narrative theory has been integrated with other theoretical and practice approaches; next we will explore using a narrative approach blended with a solution-focused approach.

Solution-Focused Approach in Group Engagement and Assessment

The solution-focused approach is becoming increasingly relevant to group practice. You will recall from earlier discussions of using solution-focused approach with individuals and families that this approach emphasizes brief, targeted interventions. A solution-focused approach "encourages more purposeful interaction among group members" (De Jong & Berg, 2013, p. 286). With its grounding in strengths-based perspective and emphasis on solutions, this approach can quickly focus the members on the issues that brought them to the group, aid them in collaborating on the development of a plan for change, and activate the planned change—all with the input and support of other group members and the social work facilitator.

Group interventions are often intentionally time-limited because of the nature of the work (e.g., mandated groups or psycho-educationally focused groups), financial or agency resources, or characteristics of the group members (e.g., children or adolescents). In engaging potential group members, the social worker can emphasize the time-limited, targeted, future-oriented nature of a solution-focused group. This orientation clearly sets the stage from the engagement phase that your work together will be purposeful, occur within a specified time period (ideally 6 to 12 meetings), and emphasize concrete, achievable outcomes. Such an approach is likely to appeal to many potential group members who may be reticent about joining a group. Solution-focused strategies have been shown to be particularly helpful with children and youth in addressing bullying behaviors (Young, 2013) and clients mandated for intervention (e.g., prison inmates and offenders of intimate partner violence) (Uken, Lee, & Sebold, 2013; Walker, 2013).

Because of the pragmatic, outcomes-oriented nature of the solution-focused approach, the assessment phase of solution-focused group work promotes a range of helpful techniques, such as creating individualized therapeutic goals, the use of scaling questions gauge the initial concerns expressed by the members of the group and will enable the group members to monitor their progress throughout the intervention. Introducing assessment through the use of the standard series of solution-focused questions highlights previous successes, strengths, and resources while focusing the client (and the group) on viable solutions. For example, returning to the group of Riverton residents who have lost someone to substance abuse, the social worker can begin the assessment phase by asking individual members the "miracle" question: "How would your life be if you were no longer acutely grieving the loss of your loved one?" The worker can then ask the group member to recall a time when they were successfully coped with a challenge or crisis. While the social worker recognizes that grief is not easily resolved, she or he can guide the group members to consider alternative strategies for coping with their loss. The benefit of using such an approach in the group setting is that group members can share ideas and strategies, help to identify strengths in themselves and others, and support and nurture one another.

Solution-focused approaches can be effectively integrated with other intervention approaches. For example, incorporating strategies from the strengths- and narrative-based schools of thought can serve to enhance the impact of the intervention (Kelley, 2008). All three approaches emphasize engagements and assessments focused on the resources of each person with the goal to empower and change. Narrative-focused techniques can elicit the stories of the group members and help develop alternative and unique change outcomes for the individual and the group.

There is an array of effective theoretical or philosophical frameworks available for your work with groups. Regardless of the orientation(s) to which you subscribe, remember that your client in group work is, in fact, the group itself, and the group experience can be a powerful one for both you and the group members.

CONTEMPORARY TRENDS AND SKILLS FOR THE BEGINNING PHASES OF GROUP WORK: ENGAGEMENT AND ASSESSMENT

As with social work practice with individuals and families, pre-planning, engagement and assessment, and planning are critical to an effective social work intervention with a group. These areas coincide with the phases of the group intervention—planning, beginning, middle, and ending phases. Group practice skills build on the skills and knowledge that you have gained for working with individuals and families; here we will discuss new skills for pre-group formation planning, engaging and assessment, group logistics, and process (Ephross & Greif, 2009, p. 681).

Pre-group Planning

A successful social work group intervention requires planning prior to the first meeting. There are many considerations that you should address before developing a group in social work practice. As the practitioner, there are nine areas you need to consider before organizing a group. These nine areas (adapted from Kurland & Salmon, 1998, p. 24) provide a useful guide:

- Need

- Purpose

- Composition, eligibility, and appropriateness

- Structure

- Content

- Agency context

- Social context

- Pre-group contact

- Contacting prospective group members

You should think about each of these areas within the context of the agency, your supervisor's input or direction, and the larger social environment. These areas are interrelated, and decisions in one category may influence decisions in another. While there is room for multiple approaches in group work practice, the considerations here do not presuppose certain answers. They are simply areas to which you can give thought, as they are likely to be the source of unexpected obstruction later if ignored in the beginning. See Exhibit 8.6 for schematic drawings relating to pre-planning models, while Exhibit. 8.7 presents an example of the operationalization of the pre-planning process. Let us return to Jasmine Johnson's situation in which she requests your help with learning alternative strategies for interacting with her teen son. A component of her contract with you was to participate in a Parents of Teens Support Group. Exhibit 8.7 may be viewed from your perspective as the social worker who will create and lead that group.

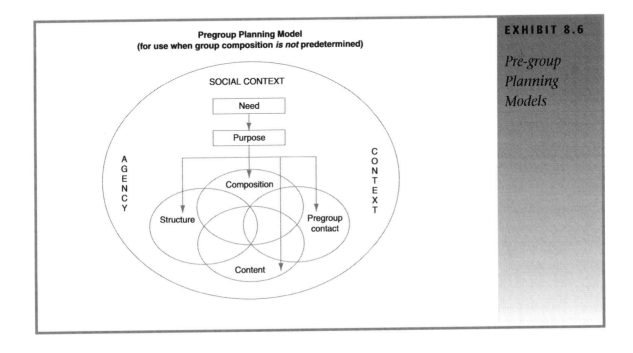

Pregroup Planning Model
(for use when group composition *is not* predetermined)

EXHIBIT 8.6

Pre-group Planning Models

EXHIBIT 8.6

Continued

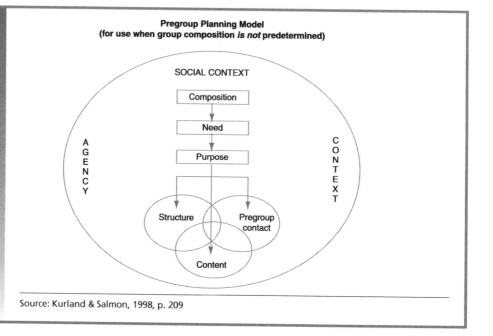

Pregroup Planning Model
(for use when group composition *is not* predetermined)

SOCIAL CONTEXT

Composition

Need

Purpose

Structure

Pregroup contact

Content

A G E N C Y

C O N T E X T

Source: Kurland & Salmon, 1998, p. 209

EXHIBIT 8.7

Pre-Planning for a Group Intervention: Parents of Teens Support Group

Your agency has experienced an increase in the number of parents of teens seeking services due to their concerns about their relationships with their adolescent children. In consultation with your supervisor and colleagues, a decision is reached to form a support group for this population. You have been asked to lead this effort. Using Kurland & Salmon's (1998) list of pre-planning tasks, you consider the following:

Pre-Planning Issue/Task	Consideration for Parents of Teens Support Group
Need	62% increase in the past six months of parents of teens seeking services due to concerns about their relationships with their teenage children.
Purpose	After discussion at staff meeting, family service staff agree that the parents can benefit from a reciprocal, psychoeducationally-focused group intervention
Composition, eligibility, and appropriateness	*Composition*: The group will be targeted to parents of adolescents aged 12–19 years and will not have a minimum or maximum number of participants required. *Eligibility*: Based on the changing needs of the target population, the group will be open to any interested parents of teens. The participants are not required to be currently receiving services from the agency. *Appropriateness*: Due to the psychoeducational/support orientation of the group, any parent feeling they are in need of support will be appropriate for the group. This type of group is consistent with other services offered by your agency.

Pre-Planning Issue/Task	Consideration for Parents of Teens Support Group
Structure	The group will meet monthly for 90 minutes in the agency's multi-purpose room. You will serve as the primary facilitator with the social work student completing practicum with you this year serving as the co-facilitator. The agency will provide refreshments. Child care will be offered for any parents with young children. Service learning students from a nearby university will oversee the childcare area.
Content	As the aim of the group intervention is focused on provision of mutual aid and education, each session will begin with a brief presentation by one of the facilitators or another professional. The parents will collaborate with the co-facilitators to determine topics of interest. Following the presentation and discussion, the members will be given the opportunity to "check-in" with one another, raise issues, and ask for input from the group regarding concerns they are experiencing.
Agency context	With support from your supervisor, agency administration, and your co-workers, this group intervention helps to promote the agency mission of providing services to families and children.
Social context	A psychoeducational, reciprocal support group meets a need within the community that no other agency or institution is currently meeting. Should members need additional support, your agency provides individual and family services.
Pre-group contact	Your social work student and you will develop a program flyer that will be circulated among agency staff and posted on agency bulletin boards and website. The program will also be promoted to other social service agencies serving this population, school social workers, a community service website, and in the organization section of the local newspaper.
Contacting prospective group members	Prospective group members may be referred by social service professional or contact the agency directly. You and your social work practicum student will conduct a brief intake interview with each potential member to determine her or his appropriateness for the group. If the group is appropriate for the group, she or he will be invited to the first meeting.

Need   To determine if there is a need for a group experience, you may begin by identifying the major and relevant issues that confront the population you would work with. You want to know your clients well and be aware of the needs as perceived by potential members. Establishing a vital, functioning group is dependent on having an understanding of members' lives and struggles and being able to focus on some aspect of their lives that is important to them. In-depth knowledge of your target group can influence your recruitment and retention strategies, meeting location, group agendas and activities, and the impetus for potential members to participate (Finlayson & Cho, 2011, p. 491). For example, if you work with several young mothers who live in poverty, consider the decisions you will make regarding the scheduling and location of meetings and the need to offer transportation and child care. You will need to consider the direct dimension of the battle of living on a limited income (e.g., managing a meager household budget, taking an assertive stand with landlords, or meeting children's needs) rather than offering a group whose activity is based on an issue that is not relevant for the members (e.g., needlework skills). On the other hand, needlework skills may be very appealing to women who have little outlet for creativity or companionship and seldom feel as if they accomplish much through the day. The point is to know your clients' needs and respond to them in a way that is consistent with your agency's purpose. Sources of data that may prove helpful include a community needs assessment, agency service statistics, and interviews with staff and clients.

Purpose   Consider both collective and individual objectives: What hopes will the group as a whole have? What expectations will individuals have? Ask yourself, what is the function of the group and what will your role be? The focus may be on, for example, counseling, teaching, or facilitating social action. Consider ways in which member interaction will contribute to the purpose of the group. The primary focus of participation in a structured group intervention should always be maintained on meeting the goals of gaining knowledge and growth that can be applied to the members' lives (Ephross, 2011).

Composition, Eligibility, and Appropriateness   The number of members and their characteristics, such as gender, age, experience, skill, beliefs, and values, serve as the group's composition. The major concern in determining the composition of a group is the degree of homogeneity or heterogeneity that will be preferable and conducive to the group achieving the desired outcomes. In general, scholars agree that some common characteristic or situation optimally provides a unifying focus, but there should also be some difference to sustain interest and the potential for growth through exposure to different ideas. Frequently a particular condition, such as living with cancer, can bridge many differences on other dimensions, such as age or ethnic background, but these aspects should be evaluated carefully in each situation.

In addition to individual descriptive variables, behavioral characteristics are also important. The group has the potential to be more successful if members have a compatible (among each other) interpersonal style, level of verbal development, and understanding of the potential for groups. This does not mean the same level, but ideally the variation should not be so great as to present overwhelming obstacles. Different types of groups will vary on the balance of these components—for example, similar ages in children's groups would probably be more important than in most adult groups.

The need and purpose of the group intervention will help to determine the eligibility criteria and type of members that are appropriate for the group. As you are exploring the potential for forming a group, take into consideration the impact of the focus of the group and the ability of members to connect to one another. For example, consider these questions. Will caregivers of spouses with Alzheimer's disease have issues that are similar or different from caregivers of adult children with a developmental disability? Will people in recovery from an addiction be eligible to remain in the group if they are found to have relapsed? Staying focused on the intended goals of the group intervention will help you answer these questions and create a group of people who will be able to help each other.

Structure   Determine if a group will be open or closed and if there will be any "trade-offs" for your particular group. What is the agency's position on this question? What are the challenges to you with either form? What type of group will best address the short- and long-term needs of the members?

Group leadership is an area to be addressed as you begin developing a group intervention. Will the group have a sole facilitator or will co-facilitators better meet the needs of the group. While a single facilitator may be more economic in terms of time and financial resources, there may be compelling reasons for co-facilitation, including: physical safety for members and facilitators, opportunity for a student to gain group experience; and the benefits of role modeling by the facilitators (Ephross, 2011).

Structure also refers to the logistical arrangements of the group: location, frequency of sessions, time of meetings, and duration. Other practical questions include: What type or size of room will be optimal? Will members require transportation or child care? Will there be a fee? How will members maintain confidentiality? What level of agency coordination will be required?

Content   You should arrive at the content of group through analyzing the purpose of the group, the members' needs, and agency and personnel resources. The activities or other means used to accomplish the group's purpose may require special equipment or educational or art materials. Consider the agenda and content of the meetings. Who will be responsible for making arrangements for the group, establishing timelines, creating an agenda, and developing a group purpose? If the group will use discussion, will the content facilitate interaction among members?

Agency Context   Consider how the agency will affect the group and how the group will affect the agency. Specifically, do the agency administration and personnel endorse group work for the population served, and is group work consistent with the agency's mission and emphasis? Do not assume support without confirming it. Your group is likely to have repercussions for others. For example, a children's group is often noisy and may be disruptive to other staff and clients. The support staff may inherit increased administrative responsibilities with the addition of group work to the agency's repertoire of service. Individual social workers may feel possessive of their clients and may be reticent to refer current clients to a group experience. It is to your advantage to address these and other concerns as directly as possible prior to creating the group.

Social Context   Finally, consider social and cultural influences that may influence the group's bonding and functioning. Will the group compete with other community services? Are there appropriate resources for members after the group? Do the cultural contexts of the members support group participation? For example, if you want to facilitate a group for adolescent girls, you will want to consider whether their families will approve of that kind of activity.

Pre-group Contact   Prior to a first meeting, consider these issues related to contact with potential group members: How will members be recruited or referred? What will you use to promote the group and how will you promote it? Will you conduct individual pre-group screening interviews to determine if someone is appropriate for the group? How will members prepare themselves for the group experience? How will you facilitate the members' orientation to the group process so they can experience maximum participation and benefit? While each group and each potential member is unique, developing a plan to address these questions can enable you to assemble a group composed of members with whom you are familiar and who are already oriented to the purpose, structure, and format of the group they may be joining.

Contacting Prospective Group Members   There are many ways to build up the membership of a prospective group and to connect with potential group work clients, including outreach and on-site service referral. **Outreach** is a method for contacting people in their homes and communities to inform them of services and information about which they may not have been aware (Barker, 2003). Reaching out to potential group members may be accomplished through connections with other professionals in the community (e.g., school guidance counselor). Other times, outreach may require a more concerted coordination campaign (e.g., advertising and individual contacts), particularly if potential clients fear discrimination or barriers to eligibility.

Contacting prospective group members directly through **on-site service** referral is a frequently useful way to connect with potential members. You may, for example, recruit members from your caseload of individual clients, or you might ask your colleagues for referrals after they give you their support. Postings and announcements are helpful, but they must be paired with personal contact, such as another staff member's enthusiastic recommendation, to be effective.

In nearly all scenarios, a pre-group interview is ideal. First, it allows you to get an in-depth sense of the potential member and her or his "fit" with the goals and purpose of the group and if she or he is an appropriate member. A pre-group meeting also provides an opportunity to assess the potential dynamic components in relation to other members of the group. At least as important, it provides the opportunity for the prospective group member to air any anxieties and develop a sense of this new experience, to ask questions, and to make a more empowered choice about joining the group. A pre-group meeting also is a time to raise questions or concerns regarding fees or associated costs of joining the group. Finally, you can recognize this contact with group members as a form of engagement, assessment, and planning that carries with it all of the requirements in the way of knowledge and skills that engagement and assessment and planning with individuals entails.

Providing the potential or new group member with printed information regarding the group experience can be an important aspect of the individual's entry into the group. Such a document may contain information on (Brown, 2013):

- Group purpose and goals;
- Techniques, activities, procedures, and format that will be included in the group experience;
- The individual's right to refuse participation;
- Limitations of the group intervention;
- Potential risks and benefits;
- Leader's credentials and group experience;
- Leadership of the group if leader is not available;
- Implications of any diagnoses that may have been made and the role of testing, if it occurred;
- Documentation, including recordkeeping, reports, and client access to records;
- Payment process, if applicable (pp. 19–20).

Engagement

Overlapping with the important pre-group planning phase, engagement is the beginning phase of the group intervention. The *Standards for Social Work Practice with Groups* (IASWG, 2006, pp. 10–17) provides practice behavior guidelines for the practitioner working in the engagement or beginning phase of the group work intervention, including such pre-group activities as:

- Identify member aspirations and needs as perceived by the member, agency, and yourself.

- Clarify member goals and expectations along with the person's feelings about joining the group.

Following the pre-group phase of work, practice behaviors needed for continuing the engagement and assessment of group members include:

- Develop contracts for explication of individual and group goals, tasks, and activities for the duration of the group and beyond.

- Following your own introduction and clarification of your role in the group, invite each member to introduce themselves and share their reasons and hopes for joining the group.

- In collaboration with the group members, develop a clear statement of purpose, rules and norms, and roles that incorporates the individual and group member and agency goals, needs, and perceptions.

- Develop, as appropriate, content, activities, and resources that are relevant for the group purpose.

- Promote group cohesion among members and between the members and you by establishing rapport with each member and the group as a whole by high-lighting common interests and goals, direct interactions, and potential link-ages to one another and you.

- In cooperation with the group members, establish the work plan for the group for the rest of the beginning phase as well as the remainder of the group planned time together (or for the individual's time in the group if the group is open-ended and not time-limited).

- Awareness and overt recognition of the unique characteristics of each group member, including but not limited to cultural and ethnic heritage, age, gender, sexual orientation, presenting concerns, and noting that each person brings strengths to the group process.

A first session ideally begins with you and members sharing their expectations for the group. Be transparent about what you (you alone or with a co-facilitator) hope to accomplish. Likewise, members are encouraged to talk about their perceptions of their roles. Confidentiality is often one of the first dimensions discussed, and, as you can imagine, unless all members feel safe in revealing their struggles and feelings, it is not likely that many will participate fully.

Establishing **norms**, or expected rules of conduct, creates a productive group climate and requires active participation from members so the social worker is not in the position of dictating regulations for the group. The actual norms for the group will depend on the type of group. For example, a socialization group for seven-year-old boys in residential treatment may include "no hitting" as the major expectation. "No shouting" might be applicable to an anger management group, or "celebrating holidays" to a single parents' group. Some groups also discourage contact between members outside of the group, because it may dilute the group process, and others encourage it, because it fosters translation of group benefits into the "real world." The primary emphasis here is to facilitate group members' involvement through a relatively clear set of behavioral expectations that in turn will increase their comfort in being in the group and will encourage their maximum participation. If, for example, group members have differing cultural heritages, and some members interpret lateness as disrespectful while others view it as culturally appropriate or simply flexible, the social worker may opt to explore timeliness as an area for negotiation. Knowing the membership can help you anticipate particular issues that may affect group process. All of these early negotiations with group members serve, like the interview, as important opportunities for both engagement and ongoing assessment.

The engagement phase can be challenging for both the social worker and the group members. The social worker is trying to engage with each individual member and the group as a whole as well as promoting cohesion among the members themselves *and* establishing the group structure and format *and* keeping the group on task and target for the previously stated goals. Creating an environment that is safe, comfortable, and supportive is essential to the members' ability to establish rapport and engagement with the process and you as the facilitator (Furman et al., 2009). Achieving the desired level of engagement with and among group members can then empower the members to begin sharing with and supporting one another, thus alleviating the full responsibility for leadership from the social worker. Also challenging is the engagement of new members or facilitators who join an established group. The social work facilitator is responsible for engaging the new member and encouraging the group to do the same or if she or he is the new member, reaching out to the members. Attrition is a particular concern if members do not feel engaged in the first meeting. Members who are in a group voluntarily but who do not feel connected to the group or the facilitator may feel reticence about returning to the group.

The beginning phases of group work can present challenges for group members as well. Despite your best efforts to orient members to the purpose, structure, and format of the group, members may still be uncertain or even resistant about participating in the group, their role in the group, perceptions of others about them (as well as their perceptions of others), and concern that the group will not meet their individual needs (Yalom & Leszcz, 2005). Being attentive to individual reactions and responses will ensure that individuals are not "lost" or deterred from investing in the group experience.

Assessment and Planning

As with social work practice with individuals and families, the transition from one phase of work to another is rarely linear or clearly delineated. Just as engagement can be an ongoing process, assessment and planning may also be revisited throughout the duration of the group experience. Assessment and planning both logically and naturally occur as potential members are recruited and screened for membership and again as the group is forming and collaborating on the development of individual and group contracts. The need for assessment and planning can recur throughout the life of the group as individual and group goals change and evolve, as members arrive and depart, and unanticipated events influence group interactions (e.g., conflict, change of facilitator, or termination).

Within the context of group practice, assessment is a strategy for determining if the issues and characteristics presented by the group member are consistent with those of other members as well as a tool for monitoring individual and group progress toward goals. Recall the earlier example of the group for Riverton children who had lost a family member to substance abuse. As the facilitator of this group, you may have to determine if an individual who has lost a close friend is an appropriate candidate for membership in this group.

Assessment can also be employed to measure such group-related issues as cohesiveness or group facilitator skills (Macgowan, 2009b). Upon determining the area of assessment that you want to measure, you can opt for assessment by using standardized measures, observation, group member self-reports, or feedback from an external source (e.g., person or video-/audio-recording).

As with any area of social work practice, group leaders must be cognizant of the ethical obligations associated with engaging and assessing members of a new group. Such ethical considerations include (Brown, 2013):

- All assessment techniques and instruments must have sufficient and appropriate validity and reliability.

- Group leaders must have formal training and supervised practice for assessing group members.

- Group leaders must always practice within their areas of competence.

- Group members must provide informed consent for participation in the group experience and be informed of any information resulting from the assessment that will be shared with others (p. 23).

Planning within the assessment phase of group work often requires attentiveness and flexibility. While most group facilitators spend considerable time and effort in the pre-group planning phase and in developing an agenda or plan for each group session, the experienced group practitioner can attest to the need to be able and willing to adjust quickly and creatively to a need to shift plans. Regardless of the type of group you are facilitating, it is likely that at any meeting a member(s) will have an issue, crisis, request, or behavior that will need to take precedence over your plans for that session. While you will want to be responsive to the needs of the individual(s), you must try to balance the needs of the group. You may be able to set aside your plans for that session to devote time to the individual, but use caution to ensure that the other members or agenda items are not sacrificed in the process.

As noted, flexibility is an essential aspect of the social work practice with groups, particularly the beginning stages of group work. Despite the need for adaptability, the social worker may find that the engagement and assessment processes of most group experiences will include comparable and expected areas of emphasis.

STRAIGHT TALK ABOUT GROUP ENGAGEMENT AND ASSESSMENT

For many students and new workers, learning to trust the group process and to maintain a stance of **facilitator** (not necessarily "leader" and certainly not "runner of") can be challenging. Learning to share the control of the relationship(s), to share the helping role with group members, and to allow the group its own path will help you develop important practice skills. Such a position, however, can create challenges for the social worker. A tolerance for relinquishing control will place you in good stead. Despite your best efforts to refrain from controlling the group, it is important to recognize that you will, in fact, influence and shape the norms of the group simply due to your role as a facilitator/convener (Yalom & Leszcz, 2005). Fortunately, early anxieties regarding control and its management abate substantially with experience.

When embarking on an experience in which you will serve as a group leader or facilitator, it is particularly important to think about the experience within the context of the members' participation. With that in mind, consider the following assumptions one can make about group members and their roles (Brown, 2013):

- Each group member has a unique personality and history and can make a unique contribution to the group.

- Members are not always aware of the fantasies and fears that may be influencing their lives.

- Some group members may be at a crossroads in their lives that prompt fears and anxieties about group participation. Such dilemmas may present in the form of defensiveness within the group.

- Group members use different strategies to make sense of their experiences (p. 59).

Surprisingly, many workers fail to attend thoroughly to the logistics, or the detailed mechanics, of group preparation and implementation. While you consider the philosophical dimensions of launching a group intervention, also make sure there are enough chairs, the meeting is not scheduled on a religious holiday, all members have transportation to the group, and child/adult care is provided as needed. Ensure, for example, that the group for male perpetrators of violence does not meet at the same time and place as the group for their survivors. Consider competition with other known schedules, so that the parenting group does not conflict with the mothers' and children's group. While it is not possible to avoid all conflicts or awkwardness, giving thought to as many of these aspects as you can is worth the effort.

Particularly important to the engagement and assessment phases of group work is actively listening to the messages and communication being conveyed to you by group members (Shulman, 2009b). This requires you to have awareness of and empathy for the thoughts, feelings, and reactions that are held by you, group members, and others (e.g., family, staff, or referral sources). For example, if you are facilitating a group for Riverton residents concerned about the use of alcohol and drugs by local teens, it is crucial that you "tune in" to your own experiences and feelings related to substance use and abuse and the origins and meanings of the statements being made by the Riverton residents. Listening is important for your ability to work with any population as it will enable you to determine if you have biases, unresolved personal concerns, or conflicted values that may prevent you from objectively and empathetically serve a client system. In keeping with being in tune with the needs of your group members, be mindful of such additional facilitative strategies as (Ephross, 2011):

- Ability to say less (as opposed to more) to avoid interfering with the group's process—your role may need to be more active in the beginning, but should decrease as the group process unfolds (i.e., group members should be doing approximately eighty percent of the talking);

- Recognition that the power of the intervention comes from the group inter-action, not the social worker;

- Summarizing group members' discussions and providing a bridge to the next topic or area of work;

- Limit-setting through the clear and transparent expectations and policies, negotiating individual and group contracts for work, and transitioning the group through the various phases of the group process.

An issue related to attending to logistical details and "tuning in" is documentation of the group experience. While documenting the process of the group experience

© Yuri Arcurs

presents a unique set of challenges, it need not be an overwhelming or complex task. Documentation of any group experience serves a range of purposes, including: (1) insights into the positive and challenging events that occurred during the group session; (2) recording gains and potential future challenges; (3) negative interactions among group members; (4) interpretation of behaviors and interactions (including cohesion, process, norms, new directions, and gaps); (5) the termination and evaluation process; and (6) accountability for billing, planning, and referral sources (Yalom & Leszcz, 2005). Typically, the facilitator maintains two separate records of the group experiences. The group's record includes information on attendance, general themes, cohesion, interactions, and plans, while documentation in the individual group members' record includes only information regarding that client and her or his goals, needs, etc. In order to protect individual client confidentiality, the names of other group members should not be included in the individual client document. Documentation should reflect the tenor and flow of the session itself. For example, if you are using a solution-focused approach, your assessment documentation can replicate the focus on solutions versus a focus on problems (De Jong & Berg, 2013). Exhibit 8.8 provides sample items of documentation that may be included for a client-oriented group session and Exhibit 8.9 includes a list of questions the social worker can ask the client to assess and document if she or he is appropriate for membership in the group.

EXHIBIT 8.8

Information to Include in a Group Assessment/ Intervention Plan

AGENCY/ORGANIZATION NAME

GROUP NAME

Demographic Data:

- Name
- Contact information
- Legal status and needs
- Group participation needs (e.g., child or adult care needs, transportation, etc.)
- Presenting concerns as they relate to the group purpose or focus
- Current living situation (level of stability, support, and safety)
- Social environment (level of activity, satisfaction, and relationships with others)
- Cultural environment (client satisfaction and view on helping-seeking; and cultural view of help-seeking, particularly in the group environment)
- Religion/spirituality (statement of beliefs and levels of activity and satisfaction)
- Military experience (branch, time in service, discharge status, coping with experience, and view of experience)
- Childhood (supportive, strengths, and significant events, including trauma)
- Family (composition—parents, siblings, spouse/significant other(s), children, and others; level of support; and family history of mental illness)
- Sexual history (activity level, orientation, satisfaction, and concerns)
- Trauma history (physical, sexual, and/or emotional abuse or neglect and experience with perpetrator(s))
- Financial/employment circumstances (employment status, satisfaction, financial stability, areas of concern or change)
- Educational history (highest level achieved, performance, goals, and challenges)
- Substance use/abuse (history of addictive behaviors—alcohol, drugs, gambling, sexual, or other)

History of Emotional/Behavioral Functioning:

For each of the following areas, gather information regarding: current status (current, previous, or denies history); description of behavior; onset and duration; and frequency

- Self-mutilation
- Hallucinations
- Delusions or paranoia
- Mood swings
- Recurrent or intrusive recollections of past events
- Lack of interest or pleasure
- Feelings of sadness, hopelessness, isolation, or withdrawal
- Decreased concentration, energy, or motivation
- Anxiety
- Crying spells
- Appetite changes
- Sleep changes
- Inability to function at school or work

- Inability to control thoughts or behaviors (impulses)
- Irritability or agitation
- Reckless behavior, fighting, or fire setting
- Stealing, shoplifting, or lying
- Cruelty to animals
- Aggression

Past and Current Behavioral Health Treatment History (i.e., individual, family, and/or other group experiences):

- Date(s)
- Program or facility
- Provider
- Response to treatment

Mental Status Exam:

- Attention (rate on scale of: good, fair, easily distracted, or highly distractible; and describe behavior)
- Affect (rate on scale of: appropriate, labile, expansive, constrictive, or blunted; and describe behavior)
- Mood (rate on scale of: normal, depressed, anxious, or euphoric; and describe behavior)
- Appearance (rate on scale of: well groomed, disheveled, bizarre, or inappropriate; and describe behavior)
- Motor activity (rate on scale of: calm, hyperactive, agitated, tremors, tics, or muscle spasms; and describe behavior)
- Thought process (rate on scale of: intact, circumstantial, tangential, flight of ideas, or loose associations; and describe behavior)
- Thought content (note: normal, grandiose, phobic, reality, organization, worthless, obsessive, compulsion, guilt, delusional, paranoid, ideas of reference, and hallucinations; and describe behavior)
- Memory (note: normal, recent (good or impaired), past (good or impaired); and describe behavior)
- Intellect (note: normal, above, below, or poor abstraction; and describe behavior)
- Orientation (note: person, place, situation, and time; and describe behavior)
- Judgment and insight (rate on scale of: good, fair, or poor; and describe behavior)
- Current providers (including psychiatrist, primary care physician, therapist, caseworker, etc.)
- Community resources being used (including support groups, religious, spiritual, other)
- Client goal(s) for treatment
- Summary—including social worker's assessment of client "fit" with the group (see Exhibit 8.9 for assessment questions).

Adapted from St. Anthony's Medical Center, St. Louis, Missouri; Women's Support and Community Services, St. Louis, Missouri

EXHIBIT 8.9

Screening Questions for Group Assessment

A component of the assessment process for a group intervention is to determine a client's appropriateness for membership in a group. This phase of assessment can also help to ensure emotional and physical safety for all group members. The following list of general questions can aid in evaluating client appropriateness and safety:

- How does the client respond to opinions, thoughts, and insights that differ from her or his own?
- When the client becomes angry or upset, what is her or his reaction and thought process?
- Is the client able to express her or his emotions in an appropriate way and to assume responsibility for the emotion?
- How are the client's emotional responses triggered?
- What is the developmental age of the client? Is the client able to cope with negative emotions and thoughts at an appropriate developmental level with other group members?
- Does the client demonstrate:
  - Impulse control challenges?
  - Appropriate boundaries?
  - Self-awareness?
  - Self-destructive behaviors?
  - Potential to monopolize or disrupt the group?
  - Ability to respond to social cues?
  - Sensitivity toward others?
  - Potential for personal growth?
  - Appropriate group interaction behaviors?
  - Difficulty making decisions?
- Is the client's behavior potentially going to limit group participation or benefit?
- If the client is currently experiencing a crisis, will the benefits of the group outweigh risks?

Adapted from Women's Support and Community Services, St. Louis, Missouri

While documenting the work of non-client groups—social goals/action and task groups—may include some of the information found in a client group (e.g., attendance, themes, and plans), the focus is more typically directed toward creating a record of actions, decisions, and plans. Often compiled in the form of minutes or notes, documenting group process and outcomes for social action/goals or task groups emphasizes the work being completed as opposed to the interactions among the group members. See Quick Guides 25 and 26 for templates that you can use to record the work of a non-client group. Quick Guide 25 provides a template for a matrix-style record, while Quick Guide 26 provides an outline for a narrative-style document.

The early phases of a group experience can bring unique and possibly unexpected challenges for the social worker. In fact, your group experience may serve to dispel some of the myths associated with creating and facilitating a group regarding potentially conflicting agendas and roles and the perception that all members will be committed to supporting other members (Zandee-Adams, 2013). Specifically, you may encounter situations in which your goals in establishing the group differ from that of group members, your role as a provider of individual and family services creates a conflict with your role as a group facilitator, or you find that some members of the group are not able or interested in productively engaging with other group members. Four examples of challenges specific to a group experience include: (1) perceived goal incompatibility; (2) member turnover; (3) delayed results; and (4) sub-groupings (Yalom & Leszcz, 2005, pp. 298–299). Somewhat interrelated, each of these situations relates to group member expectations and dynamics. Group members may struggle to view the group process as being helpful to them, particularly when compared to an individual helping relationship or in an immediate time frame, thus they may then leave the group. Group members often find that the common experiences they share extend beyond the group and lead to alliances within the group session and/or socializing outside the group. While not necessarily negative, such relationships can be disruptive to the group process.

QUICK GUIDE 25 TASK GROUP DOCUMENTATION TEMPLATE

AGENCY / ORGANIZATION NAME
GROUP NAME

Date
Present:
Absent:
Minutes submitted by:

ISSUE	DISCUSSION	FOLLOW-UP / RECOMMENDATIONS	PERSON(S) RESPONSIBLE
Call to Order			
Minutes			
Announcements			
Old Business			
New Business			
Adjournment			
Future Meetings			

QUICK GUIDE 26   TASK GROUP DOCUMENTATION
                 TEMPLATE

Agency / Organization Name
Group Name
Date

In attendance:
Absent:

1. Call meeting to order
2. Review meeting agenda
3. Review minutes from previous meeting
4. Announcements
5. Old business
6. New business
7. Adjournment and next steps

Respectfully submitted,
Note taker's name and title

Regardless of the challenge that may present itself to you as a group facilitator or leader, maintaining a transparent, open, and equitable style will best serve both the group and your own sense of competence. Remember, the "basic reason for doing group work is the power of the group, *not the worker*" (Ephross, 2011, p. 13). Gaining as much group experience as possible, particularly facilitator or leadership experience, throughout your social work education can also prepare you for being a contributing member and capable leader in your social work career. As we continue the exploration into social work practice with groups, consider the valuable learning that you can gain by experiencing different roles within a group, including member, facilitator, and observer.

CONCLUSION

This chapter advocates for practitioners to mediate the culturally imposed isolation of many individuals through groups. There are many exciting adventures into group work in the service of contemporary theoretical perspectives, social justice, and diversity that we could not delve into depth here. Scenarios relating to cultural inclusion, gender and disability, collaboration, and spirituality in models all point to the empowering direction that social group work is taking. Group work has renewed a significant potential for the future and particular relevance for the social justice, diversity, and human rights connections that give social work its meaning.

The focus will now turn to the next phases of social work practice with groups. Building on the pre-planning, engagement, and assessment work that has been completed, the social worker–facilitated group moves into the intervention or middle phase of work followed by the termination and evaluation (or ending) phases of the group experience.

MAIN POINTS

- All people are members of groups that provide meaning and critical human connections. Western philosophy tends to underemphasize the gifts and power of group connection.

- Group work in the social work profession has been a controversial topic but remains a vital part of practice that lends itself especially to social justice, diversity, and human rights perspectives.

- Organizing a group requires careful planning and continuous consideration for the value of the group as a whole.

- Traditional theoretical models for group work include the task group, social action or goals model, the reciprocal model, and the remedial model.

- Social work group practice employs a variety of theoretical frameworks. The approaches highlighted in this chapter include: strengths and empowerment, narrative-focused, and solution-focused perspectives.

- Engaging and assessing group members individually and collectively is the beginning phase of group formation.

- While primarily completed during the beginning phases of group work, engagement and assessment can be ongoing aspects of the group experience. The fluid and evolving nature of group work can result in changing membership and leadership, new and unexpected issues, and interpersonal dynamics and conflicts that can all influence the course of the early (and later) stages of the group intervention.

EXERCISES

a. Case Exercises

1. Go to www.routledgesw.com/cases and review Carla Washburn's video vignette and complete the following:
   a. Summarize the group's activities as they are depicted in the vignettes.

    b. Document the group practice behaviors that the social worker, Shannon, is utilizing.

    c. Identify any challenges you anticipate that may occur in completing a group level intervention with the members of this group.

    d. Brainstorm about the next steps that you would initiate as the social worker facilitating this group.

2. Review the Carla Washburn video vignette and explore options for facilitating this group using a range of different approaches, including:

    a. Psychoeducational group

    b. Reciprocal group

    c. Remedial group

    After you have considered strategies for facilitating the group using the three different models, respond to the following questions:

    a. How does each group differ in its focus?

    b. How does the social work role differ in each group?

    c. What engagement skills did the social worker utilize?

    d. Utilizing the case vignette as an example, role-play the group as a one of each of the following: (1) psychoeducational, (2) reciprocal, (3) remedial

3. Go to www.routledgesw.com/cases and review the case for Brickville, focusing on Virginia Stone and her family. In the Intervention section, review Vignette #3 which describes the use of a social action group intervention focused on Virginia's efforts to save the park that was created in memory of her family members who were lost in the apartment fire twenty years earlier. Using the information that you have available to you, develop a written plan for:

    a. Determining the need for this group

    b. Identifying the purpose a task group would serve in this situation

    c. Propose appropriate group composition and their potential contributions

    d. Develop your thoughts regarding group structure and content

    e. Reflect on the meaning of such a group forming within the context of the agency and community context

    f. Describe your plans for initiating pre-group contact, engaging group members, and assessing members' potential commitment and contributions

    g. Assess available and needed resources and potential barriers to success

4. Go to www.routledgesw.com/cases and review the case for Hudson City. Recall from Chapters 6 and 7 that the Patel family experienced significant impact from Hurricane Diane. Several weeks after the hurricane, Sheetal (wife of Hemant and mother of Rakesh, Kamal, and Aarti) confides in you that she is concerned that her 12-year-old daughter, Aarti, is not coping well with life following the hurricane and their displacement from their home and restaurant. They have been able to return to their home and are working on getting the restaurant re-opened. Aarti has returned to her school, but continues to have nightmares about the storm, is uncomfortable being away from her parents, and her appetite seems to have lessened. Both your co-workers and you

are hearing similar concerns being expressed by parents whose families were affected by the storm. Describe in writing your plan for developing a group intervention to address the needs of children who survived the hurricane, including:

- Type of group approach (include format and structure)
- Plans for member eligibility, recruitment, and parent involvement
- Strategies for engaging group members in a culturally competent manner, keeping in mind that the community is comprised of a diverse and large immigrant population
- Strategies for assessing group members' appropriateness for the group.

5. Go to www.routledgesw.com/cases and review the case for Riverton, then, referring back to Exhibits 8.3, 8.4, and 8.5 in this chapter, conduct a search of the literature on group-level practice in order to determine the following:

   a. Riverton Against Youth Drinking (RAYD): evidence-based practices for facilitating social goals groups on teen drinking.

   b. Riverton Children's Grief Support Group: evidence-based practices for facilitating reciprocal groups with children.

   c. Riverton Mental Health Center Groups for Persons with Co-Occurring Diagnoses: evidence-based practices for facilitating a treatment group for this population and for incorporating new members into an existing group.

b. Other Exercises

6. As a skilled individual and group practice social worker at a local community health center, you have several young clients who have been diagnosed with attention deficit hyperactivity disorder (ADHD). The clients are Hispanic children who range in age from six to eight years of age. Although you usually meet with the children individually, you notice that when their parents pick them up from appointments, some of the parents appear sad about their children, while others appear anxious, frustrated, or angry. The children themselves seem somewhat isolated and all are experiencing social, academic, and behavioral problems in school.

   Assume that you have the time, interest, and agency support to offer a group. Choose one of the following interventions from the list below that you think will be the most helpful:

   a. A play/social skills group for the children.

   b. A support group for the parents.

   c. A psychoeducational group for the parents.

   d. An empowerment group for the children.

   Be prepared to provide a rationale for your choice to your classmates. How might one choice intersect with another? Compare with peers.

7. You work for a child welfare organization and are facilitating a support group for adolescent females who have recently given birth and are preparing to

return to their high schools. Some of the babies are being partially cared for by their grandparents, and some have been adopted through the agency. Some of the group members have concerns about returning to school and others are eager to get back into a "normal" social life again. Most members are participating well, although one member, Janine, has said almost nothing in the three meetings that have already occurred. All the members of the group are African American. You are a white, female social work practicum student, 23 years old.

At the beginning of the fourth meeting, the mood of the entire group seems contentious. After brief preliminary pleasantries and a restatement of the agenda for this session (hoping that would bring everyone on board), you realize that Janine is quietly crying in the corner. At the same time, two of the other members start calling your name angrily, competing for your attention. They tell you they are annoyed at the group, at the plan for today, at the agency, and at Janine who is sitting there acting like a "baby."

Respond to the following:

a. Identify two skills from the chapter that you would use and provide an example of the way in which you would perform the skills.

b. Provide a rationale for your selection of these particular skills. What are the expected results from the use of the skills?

c. Which of the models described in this chapter offers the best explanation for the group dynamics?

8. Attend a mutual aid group in the community and write a reflection about your experience, including:

a. Describe the group type, purpose, and structure.

b. Identify group leader and member roles.

c. Reflect on your previous experiences as a group member. What role do you often play? Why? Do you want to do things differently?

9. In small groups of three or four, create your own social action group.

a. Identify an issue that is of mutual interest to group members.

b. Determine the roles for each member.

c. Develop a plan of action for the group. Prepare as a presentation for the class.

10. Your field instructor at your practicum has invited you to join her in co-facilitating a psychoeducational support group for persons who serve as caregivers for a family member experiencing Parkinson's Disease. In addition to co-leading the group each session, your field instructor has suggested that you assume responsibility for leading one session on a topic of your choice that will be relevant for this group of primarily wives and adult daughters. This is your first group work experience and you are unfamiliar with this medical condition. To accomplish your task:

a. Review the literature to learn about Parkinson's Disease.

b. Develop a plan for the session that you will lead, including identifying a relevant topic.

CHAPTER 9

Social Work Practice with Groups: Intervention, Termination, and Evaluation

I found myself slipping into that self trashing thing, man, you know, putting myself down, thinking and saying I'm a dumb broad, ugly and worthless, just like J. used to tell me. But they got on me, those awesome women! They told me I was breaking the friggin' rules! Me! Breaking the rules, and then I remembered what they meant. We're not doing that stuff in this group. The end. Not okay. They are really the most awesome! What would I be without them?

Marcy (of the Debbie, Joan, Marcy,
and Kate Group for Survivors of Intimate Partner Violence.)

Key Questions for Chapter 9

(1) What competencies do I need to intervene, terminate, and evaluate with client systems at the group level of social work practice? (EPAS 2.1.10(c & d))

(2) How can I use evidence to practice research-informed practice and practice-informed research to guide the evaluation of a group I am facilitating? (EPAS 2.1.6)

(3) What is the appropriate response for a social worker leading a group if one group member violates the confidentiality of another member of the group? (EPAS 2.1.2)

(4) What is distinction between the appropriate social worker role in facilitating an intervention with a self-help support group and a therapy group? (EPAS 2.1.3)

THE EFFICACY OF SOCIAL WORK PRACTICE INTERVENTIONS, terminations, and evaluations with groups stems from the engagement and assessment phases. The middle and ending phases of work, interventions, are the period of the group experience in which the "majority of the work of the groups gets accomplished" and endings are "the time to consolidate the work of the group" (Toseland & Horton, 2008, p. 302). Terminations and evaluations are complex because the dual focus is on both the individual as well as the group.

To complete our exploration of work with groups, this chapter continues the group experience from the development of the intervention process through the termination and evaluation phases. We will also focus on theoretical frameworks for group interventions and models of group intervention and look at the social work practice behaviors needed for groups. The chapter will continue with a look at the final phase of the group intervention: termination and evaluation. To set the stage for delving into the middle and ending stages of group work practice, let us first consider the key issues of social justice, diversity, and human rights.

INTERFACE: SOCIAL JUSTICE, DIVERSITY, AND HUMAN RIGHTS

Social work with groups is a natural setting for practitioners who are committed to social justice, diversity, and/or human rights concerns. As discussed elsewhere in this book, much of social injustice is rooted in exclusion—from resources, opportunities, respect, supports, and so on. This kind of exclusion is especially evident in the experiences of those considered "other" or different. Even in our current culture, that can mean people with disabilities, people of color, groups living in poverty, older adults, persons who are gay, lesbian, bisexual, transgender, or questioning; unfortunately the list is very long (see Greif & Ephross, 2011). An ongoing debate within group work practice is the social worker's response to issues of diversity within the group intervention. Are group interventions more effective if the group is heterogeneous or homogenous? Most scholars agree that evidence-based practice is critical for group work, particularly the need to identify evidence to support the intervention(s) and inform the decision to offer a heterogeneous or a homogenous group structure (Toseland & Horton, 2008). Diverse groups are reflections of the world in which most people live, but not all individuals may feel comfortable or safe taking personal risks with others whose reasons for joining the group are different from their own. In addition to consulting research on group diversity, social workers can also benefit by examining their own views (including their own "isms") on the groups they will be bringing together for a group intervention (Toseland & Horton, 2008).

Group work practice brings people together in meaningful ways that can serve as a forum for increasing understanding, appreciation, and respect for others. In short, group membership can reduce the effects of exclusion and the injustices associated with those feelings of marginalization. When working with groups, you can identify, establish, articulate, and mediate the rights, as well as needs, of group members within the microcosm of the group. This can be an important and empowering experience for many people who may have rarely (or never) understood their own social contexts in terms that affirmed their rights as human beings (Kurland et al., 2004). This arena—human rights and social work with groups— holds great promise for the further integration of human rights practice into the profession.

Approaching group work with an orientation to social justice requires a commitment to learning about and embracing a number of conceptual foundations. Singh and Salazar (2011) suggest the social justice-oriented group work is based on the following foundations:

- The centrality of multicultural competence—integral to competence for group facilitation and social justice, multicultural competence is essential, but recognizably a skill set that the social worker will strive to achieve throughout her or his entire social work career. The diversity of our contemporary society means that, as a social worker, you will routinely interact with and serve a wide range of individuals who are members of groups, thus, the need for not just cultural competence, but *multi*cultural competence becomes paramount to your practice.

- The interplay between content and process—the commitment to a social justice orientation enables the social worker conducting groups to address social inequities and oppression within any group setting and among group members.

- The influence of privilege and oppression—delving into the impact of group leader and members' experiences with privilege and oppression is critical for social justice-oriented group work. Questions to consider may include: "What are group members' needs, perceptions, experiences, and wants with regard to the injustices they face and their efforts toward empowerment and freedom from self-blame? How are these injustices experienced in the community? How is empowerment defined and perceived individually and collectively by community members?" (p. 218).

- Effects on power dynamics within and outside groups—emphasizing issues of power within the group can and should have the added benefit of empowering group members to engage in advocacy and change in other areas of their lives.

THEORETICAL APPROACHES TO INTERVENING WITH GROUPS

Just as there are many theoretical models for social work intervention with individuals and families, there is also a full legacy of theory related to group interventions, processes, skills, and ending points. Subscribing to a specific theoretical

© Glynnis Jones

perspective can influence the group intervention in terms of guiding the formation of the group, defining roles, and impacting group dynamics (Macgowan, 2008).

In this section, we will continue our examination of theory-driven approaches to group practice. Following an overview of theoretical applications, we will explore several classic, contemporary and developmental models. Later, we will look at intervention skills, examples of current groups, and finally, contemporary innovations in group work.

Strengths and Empowerment Perspectives on Group Intervention

As you recall from Chapter 8, this book is grounded in the premise that social work practice with groups should be approached from the position that all group members bring strengths to the group. A strengths-based perspective integrates easily with other theoretically driven intervention approaches. Within the intervention itself, the social worker can use the strengths for a range of purposes, including developing individual and group goals and sharing resources. Strengths can affirm and motivate the individual's change process through the focus of "possibilities versus problems," enable the individual strengths to serve as models for other group members through the sharing of ideas and resources, and help identify and integrate the individual members' strengths into strengths for the group. Approaching the group intervention from a strengths-based perspective requires the social worker to help create an environment in which the following three norms are accepted by all the group members (Benard & Truebridge, 2013):

- Participation—all group members are recognized as being equal participants with each having the right to the same opportunities for voice.

- Communication—interactions among group members and the facilitator must be respectful (e.g., allowing everyone to speak without interruption or side conversations).

- Interactions—in order for all members of the group to contribute equally, members and the leader should be committed to arriving on time and staying for the duration of the group (p. 215).

One of the theoretical models that can help incorporate a strengths perspective into a group intervention is empowerment. With origins in an ecological perspective and aimed at addressing social injustices, an empowerment-focused group intervention emphasizes reciprocal connections with members' environments (Hudson, 2009, p. 48). Within this context, empowerment as a principle generally incorporates three major areas of concern: (1) the personal, including attitudes, values, and beliefs; (2) the interpersonal, including knowledge, skills, and networks; and (3) the sociopolitical, including individual and collective action (East, Manning, & Parsons, 2002). These components are well-suited to **empowerment groups** because membership itself can support the personal and interpersonal dimensions of empowerment. The critical analysis of the political environment and individuals' participation in change efforts is also an important component of the empowerment process. This means that group members are empowered from the earliest planning and participate in such processes as the identification of needs, as discussed earlier (Breton, 2004).

In helping to negotiate a change between the group members and their environment, the role of the social worker is to collaborate with the members to mediate between the members and the entities or issues within their environment that creates oppression or injustice (Hudson, 2009). For example, the social worker is thus viewed as a "co-activist" working along with the group to achieve their goals. Such an approach works with many types of group interventions, including social goals/action and reciprocal mutual aid groups.

Recall Georgia's situation from Chapter 1; Georgia experienced intimate partner violence and after working with a social worker individually, she joined an empowerment group with other women who had been in violent relationships. This group supported Georgia's personal needs for esteem and dignity, offered her the opportunity to expand her interpersonal skills and connections, and opened the door to analyze and take action in the wider context of societal institutions that both sustain and challenge the status quo (see Donaldson, 2004). The quote from another survivor of intimate partner violence, Marcy, which appears at the beginning of this chapter, shows us just how powerful the group process can be.

Narrative Theory and Group Interventions

Building on a strengths- and empowerment-focused engagement and assessment process, a narrative approach in intervening with groups continues to emphasize not only the collaboration between the client and social worker, but the collaboration among group members as well. A narrative-oriented group intervention requires the social worker and members to listen to the voices of each member and aid in the deconstruction and reconstruction of the individual or group story. In the case of a mutual aid or therapy group, the stories will be individual, but in a social goals/action group, the "story" may be the group's story. Reshaping individual or group perceptions sets in motion a plan for members to achieve the unique outcome desired by the individual group member(s). The group members can then contribute to individual or group change process by brainstorming and processing the members' motivations, options, and behaviors.

One of the hallmarks of the narrative approach is the use of witness groups and community supports. **Witness groups** are people called together by the social worker to serve as "witnesses" to discussions between the social worker and the client and/or among the group members. In the case of a group intervention, the witness group is already in place to serve in this capacity. Known as the outside-witness group, these people provide feedback to the social worker and individual group member based on the dialogue they have just heard (Morgan, 2000). Such feedback can include questions, observations, and interpretations. The individual receiving the feedback then has the opportunity to ask questions and respond. This process aids in the development of an alternative approach to the client's current dilemma or concern.

The strategy of using "insider" knowledge (i.e., hearing from others with similar life experiences) is a staple of the narrative approach. This practice strategy is well suited for use with a group intervention, particularly if the group members share similar life experiences and are at different phases of their experiences. For example, Hall (2011) describes a narrative approach in use with a group of males who have battered their partners. Using narrative strategies, the group leader was able to work with the group members to address issues of male power, privilege, and entitlement by externalizing the violence outside of the individual. Using this technique, the males in the group were able to gain insight into the origins of their belief systems (also known as principle of least contest), thus freeing them to determine if they wished to continue their behavior or change (Hall, 2011, p. 180). Such understanding promotes responsibility for choice and, ultimately, assuming responsibility for one's choices. As noted in Chapter 8, narrative approaches are also well suited for application with other theoretical frameworks.

Solution-Focused Group Interventions

Solution-focused interventions with groups are similar to family interventions. While a group of family members and a group of unrelated people may be of similar size, have a common area of concern, and identify similar goals, the dynamics of interpersonal interactions will likely differ. Family members have a history together, while the members of a group intervention do not typically have an existing relationship that shares the intensity, commitment, or future orientation of a family group. Nonetheless, much of the knowledge and skills that you can attain for working with families can be applied to a solution-focused group intervention with a formed group.

To set the stage for implementing a group intervention from the solution-focused perspective, think about the work accomplished during the individual client engagement and assessment phases of group work. During the beginning phases of group work, you collaborated with the clients through a series of questions to identify desired new realities and available strengths and resources that can be mobilized to achieve the clients' goals for change (De Jong, 2009). For the intervention plan, you can continue to build on the questions from the assessment phase by asking the clients to consider again the "miracle," "exceptions," and "scaling" questions to solidify the plan for change. While the questions are posed to individual group members, the entire group is a resource for development of a plan for change. Not only can the members contribute to the development, implementation, and evaluation of individual change plans, they can continue to be a resource throughout the change process through their own questions, observations, and experiences. Once the plan is developed and underway, you can incorporate questions to monitor the members' progress by asking group members to describe changes they are experiencing (i.e., "what's better?").

As noted throughout the discussions of solution-focused interventions with individuals, families, and groups, this approach is used in conjunction with other approaches (e.g., narrative therapy and cognitive behavioral approaches) to enhance the effectiveness and accountability of interventions. De Jong and Berg (2013) suggest that social workers implement a solution-focused intervention with a group after becoming competent with solution-focused work with individuals and families. In practice, it may be easier and more effective to start by using this approach with individual or small family client systems before attempting to manage a larger scale group intervention with which you are not yet comfortable or proficient.

The solution-focused group intervention is particularly well-suited for a variety of client populations and settings. With an emphasis on highlighting positive changes in the client's life and individualized treatment plans developed by the client, this intervention has shown promising outcomes with adults, adolescents, and children and with clients who are not voluntarily participating in the group (Greene & Lee, 2011). Used with adults who are incarcerated, in mental health settings (in- and out-patient), and substance abuse treatment programs, solution-focused interventions "can often be like doing individual therapy in front of a group" (Greene & Lee, 2011, p. 203).

Equally as promising is the integration of solution-focused group interventions with adolescents and children. Attributes of the solution-focused intervention that make it a desirable choice for teens and children are the brief time-limited format, its flexibility, future-oriented focus, de-emphasis on problem "talk," and the ability to build the intervention around a specific topic or theme (Greene & Lee, 2011).

Developmental Models

One of the classic theoretical perspectives on group work, the **developmental model**, is defined by the assumption that the group members (individually and collectively) grow and change as the group process unfolds. Developmental models assume that the group changes and grows in semi-predictable ways. This assumption does not mean the group goes through a rigid progression but rather a series of ripening relationships in which members are perhaps ambivalent about joining at the beginning, then jockey for position within the membership, grow closer together through the work of the group, establish differences from one another, and finally separate at the group's ending. This perspective reflects the idea of stages (also referred to as phases) and has been extremely influential in contemporary group work. Developmental models are still the norm in many practice contexts and are frequently very useful in alerting the worker to possible dynamics, gauging what is happening, and thinking about how to intervene. Two different models—the Boston Model and the relational model—are examined here.

Boston Model   First developed at Boston University's School of Social Work, the **Boston Model** (Garland, Jones, & Kolodny, 1965) has remained a prominent feature in social work education and particularly in practice. The Boston Model outlines five stages of group development: preaffiliation, power and control, intimacy, differentiation, and separation.

- During **preaffiliations** members may feel some ambivalence or reservations about joining the group as well as excitement and eagerness. For example, someone joining a support group for people diagnosed with an illness may be eager to connect with others who have a similar experience, while wondering if she or he will find others who share experiences, fears, and needs.

• In the **power and control stage**, members vie with each other and with the social worker for influence and status within the group. Continuing with the support group for the newly diagnosed person, members who are further along in their illness, treatment, or recovery may perceive themselves as having more status and influence within the group than those members who are recently diagnosed.

• **Intimacy** occurs when the members, having worked through their power issues, become closely connected; they may seem more homogeneous than at any other time in the group. Having processed the issues of power and control, the support can begin to bond around their common life experiences. Members will often share coping strategies and develop relationships outside of the group sessions to help each other through crises.

• During **differentiation** members feel they are safe enough to express and value the differences among each other and the worker; the homogeneity of the former phase matures into a respect for difference. Returning to the illness support group, members may gain enough comfort with one another that they can confront one another on such issues as difference of opinion, coping behaviors, or lack of compliance. Such confrontation can occur successfully only when members have reached a point of mutual respect for one another.

• In the final stage, **separation**, members begin to withdraw from the group in anticipation of its ending. Members of an illness support group may separate as they finish treatment, recover, or learn the illness is terminal.

Although the creators of the Boston Model propose a general progression through these stages, they do not assume that progress will occur as a rigidly linear sequence. There are likely to be points in the life of a group in which one or more members seem to loop back to the behavior common to a previous stage or tend to jump ahead to another one. See Quick Guide 27 to learn how the developmental stages have been applied to three different group populations. While these phases of group process are not typically associated with task groups, one could argue they are in fact, relevant for working with tasks groups as task groups form, bond, and progress through similar relationship-building stages as client groups.

Other authors have created models of group development in which the stages divide slightly differently, and some have additional substages. The group population also influences the degree to which members progress through the phases and the way in which they progress. For example, in an adaptation applied to older institutionalized residents in a group, Kelly and Berman-Rossi (1999) found that

QUICK GUIDE 27 THREE MODELS FOR STAGES OF GROUP DEVELOPMENT BASED ON THE BOSTON MODEL PROTOTYPE

	BOSTON PROTOTYPE	FEMINIST	FEMALE ADOLESCENT FOSTER CARE GROUP	OLDER INSTITUTIONALIZED PERSONS: FLOOR GROUP
	Garland, Jones & Kolodny, 1965	*Schiller, 1995, 1997*	*Lee & Berman-Rossi, 1999*	*Berman-Rossi & Kelly, 1997*
Stage 1	Preaffiliation	Preaffiliation	Preaffiliation: • Approach-Avoidance • Power and Control	Approach-Avoidance
Stage 2	Power and Control	Establishment of a Relational Base	Intimacy and Flight	Intimacy
Stage 3	Intimacy	Mutuality and Interpersonal Empathy	Differentiation	Power and Control 1: Challenging the Institution
Stage 4	Differentiation	Challenge and Change	Termination	Power and Control 2: Challenging theWorker
Stage 5	Termination	Termination		Differentiation & Empowerment

Adapted from Berman-Rossi & Kelly, 2003

separate stages emerged in which the members first challenged the institution and then challenged the worker. In an empowerment-oriented group (Lee & Berman-Rossi, 1999), adolescent girls in foster care demonstrated an impulse to take flight rather then enter the intimacy stage which may be a result of their family history of chaos and separation).

As with the selection of any intervention approach, professionals must consider the needs of the group and the model or approach that will best serve those needs. With its emphasis on power and control, the Boston Model may be most appropriately used with group members that are more comfortable with competition, power, and conflict (e.g., younger groups) and groups that can move quickly and with independence (Schiller, 2007).

Relational Model This model derives from feminist theorists and practitioners who have objected to the exclusion of women in developmental theory-building. For example, many feminists challenge Erik Erikson's famous male-normed psychosocial sequence of life stages on grounds that he has stereotyped girls as being concerned with "inner space" and boys with "outer space." Some feminists believe the intimacy stage, a clearly relational dimension, actually precedes the identity stage in girls, which reverses Erikson's order. Over two decades ago, Carol Gilligan (1993) suggested that the identity and intimacy stages are intertwined in girls.

The feminist orientation to the importance of relational aspects of development offers a different emphasis for women and girls and appears in group work models as well. Although the **relational model** incorporates stage development, the model also proposes that women go through stages that are different from those of the Boston Model. The second and third stages reflect the emphasis on relationships that are established before the conflict, or challenge, stage. The original model is posed as follows (Schiller 1995; 1997; 2003):

- *Preaffiliation:* Members experience ambivalence about joining.

- *Establishment of a relational base:* Members build strong, affective connections with others.

- *Mutuality and interpersonal empathy:* The connections deepen into a commitment to mutual aid.

- *Challenge and change:* Differences are recognized, and the connections may change in nature.

- *Termination:* Members conclude their work and separate.

This model is useful in feminist groups or in groups composed mainly of women because it supports one of the more accepted gender constructions relating to women's development and theory (Lesser et al., 2004): the importance of established relationship and relational patterns as a precursor to engagement in challenge, such as self-advocacy, or taking risks previously not attempted. Specifically, women benefit in a group environment when they are able to develop relationships with other women who share life experiences and/or are similar to one another. Creating connections can enable women to feel secure and safe within the group, leading to a comfort in sharing with others (Lesser et al., 2004). A relational approach may also be applicable for other groups who may have experienced oppression or displacement, and for which confrontation is not motivating (e.g., immigrants and refugees) (Schiller, 2007).

Relationships and connections are clearly at the heart of this model of group intervention. Thus, a key role for the social worker leading a relational group is to help empower group members to feel safe so they may then move into the phases of the group process in which they take risks and address areas of concern (Schiller, 2007).

There are many valid theories and perspectives that can be used to guide group interventions. Each social worker must determine the theoretical perspective that is

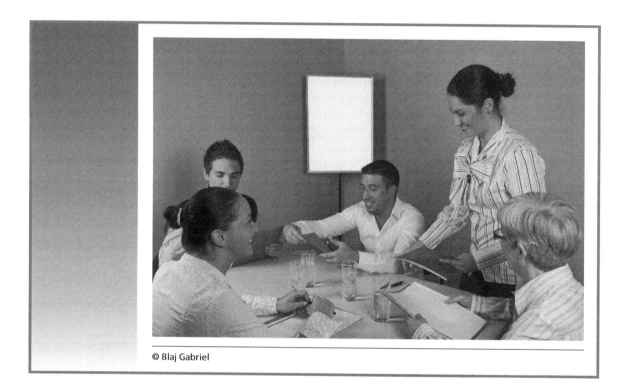

© Blaj Gabriel

most compatible with her or his philosophy and professional and personal value systems, given the agency structures and guidelines and funding sources. Along with comfort level, the practitioner must develop competency in the approach(es) they choose. Regardless of which theory you choose, demonstrating competency through practice behaviors is essential.

CONTEMPORARY TRENDS AND SKILLS FOR THE MIDDLE PHASE OF GROUP WORK: INTERVENTION

The middle phase of the group experience is when the social worker, the client, and the entire group implement the plan to work toward their goals. The social worker and group move into a pattern of interaction in which cohesion, unity, integration, trust, and communication are all enhanced (Macgowan, 2008, p. 284). The primary function of the middle, or intervention, phase of group work is to carry out goals. The *Standards for Social Work Practice with Groups* (IASWG, 2006) provides guidelines for organizing this phase of work and identifying skills needed:

1. Support progress toward individual and group goals—having established both individual and group goals in the assessment phase, the members can

plan and implement the steps needed to accomplish the goals. The social worker must be attentive to the need for goals to be re-negotiated during this phase of work.

2. Attend to group dynamics and processes—the social worker must be vigilant in her or his ongoing observations of group dynamics and processes. As group members become familiar with one another, they may feel more confident confronting one another, which can create conflict within the group. Moreover, the social worker must be mindful of alliances that form within the group and outside the group and the impact of those relationships on individual and group functioning.

3. Identify and access resources within and outside the group—as the work phase progresses, the social worker should know of and have access to resources that may be helpful to the members of the group or the entire group.

4. Have knowledge, skills, and other resources of group work, group members, and sources outside the group—the social worker may encounter situations, dynamics, and needs (e.g., group member conflicts, non-compliance with rules, or needs unable to be met by a group experience) within the intervention phase that require additional knowledge, skills, or resources that can be gained through researching, consulting with colleagues, and even conferring with the group members themselves.

5. Use evidence-based practice techniques in facilitating the group—the social worker is responsible for familiarizing herself or himself with the research available for the type of the group intervention with which they are working.

Examining the literature for evidence-based group interventions can help your group practice. Having both quantitative and qualitative evidence to support the "best available" practices is known as **evidence-based group work** (EBGW) (Macgowan, 2009a, pp. 132–133). Using rigor, impact, and applicability as the criteria for determining the strength of the evidence, EBGW enhances practice and policy accountability, enables social workers to improve practice competencies using empirically validated tools and research outcomes, and ultimately bolsters the efficacy of the group intervention. Crafting an evidence-based approach to implementing and evaluating a group intervention includes seven principles outlined in Exhibit 9.1. While the group format and the social worker's role can vary during this phase of work, a set of practice behaviors exist to facilitate the "work" phase of group practice.

Social Work Group Interventions

As we discussed in Chapter 8, there are four types of groups within which practitioners often work: task groups; social action/goals groups; reciprocal groups (including psychoeducational groups and support groups); and remedial groups. These groups often have overlapping outcomes. For example, the support group educates, the psychoeducational group empowers, the social goals group supports, and all deal with some aspect of social justice, diversity, or human rights, as each issue and

EXHIBIT 9.1

Principles for Evidence-based Group Work

When reviewing the research on approaches to group interventions, consider the following principles:

(1) The way in which client needs and strengths were assessed;
(2) Identification of desired outcomes;
(3) Risks involved in various approaches;
(4) Compliance with the intervention plan;
(5) Client responses to intervention;
(6) Assessment of outcomes; and
(7) Distinction between individual and group outcomes.

Source: Comer & Meier, 2011, pp. 464–470

population represents some dimension of exclusion, which in turn leads to unmet needs and violation of rights (see Goodman, 2004).

At the same time that group work has many traditional approaches in full use today, it also reflects, as does the profession as a whole, the sociocultural context of the times. Accordingly, several innovations in working with groups reflect current theoretical, political, and social issues. Two contemporary issues that the profession has addressed through group work models are intimate partner violence, with constructionist groups, and new approaches to corrections or crime restitution, through restorative justice groups. Each of these will be discussed as an example of a constructivist approach to group intervention.

Each of the efforts described here represents a vital, responsive attempt to counter the negative effects of a contemporary social issue, and each demonstrates creativity and courage. Note that these are living works in progress and as such may not be proven effective, and many conclude with recommendations to improve the experience. Although they are based on recognized social work perspectives and guided by research inquiries, they will no doubt evolve and be fine-tuned as they undergo evaluation procedures to gauge effectiveness and pinpoint the need for change. They take risks in forging new territory and reflect group work's potential.

Constructionist Groups for Women Experiencing Intimate Partner Violence
A **constructionist group** is a group intervention that is facilitated from a social constructionist perspective. This approach requires the facilitator to recognize that reality is created through shared meanings, and offers members the opportunity to develop new understandings of themselves through the group process. A constructionist group intervention embodies feminist and narrative theories as well as the postmodern notion of the way in which a person develops a new and preferred **representation of the self**, or a new view of her or his own worth and identity. In this feminist group, the members accomplish their new representations of the self

by resisting and protesting the male violence they have experienced. The work of the group includes three processes: (1) revealing and undermining the oppressive discourse relating to women experiencing violence, which is a *political* process; (2) identifying and detailing the protest that women actually use in response to violence, the recognition of which reflects *change*; and (3) reconstructing the identities of participants based on the protest. These activities work together to promote first the seeking of resistance (i.e., confronting difficult issues) then an anchoring of resistance (i.e., identifying potential change), culminating in the telling of a new story that elaborates a new identity (Roche & Wood, 2005). This last process is celebrated in an empowering **"definitional ceremony"** (Wood & Roche, 2001a, p. 17), which allows the women to present to an audience of people important to them their new understandings of self. The definitional ceremony includes a first telling of the story by the group member with a response from a witness, followed by the witness re-telling the story, and finalized by the original speaker re-telling the story incorporating the new insights provided by the witness (Leahy, O'Dwyer, & Ryan, 2012).

To illustrate, the social worker in this group points out the common themes of the women's conversation relating to their reactions to violence. For example, some women adopt a socially imposed understanding, which incorporates shame and guilt when male partners are violent toward them. They believe that their own shortcomings cause violence against them and that they are responsible for changing their behaviors in exchange for safety. After a period of time in which the social worker expresses support for the woman, the worker can then help to counter the woman's feelings of shame and guilt by asking perspectival questions that help to break the logic of self-deprecation (for example, "What would your sister say about the way Mike treats you?" "What did the court say about this?"). Such questioning over time encourages a focus on multiple realities by helping women see that others would not think they "deserved" violence or "had it coming," or should "just put up with it."

At this point the social worker seeks descriptions from the women in the group regarding their actual responses, that is, the ways they have resisted and protested. Protest may be in the form of simply not accepting the negative statements made by the batterer, or it may be considerably more confrontational, such as obtaining a restraining order. Some protests may be viewed as passive (giving older bread and milk to an abusive partner while saving fresher food for a child). These incidences of protest, however they are expressed, begin to form the basis for a new understanding of the self as a person of agency who can make real and meaningful life changes.

Group members ask where a woman got her ideas for the protest or the courage to carry it out, and they also consider what the protest says about her. These explorations challenge the woman's identity as helpless and worthless as they lead to a new view. The social worker and other group members then anchor this new more positive representation through reinforcement. The members do this by seeking to enrich the story through the woman's further detailed description, and finally they celebrate her new identity as she sees it through a definitional ceremony to be created collectively by the woman, the group members, and the social worker.

Through an emphasis on process rather than group stages, this group is committed to helping the women in its membership discover the other side of their survivorship and become who they want to be.

New models like this one, based on narrative ideas of the story and constructionist ideas of self, are highly useful in political contexts that highlight contemporary views on gender and power relationships. They are especially applicable with groups addressing sexual assault, intimate partner violence, relationship issues, and in community mental health centers.

Restorative Justice Groups for Combating Crime   In another response to a contemporary phenomenon, in this case the climate of punishment and stricter approaches to criminal offenders, social workers have been among those advocating for a different strategy. Seeing the criminal justice system as bogged down in practices that neither heal nor rehabilitate, scholars and practitioners have developed an approach thought to be both more relevant and responsive to the issues of offenders as well as survivors, particularly in cases involving gendered violence against women (see van Wormer, 2009). A loosely associated collection of strategies called **restorative justice groups** focus on crime as an interpersonal conflict that has repercussions on the victim, offender, and community at large. The emphasis is more on the harm done to the relationships of those hurt, and their restoration (see, for example, Boyes-Watson, 2005), than on the violation of the law (Lovell, Helfgott, & Lawrence, 2002) or on the impact on women (van Wormer, 2009). The involvement of the community as an invested party in the occurrence of crime is an important focus: the community suffers when its members are engaged in crime through damage to property and relationships, and the community benefits when relationships are restored.

Based on an actual series of groups conducted at the Washington State Reformatory, the purpose of the groups was to address: (1) offender accountability, (2) the rights of victims, and (3) citizen involvement in the justice process in a way that balanced all three. The major work of the three groups was accomplished through the story of each participant's personal crime experience. Each week one victim, one offender, and one community member shared their personal accounts. Such storytelling increases understanding, validates experience, reduces isolation, and increases the vision for change. Group participants then determined how offenders could respond to the needs of individual victims and what needed to be done to repair the harm done.

The group progress and process variables of these groups were seen as largely consistent with classic models of developmental group work theory (that is, there was initial anxiety and a stage of conflict, followed by greater connectedness) but were also influenced by individual members so that each of the three group meetings reflected different stages of development. A number of additional obstacles to the development of group unity were noted, such as the emphasis on crime, the large number of participants, emotional fragility of participants, problematic group dynamics at times, safety concerns, confidentiality issues, and the implications of diversity, among others. This emphasis on an alternative strategy to respond to crime that heals and helps people reconnect with each other holds encouraging promise in a society struggling with the alienation of both victims and perpetrators. A recent addition to this concept is the enactment of Neighborhood Activity Boards. In many communities, groups of volunteers come together to meet with first-time, non-violent offenders and those people victimized by the criminal activity to discuss the impact of the crime. The offender is typically required to complete community service along with participating in the impact panel.

Motivational Interviewing   As discussed in Chapters 5 and 7 in the context of working with individuals and families, motivational interviewing (MI) is an approach that can be introduced into the group setting as well. Known as GMI (group motivational interviewing), implementing an MI-focused group is built on the same premise of engagement, focus, evoking and planning, GMI, in particular, requires the facilitator to emphasize collaboration, autonomy, support, and empathy through the use of reflective listening and change talk (Hohman, 2012). MI scholars, Miller and Rollnick (2013), support the use of MI with a range of group interventions but offer two cautionary notes: 1) the group leader should be competent in the facilitation of MI with individuals before attempting to incorporate it into a group experience; and 2) due to the larger number of participants, there will be fewer opportunities for change talk which may result in less predictable outcomes.

Social Work Skills for Group Interventions

While all theoretical models require skills, and group work interventions may seem different from one-to-one models in social work settings, many of the same generalist practice roles and skills of individual and family interventions are not only applicable but vital to group work interventions. When working to maintain a group-centered focus during the intervention, you will find that listening, supporting, and empathizing all have as important a place in group work as they do in work with individuals. While the following section provides a more in-depth discussion of specific skill areas needed for group interventions, Exhibit 9.2 provides a comprehensive list of general skills that are important to remember when intervening at the group level.

Here are some additional skills critical to group practice, adapted from the authors' practice experience as well as Brown, (2013), IASWG (2006) and Middleman and Wood (1990, pp. 96–102):

Leadership

- Maintaining a **"thinking group"** posture assumes an orientation in which you, as the social worker, consider the group-as-a-whole first and individual members second. This concentration on the whole can require a paradigm shift from thinking of the individual exclusively. For example, you may avoid

EXHIBIT 9.2

Skills for Group-level Interventions

When working with groups of any type, a diverse array of skills are needed, including:

1) Understand your relationship to your agency and the way in which you both fit within the context of the larger community.
2) Understand the flow of group work from beginnings through endings.
3) Interact with group members with cultural awareness and sensitivity.
4) Be prepared to advocate for individual clients, the group, and your agency.
5) Practice within the ethical guidelines of the profession.
6) Help the group to establish adaptive norms.
7) Ensure that self-disclosure is consistent with agency policy and meets the needs of the group (as opposed to you).
8) Use of self can help reflection and role modeling for the group.
9) In working with group members to establish goals, ensure they are consistent with the purpose of the group.
10) Regularly seek feedback from the group regarding members' feelings about the group and the process.
11) Collaborate with group members to identify short- and long-term goals.
12) Clarify members' perceptions of time, particularly in terms of change.
13) Provide information to group members that is relevant to the purpose of the group (e.g., medical/health information or legal processes).
14) Be able and willing to say you lack information when that is the case.
15) Incorporate a variety of strategies and techniques into the group process (e.g., art projects, role-playing, relaxation exercises, or videos, speakers, or exercises).
16) Promote expression of feelings within the group.
17) Demonstrate your respect for the group when feelings are shared—active listening, reflecting, and tracking are strategies for showing your interest.
18) Normalize group members' feelings.
19) Engage members on a cognitive level (i.e., thoughts and feelings).
20) Be willing to incorporate past experiences and family history to help group members connect with emotions.
21) Partialize the presenting issues to enable group members to avoid feelings of being overwhelmed.
22) Use confrontation with individuals and the group when needed for issues related to compliance or engagement, for example.
23) Maintain the focus on the present, including use of events in the media to emphasize human nature and social justice.
24) Offer strategies for resolving interpersonal conflicts.
25) Model empathy and use of "I" statements and contracts.
26) Promote member self-esteem and competence.

Source: Adapted Greif & Ephross, 2011, pp. 489–493

a prolonged exchange with a single group member because that focus hinders the group's communication.

- **Balanced leadership** can challenge social workers who believe they must have control of the group and its agenda or it will explode or become chaotic. In actuality, if the social worker allows the group to evolve without close attention to process, it *can* become chaotic, members may be emotionally hurt, or the group fragments and loses its meaning for the members. The social worker's ability to effectively facilitate depends on many factors: group connection, functioning, and the presence of internal or **indigenous leadership**; that is, leadership that evolves within the membership.

Generally, the social worker is more directive in the early stages of groups, in groups with lower-functioning members, in groups with little indigenous leadership, in open-ended groups, and in task-oriented groups. As the group progresses, the social worker role is to retreat and encourage growth in group ownership of the activity. The key here for any social worker is to recognize group needs and to be flexible with respect to the degree of direct leadership used. The overall goal for group workers is typically to reduce their activity to as little as possible while maintaining self-awareness and a safe environment and encouraging members to be in charge of their own group.

- **Scanning** is a strategy for maintaining visual observation of all members—the "group version of the attending skill."

- Maintaining **cohesiveness**, or connectedness, means sustaining a sense of "we" through language, encouragement of rituals (for example, marking the beginning and end of each meeting in a specific way), and recording the group's progress. When groups have too much or too little cohesiveness, the leader can address the issue in an effort to uncover the causes (e.g., group member anxiety) (Berg, Landreth, & Fall, 2013). These skills contribute to group members' spirit and facilitate a sense of belonging to something significant. Development and recording (through a chart on the wall, for example) of group agreed-upon norms or customs contributes to a sense of connection, as well.

- Assisting group members in making progress toward goals through support, programmatic activities, addressing obstacles, assessing progress, and re-contracting for goal achievement, as needed.

- Promoting development of mutual aid; may involve re-review of group norms and values and conflict resolution.

- Reviewing and reiterating definitions and rules related to confidentiality with the group, particularly related to sharing information about other group members outside of the group meetings.

Communication

- You must carefully choose the patterns of communication used in your group. If you respond only to the members who speak up, there is likely to be a subset of members who are marginalized and excluded. On the other hand, if you always go around the group, member by member, some members will feel pressed to contribute, and all will feel a certain amount of routinization. A more effective approach is to encourage a respectful balance so that all members can have their opportunity to speak without any one member dominating. Alternatively, you may choose to invite participation by all members (especially those members who remain quiet) and ask if others in the group think or feel the way this (currently speaking) member does. Remind members periodically of the group's commitment by verbalizing the norms that the membership agreed upon, and emphasize the group's accomplishments and history when appropriate.

- Responding empathetically is a critical skill in the context of the group intervention that requires the group leader to: focus on the person speaking, restricting questioning to only those areas that need clarification, allow the group member to finish speaking, and resisting the temptation to provide your own answers to client situations.

- A challenging group work intervention skill is **redirection**, or redirecting questions and concerns away from you back to the group or to individual members. For example, some members will continue to address you over time as the source of authority for the group. Given the power dynamic that many group members may have experienced as clients in other services, such behaviors are not unexpected. By the same token, some members may complain about other members through a third party (often you). In both these situations, the social worker can redirect the message. The goal is to facilitate direct, constructive, communication within the group and the environment that supports it. Exhibit 9.3 provides an example of a redirection within a group using the two scenarios mentioned here.

- Establishing both consensus and difference occurs when you invite agreement and disagreement on issues (e.g., the visitor issue). Registering dissent in a group that approves something heartily, particularly for a person who has not been highly vocal, can be challenging. Early and strong feelings of connectedness and strong group bonds can make that dissent even harder. Later, as the group matures, expressions of difference should be less troublesome to members, but continue to support difference and encourage others' capacities to respond.

- **Exercising silence** can be challenging. If the facilitator is talking, members cannot. The group should engage in most of the interchange and frequently

Following is an example that you, as the group facilitator, can use to redirect a group session in which one member of the group appears to be leading the group in a different direction:

A member asks if visitors can attend a group meeting. That issue has not been previously addressed, so you submit the question to the full membership. In this instance, you turn the question back to the group:

"How do others see this question?" or "How do you as a group want to handle this?"

Within this response you may also want to invite quieter members to participate while softening the messages of the louder voices.

A second scenario involves one member of the group complaining about another member. In this scenario, you may simply say,

"Why don't you tell Bernice that?" or "I don't think you need my help in talking to Kate about that."

EXHIBIT 9.3

When Redirection is Needed in Group Work

can be supported in achieving that by the social worker's well-placed silence, which allows the communication patterns of members to develop.

Problem Solving

- **Connecting progress to goals** Summarizing progress, identifying options, prioritizing decisions, mediating conflicts, confronting lack of progress and group interactions, and weighing potential outcomes are skills and activities that a social worker employs in problem-solving during the intervention phase of group work. On occasion, the social worker may have to negotiate an amended contract with the individual members or the entire group. The social worker may also identify the next discussion areas for future group meetings.

- **Locating resources to benefit group members** involves the mutual identification of resources for group members and accentuating inclusion of natural assets (e.g., friends, family, or neighbors) into the helping network that may also include services, and emphasizing the connections between the group and the community. Engaging in a joint discussion with and among members early in the process conveys the expectation that the group has both the ability and the responsibility to deal constructively with its own issues. As resources outside the group are identified, the potential network expands for all members and supports the interdependence between members, groups, and the environment.

- **Making use of group process and problem solving** The tension between the needs of individual group members and those of the group as a whole is the substance of social work practice with groups. Negotiating differences and the creative enrichment that is possible from the process are the greatest values of the effort. The goal then becomes the reconciliation of difference through a genuine compromise that benefits both the individual and the group. One of the group's clearest responsibilities is to establish an acceptable expression and appreciation for difference. Consider an example, described in a social worker's notes of the eighth meeting of a socialization group of 12-year-old girls, who were referred by their school as having a "rocky time" both at home and in adjusting to middle school life.

The girls were bustling around preparing crepe paper streamers and searching for birthday candles, giggling, joking about how old Lila was really going to be. Some said she was probably going to be 60 or so, judging by how glum she had seemed last week about the party they were planning. Lila was late, and when she finally showed up, she looked more miserable than ever. Finally, she blurted out, "I HATE BIRTHDAYS!!" in a voice very unlike her usual somber tones. The other girls were horrified and silent for a moment—almost unheard of in this group. Lila started to cry. Finally, she choked out the story: Her mother had died the night before her birthday two years ago, and she didn't know how to tell anybody in the group that before. The very word "birthday" was a terrible reminder. She didn't want to celebrate.

The girls seemed to feel sorry, they liked Lila, but they also really wanted to celebrate birthdays in this group. It was an important ritual for them. I confess I didn't have a clue what to do, as their facilitator. After a moment, Betsy, whose grandmother came from France, cheerfully volunteered, "Well, let's be trés français in this group and say we're celebrating our anniversaries! That's what the French call them, the anniversary of birth!" The others responded loudly, hoping their ritual was rescued from certain demise. Lila was silent. She looked up. Finally she almost smiled and said, "I think that would work." And that was that. The group took on a "French theme" ever after and was the only group of 12-year-olds I ever knew that celebrated their anniversaries!

Management of Group Function and Process Inherent in all effective social work interventions is the social worker's ability to interact competently with the client systems. Encompassed within those interactions is an awareness of the spectrum of potential roles that are represented by both the social worker and the group members. Social worker roles with groups have been highlighted throughout this and the previous chapter, but will be summarized here followed by an overview of the roles displayed by group members that social workers in group practice may encounter.

Social Worker Roles While the social worker's primary role is to provide leadership for the group intervention, this role often encompasses a range of roles and skills in order to be effective. The type, format, and goals of the group may determine the role that the social worker will play. The social work group practitioner may find her or himself needing to function in one or more of the following roles (Berg et al., 2013; Furman et al., 2009; Collins & Lazzari, 2009, pp. 299–302; Reid, 2002, pp. 435–436):

- Serving as a **facilitator** requires the social worker to invite sharing and participation, reframe and link issues, and maintaining group boundaries and rules to promote appropriate interactions. The facilitative role requires the social worker to be a skilled listener as well. In a task group, the role of the facilitator may include setting the agenda, maintaining the group's focus on the tasks, and providing documentation of the meeting. Regardless of the group setting, the social worker should strive to maintain an ongoing awareness of the "unconscious group process" (i.e., understanding issues that permeate the group's functioning) (Levy, 2011, p. 155).

- The social worker in the **synthesizer** role summarizes the group members' discussions, identifies themes and patterns, and connects content from one session to the next to promote continuity and substantive discussion.

- **Norm setting** is demonstrated when the social worker provides information regarding appropriate group member behavior through role modeling and direct feedback. For example, the social worker establishes appropriate group interaction by encouraging the use of direct interactions, use of "I" statements, appropriate challenges, and concrete examples, and helping to set the rules at the beginning of the group. Part of norm setting includes the issue of self-disclosure, which can be challenging for many, including the group facilitator. As the leader, you can appropriately share information about yourself as well as suggest group activities that focus on attitudes, values, and beliefs as opposed to more threatening exercises that emphasize sensitive content areas.

- Social workers functioning as **educators** or teachers within a group setting find themselves providing factual information and content specific to the goals of the group.

- As group leaders, social workers can empower group members through promoting **self-advocacy** that can be applied both inside and outside of the group setting. In fact, the group can serve as a place for members to rehearse their newly learned self-advocacy skills.

- As with social work practice with individuals and families, social workers may **collaborate** with another professional. In group work, co-leadership is often an effective strategy in group intervention that involves equal commitment, motivation, and vision and builds on the strengths that each of the leaders brings to the intervention.

Group Member Roles Group members bring their unique characteristics and traits to the group experience regardless of the type of group or its purpose. These qualities can be experienced by the social worker as both strengths and challenges. Ideally, group members will be open to new information, growth, and change, and will be willing and able to actively participate in the group process (Furman et al., 2009). While such characteristics and qualities as these are obvious strengths, even challenging behaviors can be reframed and used for positive individual and group outcomes. If you observe behaviors that suggest that the individual is being resistant (e.g., unwillingness to engage or exhibiting disruptive behaviors), you may be encountering a lack of trust or sense of insecurity (Berg et al., 2013). See Quick Guide 28 for a list of questions that may be helpful in managing resistance.

The social worker can set the stage for appropriate group member interactions by incorporating expectations for appropriate group interactions and responses into the beginning phases of the group intervention, but may still have to work with challenging interactions that result from personality characteristics that are likely to emerge within the group process.

There are some group member roles that commonly emerge within a group intervention. As individual personalities emerge, they will influence and interact with the dynamics of the group itself (much like the dynamics of the family interaction). The competent group practitioner can thus begin to anticipate these roles and behaviors and, having previously considered these possibilities, be prepared with an appropriate response. You must exercise caution, however, to ensure that you do not generalize or stereotype the group member behaviors, but respond to each person as unique. Four of the potentially challenging group member roles and possible social worker responses that you can expect include the following (adapted from Berg et al., 2013; Furman et al., 2009; Yalom & Leszcz, 2005, pp. 391–405):

- The "silent" group member is challenging because it is difficult to determine if the individual is not speaking because she or he is not engaged or is uncomfortable or intimidated, and thus not able to benefit from the group experience. Silence does not necessarily mean that the person is not engaged. While it is possible to experience vicarious gains without active engagement, the social worker typically strives to turn the reticent group member into an active participant. Inviting the individual to participate, noting non-verbal gestures, and speaking with the member outside of the group about her or his silence are all strategies for promoting participation. Should these strategies result in continued lack of participation, the social worker has the option to allow the individual to continue as silent in the group or to develop an alternative intervention outside the group for the individual. As you consider the way in which you are going to address the silence, take into account the responses from the other group members.

QUICK GUIDE 28   LIST OF QUESTIONS THAT MAY BE HELPFUL IN MANAGING RESISTANCE

If you encounter a group member or members who you feel are being resistant to engaging in the group process, consider the following questions:

1. What is the nature (e.g., behavior and attitudes) of the resistance?
2. Are such behaviors as monopolizing or joking disrupting group function and process?
3. How does resistance impact other areas of the individual's life?
4. How are other group members responding to the group member displaying resistance?
5. How are you responding to the group member displaying resistance?

After reflecting on these items, your role as the group facilitator is to share your observations with the group and, collectively, brainstorm possible causation and responses.

Source: Berg, Landreth, & Fall, 2013, p. 125.

- Equally as challenging for a group leader is the "monopolizer" who is perceived as talking too much. In this role, the group member may attempt to offer her or his opinion on virtually every statement made by others or may spend an inordinate amount of time describing her or his own situation or needs. Monopolizing can present itself in different forms, including the "compulsive talker," "intellectualizer," "special interest pleader," or "manipulator," all of whom may be operating out of fear or a need to control the situation. While understanding the reasons for this person's behavior is important for changing the behavior, the impact on the group process and members can be negative. As with the "silent" group member, the social worker can address the monopolizing behavior within the group her or himself or encourage the group to address the behavior, work with the monopolizer outside the group to address the reasons she or he feels compelled to speak so frequently, or develop an alternative intervention strategy.

  Groups of individuals within the group can form sub-groups or cliques which can also monopolize the group's time and energy as well as isolate or create divisions or conflicts. Allowing the group itself to manage sub-groups when they form is ideal; the social worker can ensure that the process is fair and respectful.

- The group member who appears to reject help/ideas can be viewed as both a challenge and a resource. Such avoidant behavior can signal depression or lack of problem-solving skills. As a challenge, the "help-rejecting" or complaining group member is likely to have a negative influence on the group dynamics and be unable to experience actual change or growth. As a resource, the negative perspective can be used by the other group members to see the potential possibilities (if only as a reaction to the negativity). The social worker can respond, not to encourage the individual, but to maintain a focus on concrete feedback and the group process and can encourage the group to respond to this member as well. The leader may also seek to build trust with the member displaying avoidant behaviors.

- The "caregiver" (also known as the coordinator or rescuer) is the group member who strives to take care of others, including the group facilitator. Not surprisingly, the caregiver often neglects to attend to her or his own needs, but uses others as a way to avoid addressing individual challenges. The social worker can respond to the caregiver by acknowledging her or his history of altruistic caregiving, praising the caregiver for her or his willingness to now take care of her or his own needs, and incorporating gentle confrontation when the caregiver attempts to care for others as a way to impede personal progress.

- The "attacker" can stimulate the group by her or his assaults on other members or the facilitator, but can be disruptive as well. Acknowledging the attacker's behavior is a first step toward exploring the underlying reasons for the aggressive behaviors. Confrontation is required if the attacks become personally targeted.

- Certain "dependent" behaviors can be challenging to manage in the group setting. For example, the "harmonizer" strives to maintain peace within the group; the "clown" uses humor (often to mask depression or fear); and the "poor me" member seeks constant affirmation. As a facilitator, you can initiate a discussion focused on the styles that the members possess and the function those styles serve in their lives.

© vm

QUICK GUIDE 29   SUMMARY OF INTERVENTION SKILLS FOR
SOCIAL WORK GROUP PRACTICE

The social worker engaged in the intervention phase of social work practice with groups should be:

- knowledgeable and skilled in group leadership (e.g., logistics and time management);
- facilitating group communication and group dynamics;
- competent with individual and problem-solving;
- focused on promoting progress toward group and individual goals;
- able to manage of group functions.

As the discussion of the intervention or middle phase of the group work process comes to a close and the exploration shifts to the termination and evaluation phases of group work, a review of the skills needed for competently intervening with groups may be helpful. See Quick Guide 29 for a re-cap of the skills presented.

CONTEMPORARY TRENDS AND SKILLS FOR THE ENDING PHASE OF GROUP WORK: TERMINATION AND EVALUATION

Although all of the concepts explored in terminating (i.e., ending) and evaluating social work with individuals and families can be applied to most clients in any constellation, there are some additional considerations and dynamics that often occur in social work practice with groups. As in social work terminations and evaluations with individuals and families, the intensity of the phases of ending a group and evaluating the work depends on the type and function of its purpose.

Social Work Group Endings

Social work practice with groups ends in many ways and evokes a range of member responses and interactions. Terminations may occur when a member opts to leave the group, when the group reaches a pre-determined time limit, or when the leader leaves the group (Furman et al., 2009). Regardless of the reason for the group's termination, endings have the potential to evoke emotional responses from the members; therefore, the social worker's role in termination is to "help members examine their accomplishments, review their experience together, and prepare for the future . . . and express and integrate positive and negative emotion" (Garvin & Galinsky, 2008, pp. 291–292). Group members may experience such positive emotions as success and elation and/or such negative emotions as loss, threat, rejection, abandonment, or anger—all of which may relate both to experiences from the group and their own lives (Furman et al., 2009). The group leader may notice that group members regress back to previous behaviors, withdraw from the group, panic, or begin to devalue the group experience (Brown, 2013). For example, members of an educational group are likely to experience fewer highly emotional responses than those of a treatment group. A group that has met only six times will probably not have the level of investment in the group process as a group that has met for three years. Addressing members' responses is a part of the social worker's responsibility in helping the group to arrive at its endings. In any event, ending with groups is often a complex endeavor as you deal with endings on three different levels:

- The relationship between group members and the social worker.

- The relationships among the group members.

- The structure of the group itself.

A practitioner needs to consider the termination phase of group work from the theoretical framework they are using. We will now look at endings from the theoretical perspectives discussed earlier

Endings in Group Work with Strengths and Empowerment   Continuing with the integration of strengths and empowerment concepts into the termination phase can enable the individual members and the group to review the progress made toward their goals and develop strategies for sustaining the changes. In the case of social work groups with clients, the social worker can invite each member to review and reflect on her or his individual experience in the group, including strengths brought to the group process, status in the beginning, middle, and endings phases of work, change experienced, and plans for maintaining the change(s) while using the group's strengths. Having individual members engaged in this process provides an opportunity for the social worker and other group members to contribute to this process. Other group members can also take advantage of their fellow group members' reflections for their own review and sustainability processes.

A strengths-based perspective can further enable the social worker and the group members to reflect on the group strengths that have evolved as the group moved through various phases. The social worker can use the group ending as an opportunity to provide feedback on the changes observed in the group's engagement, cohesion, and work. Additionally, the group members can reflect on their experience being part of a strengths-focused group experience. Such a reflection can serve to empower the group members and the social worker to integrate the power of the group process.

In situations in which the individual or group goals are not realized, the formal ending of a task, social action, or client-oriented group can still be oriented toward a strengths perspective. One strategy is to engage in an exercise in which the members review the strengths that existed at the outset of the group, those strengths gained or mobilized during the group, and those strengths that can be carried on by the members after the group is terminated. While the members (and the social worker) may be dismayed by the perceived failure of not achieving their goals, planning ways in which the members can continue to work toward achieving the goals can be empowering.

Endings in Narrative-Focused Group Work With an emphasis on strengths, termination of a narrative-focused group lends itself well to the use of a ritual or ceremonial activity as well as the public acknowledgement of growth and change. Group members can continue as collaborators with one another and the social worker to plan a celebration to recognize the ending of the group's formal phase of work together. This "definitional" ceremony can acknowledge the achievement of goals and the next phase of the individual and group members' growth experience as well as help individuals to reclaim or redefine themselves (Morgan, 2000, p. 121).

As with individual and family work endings, public testimonials are a part of the termination process (Morgan, 2000). Using the group members to listen to individual testimonials and provide feedback can serve to empower the members' changes and to solidify plans for maintaining change beyond the formal group experience. A process similar to that used with individuals can be employed with groups, with the group members serving as the outsider-witnesses. The definitional ceremony begins with the social worker and group members listening as the individual group member re-authors her or his work in the group. The witnesses then reflect back to the individual re-authored story, the individual member responds to the feedback, and the entire group engages in discussion about the process. This process can be helpful both as a tool for recognizing individual and group strengths and goal attainment and to evaluate the process of change.

Endings in Solution-Focused Group Work Termination of the solution-focused group intervention can be viewed as the achievement of the initial and overall goal for the work of the group. Solution-focused group interventions identify issues and plan and begin a planned change effort. In the case of a group intervention, the other group members provide a structure for vetting the issues as well as the solutions. You will recall that solution-focused interventions are grounded in the ongoing use of a series of questions to elicit strengths, thoughts and feelings regarding change, and developing plans for change. You can bring this technique into the termination phase as well; you can ask members about the progress they've made via scaling questions (e.g., "On a scale of 1 to 10, where were you when you began this group? Where are you now? Where do you need to be in order to leave this group and maintain the change?") (De Jong, 2009). The group members can involve themselves in the individual member's response by providing their own observations of her or his change process. Shifting the emphasis from the present to the future can also empower the individual and group members to perceive themselves as separate from the group and the social worker leading the group, thus enabling them to view themselves as empowered to implement and maintain the desired changes.

Regardless of the theoretical perspective employed for the group intervention, a number of competencies are needed for effectively bringing an intervention to an end. As with all aspects of the social work intervention, groups are made of unique individuals and situations, and the social worker must be attuned to those aspects. However, there is also a set of termination-related skills specific to group practice.

Skills for Social Work Group Terminations

Just as the other phases of the group intervention have a primary function and requisite skill set, so too does the termination phase. With an emphasis on consolidating the work, the social worker focuses on bringing closure for the individual group member, the group itself, and for her or himself (IASWG, 2006; Toseland & Horton, 2008). As a result of the complexity and intensity of group endings, even those that are planned, social workers need a skill set that is reflective of the unique features of the group intervention. The social worker should recognize and attend to all the meanings that evolve (Kurland & Salmon, 1998). A particularly powerful aspect of the termination comes in the form of individual and group reflection. Group members and the facilitator have the opportunity to reflect on commonalities, differences, accomplishments, and the development of relationships, all of which can promote individual and group self-awareness (Drumm, 2006). Let's now look at each of the multiple areas related to group endings.

Ending the Relationship between Group Members and Social Worker   A more extensive examination of the ending of the relationship between group members and the social worker is warranted, as this ending, more than the other two, has implications for the social worker. In this final phase of any type of group (i.e., task or client group), the social worker has several responsibilities with respect to the entire group, including (Brown, 2013; IASWG, 2006; Furman et al., 2009; Kurland & Salmon, 1998; Toseland & Horton, 2008):

- Prepare members for ending (from the mid-point of the group intervention).

- Assess progress toward achievement of group goals.

- Help stabilize member and group gains.

- Anticipate and elicit individual and group responses to ending.

- Plan timing and content to maximize the sessions/meetings left.

- Help group members express their ambivalence about the group's ending and address individual and group reactions and behaviors to individual or group accomplishments, including affirmations and confidence building regarding achievements.

- Share observations of progress and confidence in members' abilities to function successfully without the group or in the case of a task group, continue working toward identified goals (it may be helpful to identify any obstacles to success and needed connections to resources outside the group).

- Support members' efforts to begin the process of separating from the group and identify strategies for implementing change and applying new knowledge.

- Develop awareness of ways in which individual and group change will impact systems external to the group.

- Help members connect their experiences in the group to life experiences in the future.

- Develop awareness of your own feelings regarding ending and reflect on and share feelings with the group.

- Elicit feedback from the group members about the group process.

The social worker's task is to help the group end positively and help members' achievements translate into the "real world" outside the group. The social worker also has to monitor her or his own responses; after all, she or he has invested a great deal of effort in facilitating an effective experience, and more successful groups may experience more difficult endings. Recalling the overall purpose of the group and focusing on the specifics of the process can help balance the response between task and emotion.

There are also a number of typical group behaviors at ending that may be directed either at the social worker or the group as a whole. These include: (1) denial (or simply "forgetting" that the group is ending); (2) **clustering**, moving toward more connection rather than less; (3) **regression**—either claiming verbally, or acting out in behavioral terms, that the group is not ready to end; (4) withdrawal or passivity related to active participation, (5) rebellion; or (6) flight—leaving the group before it ends (Furman et al., 2009; Reid, 1997).

The responses to ending are similar to those that occur in intervening with individuals and families. The fact that they may be multiplied by the number of people in the group can make them feel quite momentous to you as the social worker. For example, when an entire collective of 13-year-old girls makes it clear, through sudden and orchestrated hostility to you, that they do not want the experience to end, you can certainly feel the power of the group. In this case, just as in individual or family work, you can view the group's reaction as a function of the process (and perhaps of the success of the group), rather than focused personal assault.

Social worker skills that are particularly useful in ending work with groups include (Middleman & Wood, 1990):

- *Focusing on group:* As always, in group work, this skill keeps the social worker focused on the processes of the entire group and the priority of its development as an entity rather than on individual members.

- *Summarizing:* Completing a review of group decisions and actions is a useful strategy for ending group work because the group can discuss their achievements.

- *Voicing group achievements:* The social worker and group members can acknowledge the group's successes and validate the members' hard work.

- *Preserving group history and continuity:* This skill involves emphasizing the entity of the group in its social location and linking its history to the members' futures. In the process of ending, the social worker can focus on the group's continuity as translation to the world outside of the group.

Ending the Relationships among Group Members In this aspect of ending, members may exhibit individualized versions of denial or flight as well as variations of these. Some members may not attend meetings that are specifically dedicated to ending activities. Others may attend but refuse to enter any group interactivity about endings, or they may simply resign themselves to rejection. Individuals may become increasingly short-tempered and impatient with other members, as if to negate the importance of their relationship and to render ending insignificant or even a relief. This behavior can occur among members who have worked the hardest at making connections with one other.

In other situations, individual members will question their ability to maintain the changes they have made without the assistance of the group and the social worker. These members will sometimes lobby for individual sessions with the worker or a reconstituted "mini group" in which only a few members of the original group would attend. In addition, some individuals may initiate more intense relationships with other group members outside the confines of the group meetings, as if to negate the need for the group. The most helpful thing you can do is articulate your observations regarding group dynamics. Staying focused on the group, rather than on the individuals, can be challenging, but it is part of negotiating a successful ending.

Ending the Group Itself This ending is at once philosophical and technical. On the philosophical level, reflect on your own feelings about ending this unit of work and this group of unique characters. How will it contribute to your professional growth? What could you have done differently? How will members benefit from it? If the group has been difficult, you may struggle with feelings of inadequacy or a sense of

© Yuri Arcurs

work left undone. When there is an overall sense of the group's having gone well, you may feel exhilarated by a sense of accomplishment, of having crossed a particular hurdle, or of entering into the realm of the skilled. When you consider a metaphor for your experience, would it be death? Divorce? Disengagement? A required course? Graduation?

On a much more practical side, you will need to close out the records of participation, complete the evaluation process (addressed shortly), and terminate the logistical arrangements such as space and place. Finally, you will need to honor follow-up commitments and successfully make any referrals or transfers.

As an example of the issues that can arise when terminating with a group, consider the following group scenario:

A community-based agency that serves new immigrants offers a group for high school-aged students focused on the students' transitions from their country of origin to their newly adopted country. The group has a secondary purpose: providing an opportunity for the students to practice their English skills in a safe environment. The group composition is mixed gender and ethnicity. The social worker who is charged with facilitating this group has developed her cultural competency through her commitment to learn as much as she can about the students' heritage and traditions, language, the rules and norms for gender interactions, and faith traditions. She personally conducts an interview with each student who is referred to the group and her or his parents/family/guardians so she can be familiar with the individual student's needs and goals for joining the group.

The current group of students has developed into a cohesive group, particularly around the issues of being "Americanized" as they are enthusiastically adopting the customs of teens in their new country. The group members also share similar struggles with their parents who are distressed that their children are abandoning their heritages. The social worker has become aware of a potential dilemma. The time-limited group is scheduled to come to an end but the social worker has been approached by a number of the parents who have asked her to continue the group for the purpose of reconnecting the teens to their ethnic and cultural roots. While the teens enjoy the group, they have already planned their "graduation" celebration and appear ready to move on with life outside the group. The social worker is conflicted— she empathizes with the parents' concerns but believes the group should terminate as planned. What options or alternatives might the social worker consider in order to meet the needs of both groups?

In sum, endings can and should be a time for reflection and celebration. Equally important for all social workers in group practice, but particularly critical for those in the early stages of their career, is reviewing the group process as it has impacted your personal and professional growth. This exploration will now come to its own ending with a discussion of the process of evaluating the group intervention as experienced by the group members and the social worker.

Evaluation of Social Work Practice with Groups

Evaluation of practice with groups serves the same purpose as evaluating practice with individuals and families: to examine the work, the process, and the social worker's skills. Specifically, an evaluation of a social work group intervention reviews the progress and reflects on the process (Furman et al., 2009). While there are similarities in the evaluations of individual, family, and group interventions, there are also differences. Unlike family interventions that focus exclusively on the unit and individual intervention evaluations that focus solely on the individual, the evaluation of a group intervention encompasses both the individual and the group, thus moving evaluation to a level of complexity not typically found with individual and family evaluations.

As noted previously, groups include individuals who arrive at the group with individual goals, personalities, needs, and expectations. Oftentimes, the social worker must consider evaluative strategies within the context of a large, diverse group of individuals who perceive their experience differently from one another. You must frame an evaluation of any group intervention within the context of the purpose, type, structure, and format of the group. To further heighten the complexity of group evaluation, the social worker must work within the agency or organizational structure in which the group is conducted. Having to address multiple needs with a group of individuals thus requires the social work group practitioner to have a clear and thoughtful approach to evaluation of the group intervention *prior* to the first meeting of the group.

Regardless of the method(s) used to evaluate the group intervention, it is important for everyone involved in the intervention to participate in the evaluative process (Garvin & Galinsky, 2008). There are many strategies available for accomplishing the goals for this phase of the group intervention (Bloom, Fischer, & Orme, 2009; Furman et al., 2009; Garvin & Galinsky, 2008):

- Review individual and group member accomplishments with an emphasis on preparing for the future, sustaining change, and ensuring the inclusion of support systems to reduce risk for failure.

- Gather group members' impressions of the group experience and the activities/programming. Data can be collected publically as part of the group process (within the group or written evaluations) or anonymously (in writing), using caution to avoid "satisfaction-only" surveys as they typically do not accurately reflect growth and change, but members' feelings about the facilitator, setting, etc.

- Administer pre- and post-group measures of behaviors, attitudes, and function. Consider the use of previously validated and standardized measures that have been administered on groups comparable to the group intervention you are evaluating. Such measures will provide you with evidence-supported data from which to interpret your findings. While standardized measures of the individual are appropriate for use in group interventions, consider also the use of standardized measurements developed specifically for group interventions (e.g., see Group Engagement Measure (originally developed by Macgowan, 1997; further psychometric testing: 2000, 2003 (with Levenson), and 2005)).

- Through direct observation by the social worker, document behaviors and changes in individual group members and the group. Data can be gathered quantitatively and/or qualitatively.

- Complete a self-evaluation, including exploration into such areas as: meeting group member needs, development of appropriate structure and interventions, and assessment of own performance as a social work practitioner. As part of reflecting on your role within the group, you may want to conduct a self-evaluation so that you can grow and evolve as a group facilitator. Quick Guide 30 provides a strategy to help you engage in a self-evaluation.

- Solicit direct observation and feedback by other professionals.

In the practice of social work intervention, termination, and evaluation services with groups, the social worker will find that each group will develop its own personality, thus making each group experience unique. There are, however, aspects of each phase of the process that you will find are often replicated when you are providing leadership to a group. Recall from Chapter 8 the examination of the engagement and assessment phases of three group models (social goals/action, reciprocal, and remedial models) used within groups consisting of parents from the Riverton community. Returning to the Riverton example, Exhibits 9.4, 9.5, and 9.6 depict the intervention, termination, and evaluation phases from the perspectives of the three models.

In addition to the type(s) of evaluative strategies for examining group interventions that we have discussed, consider using the data that you gather and analyze to develop evaluation tools that can be used for future groups (Garvin & Galinsky, 2008). For example, you and other group facilitators may find it helpful to have a menu of strategies for monitoring group progress or a manual for conducting a group intervention. Exhibit 9.7 offers a sample of a facilitator evaluation that can be completed by group members.

QUICK GUIDE 30 GROUP FACILITATOR SELF-EVALUATION

When reflecting on your experience leading a group, ask yourself the following questions:

1. How did the group experience me?
2. What feelings did I experience in this session? Did I express those feelings? Did I have some feelings with which I did not feel comfortable?
3. What were my reactions to various group members? Did I feel "turned off" to some members, rejecting? Do all members know I care about them? Do they feel accepted by me?
4. What did I communicate to each member? Did I say what I really wanted to say? Was my message clearly stated?
5. How much time did I spend focused on the content of the discussion rather than on the interaction taking place or feelings and needs subtly expressed?
6. What do I wish I had said or done? What would I do differently next time?
7. Did I dominate? How willing was I for someone else to assume the leadership role?

This reflection can be completed following each session as well as when the group comes to a close. Upon finishing this reflection, consider ways in which you may strengthen your group skills.

Source: Berg, Landreth, & Fall, 2013, p. 138.

PHASES II and III: MIDDLE AND ENDING WORK

EXHIBIT 9.4

Riverton Against Youth Drinking ("RAYD"): An Example of Social Goals/ Action Group

Background: Concerned about the use and abuse of alcohol among their adolescent children, a group of parents in the Riverton community approach a local community service agency to ask for help in addressing this problem.

Work thus far: Stakeholders and their interests and goals have been identified. The social worker's role has been agreed upon. A community needs assessment has been conducted, including strengths, resources, needs, and priorities. A plan for intervention, termination, and evaluation has been established and will focus on developing and mounting a public education campaign to raise awareness about the issue of teen drinking.

Note: While the stages of group interventions are not linear and may, in fact, overlap, the following depicts a possible approach to responding to the identified need.

INTERVENTION	TERMINATION	EVALUATION
Identify community partners who will support the education campaign and help with dissemination	Terminate intervention	Conduct evaluation
		Analyze data gathered from evaluation effort
Confirm the plan, time frame, and resources for intervention, termination, and evaluation continue to be viable		Implement plan for sustainability
		Document findings
Launch the intervention		
Monitor progress, particularly dissemination and relationships with community partners		
Adapt the intervention, as needed		
Revisit plan for evaluation and sustainability		

EXHIBIT 9.5

Riverton Children's Grief Support Group: An Example of Reciprocal Group

PHASES II and III: MIDDLE AND ENDING WORK

Background: A social worker in a local community service agency has become aware of a number of children of Riverton who have lost a parent to alcohol and substance-related deaths. The social worker takes steps toward offering to the community a support group that includes to an educational focus.

Work thus far: Based on the social worker's assessment of community need and interest, group members were recruited, screened, and invited to join the group. A first session was planned and has been held, at which time group rules and norms were determined collaboratively by the social worker and the group members. Individual group goals and needs were shared. The social worker's role as a facilitator/educator was established.

Note: While the stages of group interventions are not linear and may, in fact, overlap, the following depicts a possible approach to responding to the identified need.

INTERVENTION	TERMINATION	EVALUATION
Social worker begins each session by reviewing group rules and norms and conducting member check-in	Begin termination as planned	*Individual*
		Determine if goals were met (informal or formal)
Social worker engages in ongoing assessment of individual member needs, group interactions, and group cohesiveness	Check in with each group member regarding feelings regarding the termination of the group and the process	Administer post-group collection of data
		Group
Social worker has developed a repertoire of agency and community resources available to suggest as needed	Invite each member to talk about individual gains and continuing needs	Determine if group goals were met (informal or formal)
Revisit group needs and adapt intervention and educational programming plans as appropriate	Discuss plans for sustaining change and any perceived obstacles to maintenance	Ask members to provide feedback regarding satisfaction with the group process
Share information, as agreed upon prior to group initiation, with legal guardians	Provide resources as needed to help members sustain change	Document findings
Monitor individual and group progress and adapt as needed		
Regularly revisit time frame and plans for termination and evaluation	Conduct termination ritual or celebration	
Invite suggestions from group members regarding plans for recognizing group termination		

PHASES II and III: MIDDLE AND ENDING WORK

Background: A new social worker at the Riverton Mental Health Center has recently assumed leadership for a clinical intervention group for persons with dual diagnoses (i.e., substance abuse and mental illness) who receive outpatient services at the agency. The group is diverse in membership, including mixed genders, range of ages, and mandated and voluntary members. Membership turnover is dependent on members' "graduation" from the treatment program; therefore, the group often has entering and exiting members. Two new members have been referred to the group. This will be the first time new members have been referred since the social worker took over responsibility for the group.

Work thus far: The social worker has gathered information on eligibility criteria for group membership and integrating new members into an ongoing group. The social worker has met with the two persons who have been referred and determined they would be appropriate for inclusion. The two members have been oriented and attended their first meeting. During this session, the social worker introduced the new members to the group, revisited group rules and norms, and assessed the individual goals and needs and group cohesion.

Note: While the stages of group interventions are not linear and may, in fact, overlap, the following depicts a possible approach to responding to the identified need.

INTERVENTION	TERMINATION	EVALUATION
At the beginning of each session, social worker reminds members of group rules and norms	Ongoing as membership is open	Complete formal evaluation as required by agency
Social worker conducts check in by asking members to share with the group the events/actions since the last session	Determine termination ritual appropriate to an open-ended group	Obtain information from existing members regarding achievement of goals and experiences with group format and process (e.g., open vs. closed and time-limited format) and social worker leadership
Social worker assesses individual member needs and goals, and monitors progress towards goals (critical as each person may potentially be at a different point in their progress)	Prepare existing and remaining members for termination	
	Check in with members regarding their feelings about termination	Document findings
Social worker assesses group cohesion		
Members with longer membership serve as guides/mentors for newer members		

EXHIBIT 9.7

*Group
Counselor
Rating Scale*

Instructions: Rate your group counselor as you see her/him functioning in your group.

Respect: Shows a real respect for the group members by attentiveness, warmth, efforts, to understand and freedom of personal expression.

5.0	4.5	4.0	3.5	3.0	2.5	2.0	1.5	1.0
Very high		high		moderate		low		very low

Empathy: Communicates an accurate understanding of the group members' feelings and experiences. The group members know the counselor understands how they feel.

5.0	4.5	4.0	3.5	3.0	2.5	2.0	1.5	1.0
Very high		high		moderate		low		very low

Genuiness: Realness. Everything she/he does seems to be real. That's the way she/he really is. This person doesn't put up a front.

5.0	4.5	4.0	3.5	3.0	2.5	2.0	1.5	1.0
Very high		high		moderate		low		very low

Concreteness: "Tunes in" and responds to specific feelings of experiences of group members. Avoids responding in generalities.

5.0	4.5	4.0	3.5	3.0	2.5	2.0	1.5	1.0
Very high		high		moderate		low		very low

Self-Disclosure: Lets group know about relevant immediate personal feelings. Open, rather than guarded.

5.0	4.5	4.0	3.5	3.0	2.5	2.0	1.5	1.0
Very high		high		moderate		low		very low

Spontaneity: Can respond without having to "stop and think." Words and actions seem to flow easily.

5.0	4.5	4.0	3.5	3.0	2.5	2.0	1.5	1.0
Very high		high		moderate		low		very low

Flexibility: Adapts to a wide range of conditions without losing her/his composure. Can adapt to meet the needs of the moment.

5.0	4.5	4.0	3.5	3.0	2.5	2.0	1.5	1.0
Very high		high		moderate		low		very low

Confidence: Trusts her/his abilities. Acts with directness and self-assurance.

5.0	4.5	4.0	3.5	3.0	2.5	2.0	1.5	1.0
Very high		high		moderate		low		very low

Open-ended questions may also yield insightful group perceptions about the facilitator:

1. Of what changes have you become aware in your attitudes, feelings about yourself, and relationships with other people?
2. How did the group experience help these changes to come about?
3. What did the group leader do that was most helpful and least helpful to you?
4. Was the group experience hurtful to you in any way, or did it have any negative effect on you?
5. Briefly identify any group exercises you especially like or disliked.
6. In what ways do you wish you had been different in the group?
7. How are you most different as a result of the group experience?

Source: Berg, Landreth, & Fall, 2013, p. 143–144.

STRAIGHT TALK ABOUT GROUP INTERVENTION, TERMINATION, AND EVALUATION

The social worker's overall role and purpose is to encourage and mobilize the strengths of the group. The concern for individual well-being and growth is augmented by the social factors of the group, one member to another. Consistent with trusting the group process, the social worker should strive to avoid overinvestment in the centrality or power that may attribute to her or his role. The goal, after all, is for the group to gain its voice and develop its strength, even as individual members continue to grow. You will not be able to take credit, even in your own mind, for all of the potential successes in your group. In exchange, you will have the privilege of experiencing the power of group connection and the autonomy it ultimately can exercise as it liberates the power of its members. The emphasis on the group does not mean that your own role is any less important. You are responsible for the safety of each member in the group and for ensuring the group processes its own activity. Accordingly, your role is to evaluate group process and functioning on an ongoing basis, just as you do in other forms of social work practice interventions. This will vary according to the nature of your group purpose, goals, and format. For example, if you are working in a task group, monitoring progress in completing the group's project will be the focus of the intervention and evaluation processes. If you facilitate a group for school-aged children, you must make sure to use an appropriate developmental level. Other forms of evaluation that are especially useful come from members: Is the group meeting their social and affiliation needs? Do they continue to feel safe in it? Is it a helpful forum to address the issues they want to deal with? As always, consider the work of evaluation as an ongoing process.

CONCLUSION

In emphasizing the importance of relational components in our lives, first as people and then as social work practitioners, this chapter has presented social work practice with groups in the role of mediating a range of social and emotional issues, including isolation, oppression, and life crises. Currently there are many exciting adventures into social work practice with groups that build upon contemporary theoretical perspectives, social justice, and diversity. Scenarios relating to cultural inclusion, gender and disability, collaboration, and spirituality in models that emphasize process over stages and story over problem all point to the empowering direction that social group work is taking in the history of the profession. Social work practice with groups offers significant potential for the future and is particularly relevant for the social justice, diversity, and human rights connections that give social work its meaning.

MAIN POINTS

- Effective social work practice interventions with groups provide an interface for social justice, diversity, and human rights.

- Middle-phase (intervention) and ending phase (termination) strategies were approached from the perspectives of strengths and empowerment, narrative and solution-focused approaches.

- Developmental models, such as the Boston Model and others based on it are widely used theoretical perspectives on group development. Many applications of, and departures from, this model can be found in the contemporary practice environment.

- Social workers working with groups hone their skills for intervening with individuals and must develop additional skills for group intervention in the areas of group leadership, community, problem-solving, and management of group functioning.

- Contemporary examples of innovative, evidence-based group practice models, such as constructionist groups and restorative justice groups, help to provide vision and possibility for responding to current cultural and social issues as they unfold.

- Termination occurs in three distinct areas of group practice interventions: between the group members and the social worker, among the group members, and the group itself.

- While evaluation of group practice shares some commonalities with evaluation of individual and family interventions, evaluating group interventions is more complex as examination of the individual members of the group and the group itself is both required.

EXERCISES

a. Case Exercises

1. Go to www.routledgesw.com/cases and review Carla Washburn's video vignette and consider the roles each member plays for the following activities and questions:

    a. Gather into groups. Starting the group session from the conclusion of the video vignette, role-play the next session. What happens next? Process the group session with the class.

    b. Round robin: Each student takes the opportunity to role-play the social worker. Change roles when the "social worker" is not sure how to proceed with the group. Debrief about the experiences and practice behaviors demonstrated for each role-play. What were strengths and areas for growth for each student as a facilitator?

    c. Select a member of the group and discuss her or his role in the group process.

    d. Identify the social worker's strengths as a group facilitator along with those practice behaviors that may be improved.

2. Termination of a group intervention can be challenging. Returning to the grief support group depicted in the Carla Washburn video vignette, role-play the final session. Consider the following:

    a. What is the most important role the social worker plays at this stage of the group process?

    b. What practice behaviors are critical for the termination phase of a group intervention?

    c. Brainstorm strategies for responding to the array of possible member reactions to the ending of the group experience.

3. At the conclusion of a group intervention, the evaluation of the effectiveness of your interventions is critical. Research various evaluation tools and complete the following for the grief support group in which Carla Washburn is a member:

    a. Create a satisfaction survey.

    b. Create a pre-test/post-test.

    c. Create a six-month evaluation tool.

4. Go to www.routledgesw.com/cases and view the Riverton video vignette that depicts a group meeting of the Riverton Neighborhood Association. Upon viewing the video, respond to the following:

    a. What model of group intervention is being conducted in this vignette?

    b. Identify practice behaviors and skills covered in this chapter that the group facilitator is demonstrating in the meeting.

    c. Compare and contrast group facilitation skills needed for a group such as the Riverton Neighborhood Association and a client-focused group.

5. Go to www.routledgesw.com/cases and view the Riverton video vignette that depicts a group meeting of the Riverton Neighborhood Association or the Carla Washburn video vignette that depicts a grief support group. Using the Group

Counselor Rating Scale (Exhibit 9.7), complete an evaluation of the group leader. Upon completion of the evaluation, write a reflection identifying the group leader's strengths and areas for growth and change.

6. Go to www.routledgesw.com/cases and review the case for Brickville, particularly Virginia Stone and her family. In Chapter 8 (Vignette #3), Virginia was involved in the creation of a social action group targeted at saving the park that was built in memory of her family members who were lost in the apartment fire twenty years earlier. The exercise in Chapter 8 focused on determining the need, purpose, composition, structure, and content for such a group. Using the information that you have available to you, develop a written plan that includes:
   a. Development of the social action plan.
   b. Strategies for implementing the plan.
   c. Resources needed to implement the plan, including individuals, groups, organizations, and funding, as appropriate.
   c. Plan for determining the success or failure of the social action effort.
   d. Your reflection on the process of implementing a social action plan at the community level.

7. Go to www.routledgesw.com/cases and review the case for Hudson City. Recall from Chapters 6, 7, 8 that the Patel family experienced significant impact from Hurricane Diane. As a result of her response to the experience, the 12-year-old daughter, Aarti, was referred to a group to help her develop her coping skills. While Aarti was a regular and active participant in the support group to which you referred her, there is mounting concern that she continues to struggle with the same challenges that resulted in the referral to the group (e.g., nightmares, discomfort when required to be away from her parents for activities other than school and group, and decreased appetite). Describe in writing your thoughts about the concerns being expressed by her parents and the leader of the support group and a plan for addressing the ongoing challenges that Aarti and her family are experiencing, including:
   * Continuation in the support group
   * Alternative intervention strategies
   * Resources needed for a revised intervention plan

b. Other Exercises

8. To relate the information covered in this chapter to your own group experience, reflect on a specific experience you have had as a member of a group by responding to the following items:
   a. Describe in detail a group to which you belonged (may be a current group). Include:
      * type of group (may use one of the types described in Chapter 8)
      * purpose of the group

- structure of the group (e.g., open or closed membership, time-limited or open-ended, number of members, eligibility for membership)
- your role within the group

b. Consider the quality of your involvement by reflecting on:
  - How did you feel about being a member of the group? Your role? Your contributions?
  - Did the group fulfill stated expectations? Your expectations? If not, explain the reasons.
  - What were the strengths of the group?
  - What are areas for the group's growth or change?
  - Group leadership of the group—was it formally determined or evolved naturally? What was the style of the leader(s)?

c. Based on your experience and your new knowledge of the group process, reflect on the following:
  - Would you engage with the group differently? If yes, how would your involvement change? Explain your reasons.
  - Was the group formally or informally evaluated? What were the outcomes?

9. Develop a plan for the way in which you, as a group leader, will respond to each of the following behaviors that may emerge during the course of your experience in group work:
   a. "Silent" group member
   b. "Monopolizer"
   c. "Help-rejecter/avoider"
   d. "Caregiver/coordinator"
   e. "Attacker"
   f. "Harmonizer"
   g. "Clown"
   h. "Poor me" group member

   After developing your response plan for each behavior, reflect in writing on the challenges you anticipate facing and strategies for learning and growing as a group facilitator.

10. Recall from Chapter 8 that you, as a practicum student, were invited to serve as a co-facilitator for a psychoeducational support for family caregivers of persons experiencing Parkinson's disease. In the previous exercise, your focus was on familiarizing yourself with Parkinson's disease and develop a plan for the session that you would lead. In preparing for the intervention, terminations, and evaluation phases of group work, respond to the following items:
    a. Identify potential ongoing needs that caregivers of persons with Parkinson's disease will have for pyschoeducational support.
    b. Develop a plan for evaluating the support group with a specific emphasis on strategies you will use to gather feedback from the group members.

REFERENCES

350.org. (n.d.). *Homepage*. Retrieved form 350.org

Abramowitz, M. (2005). The largely untold story of welfare reform and the human services. *Social Work, 50*(2), 175–186.

Abramson, J. (2009). Interdisciplinary team practice. In A.R. Roberts, *Social workers' desk reference* (2nd ed.) (pp. 44–50). New York: Oxford Press.

Alissi, A. S. (2009). United States. In A. Gitterman & R. Salmon, *Encyclopedia of social work with groups* (pp. 6–12). New York: Routledge.

American Red Cross. (n.d.). *Red Cross continues to help Joplin recovery from 2011 tornado*. Retrieved from http://www.redcross.org/news/article/Red-Cross-Continues-to-Help-Joplin-Recover-from–2011-Tornado

Amato, P. R., Booth, A., Johnson, D. R., & Rogers, S. J. (2009). *Alone together: How marriage in America is changing*. Cambridge, MA: Harvard University Press.

Anderson, K. M. (2013). Assessing strengths. Identifying acts of resistance to violence and oppression. In D. Saleebey (Ed.), *The strengths perspective in social work practice* (6th ed.) (pp. 182–202). Boston: Pearson.

AP Worldstream. (2010, July 15). *Planned US mosque draws opponents, supporters*. Retrieved from highbeam.com/doc/1A1-D9GV6I8G0.html

Arrington, P. (2008). *Stress at work: How do social workers cope? NASW Membership Workforce Study*. Washington, DC: National Association of Social Workers.

Atwood, J. D. & Genovese, F. (2006). *Therapy with single parents. A social constructionist approach*. New York: The Haworth Press.

Austin, M. J. & Solomon, J. R. (2009). Managing the planning process. In R. J. Patti (Ed.), *The handbook of human services management* (pp. 321–337). Thousand Oaks, CA: Sage Publications.

Banyard, V. L., Plante, E. G., & Moynihan, M. M. (2007). Bystander education: Bringing a broader community perspective to sexual violence prevention. *Journal of Community Psychology, 32*(1), 61–79.

Barker, R. L. (2003). *The social work dictionary* (5th ed.). Washington, DC: NASW Press.

Barsky, A. E. (2010). *Ethics and values in social work*. New York: Oxford University Press.

Barth, R. P. (2008). Adoption. In T. Mizrahi & L. E. Davis, *Encyclopedia of social work* (20th ed.) (pp. 1:33–44). Washington, DC and New York: NASW Press and Oxford University Press.

Beaulaurier, R. L. & Taylor, S. H. (2007). Social work practice with people with disabilities in the era of disability rights. In A. E. Dell Orto & P. W. Power, (Eds.), *The psychological and social impact of illness and disability* (5th ed.) (pp. 53–74). New York: Springer Publishing.

Beck, J. S. (2011). *Cognitive therapy for challenging problems: What to do when the basics don't work*. New York: Guilford Press

Benard, B. & Truebridge, S. (2013). A shift in thinking. Influencing social workers' beliefs about individual and family resilience in an effort to enhance well-being and success for all. In D. Saleebey, *The strengths perspective in social work practice* (6th ed.) (pp. 203–220). Boston: Allyn & Bacon.

Berg, R. D., Landreth, G. L., & Fall, K. A. (2013). *Group counseling concepts and procedures* (5th ed.). New York: Routledge.

Berg-Weger, M., Rubio, D. M., & Tebb, S. (2000). The caregiver well-being scale revisited. *Health and Social Work, 25*(4), 255–263.

Berg-Weger, M. (2013). *Social work and social welfare. An invitation.* New York: Routledge.

Berman-Rossi, T. & Kelly, T.B. (2003). *Group composition, diversity, the skills of the social worker, and group development.* Presented at the Council for Social Work Education, Annual Meeting, Atlanta, February.

Biblarz, T. J. & Stacey, J. (2010). How does the gender of parents matter? *Journal of Marriage and Family 72,* 3–22.

Bittman, M. (2011, May 17). Imaging Detroit. *New York Times.* Retrieved from http://opinionator.blogs.nytimes.com/2011/05/17/imagining-detroit/

Bloom, M., Fischer, J., & Orme, J. G. (2009). *Evaluating practice: Guidelines for the accountable professional* (6th ed.). Boston: Allyn & Bacon.

Blunsdon, B. & Davern, M. (2007). Measuring wellness through interdisciplinary community development: Linking the physical, economic and social environment. *Journal of Community Practice, 15* (1/2), 217–238.

Bobo, K., Kendall, J., & Max, S. (2010). *Organizing for social change.* Santa Ana, CA: The Forum Press.

Boland-Prom, K. W. (2009). Results of a national study of social workers sanctioned by state licensing boards. *Social Work, 54*(4): 351–360.

Bowden, V. R. & Greenberg, C. S. (2010). *Children and their families: The continuum of care.* Philadelphia: Wolters Kluwer/Lippincott Williams and Wilkins.

Bowlby, J. (1969). *Attachment and loss: Vol. 1, Attachment.* New York: Basic Books.

Bowlby, J. (1982). *Attachment and loss: Vol. 1, Attachment* (2nd ed.). New York: Basic Books.

Boyes-Watson, C. (2005). Seeds of change: Using peacemaking circles to build a village for every child. *Child Welfare, 84*(2), 191–208.

Briar-Lawson, K. & Naccarato, T. (2008). Family Services. In T. Mizrahi & L. E. Davis, *Encyclopedia of social work* (20th ed.) (pp. 2:206–212). Washington, DC and New York: NASW Press and Oxford University Press.

Brager, G., Specht, H., & Torczyner, J. (1987). *Community organizing.* New York: Columbia University Press.

Breton, M. (2004). An empowerment perspective. In C. D. Garvin, L. M. Gutierrez, & M. J. Galinsky (Eds.), *Handbook of social work with groups* (pp. 58–75). New York: Guilford Press.

Brill, C. (1998). The new NASW code of ethics can be your ally: Part I. *Focus Newsletter.* Retrieved from http://www.naswma.org/displaycommon.cfm?an=1&subarticlenbr=96

Briskman, L. & Noble, C. (1999). Social work ethics: Embracing diversity? In J. Fook & B. Pease (Eds.), *Transforming social work practice: Postmodern critical perspectives* (pp. 57–69). London: Routledge.

Brody, K. & Gadling-Cole, C. (2008). Family group conferencing with African-American families. In C. Waites (Ed.), *Social work practice with African American families: An intergenerational perspective.* New York: Routledge.

Brookings Institution. (2011, September). *An update to "Simulating the effect of the 'Great Recession' on poverty".* Retrieved from http://www.brookings.edu/research/reports/2011/09/13-recession-poverty-monea-sawhill

Broussard, C. A., Joseph, A. L., & Thompson, M. (2012). Stressors and coping strategies used by single mothers living in poverty. *Affilia, 27,* 190–204.

Brown, N. W. (2013). *Creative activities for group therapy.* New York: Routledge.

Brown, R., & Hauser, C. (2012, August 10). After a struggle, Mosque opens in Tennessee. *New York Times.* Retrieved from http://www.nytimes.com/2012/08/11/us/islamic-center-of-murfreesboro-opens-in-tennessee.html

Brueggemann, W. G. (2005). *The practice of macro social work.* Belmont, CA: Thomson Higher Education.

Brueggemann, W. G. (2013). History and context for community practice in North America. In M. Weil's (Ed.), *The handbook of community practice* (pp. 27–46). Thousand Oaks, CA: Sage.

Buck, H. G., Overcash, J. & McMillan, S. C. (2009). The geriatric cancer experience at the end of life: Testing an adapted model. *Oncology Nursing Forum, 36*(6), 664–673.

Bullock, K. (2005). Grandfathers and the impact of raising grandchildren. *Journal of Sociology & Social Welfare, 32*(1), 43–59.

Burry, C. (2002). Working with potentially violent clients in their homes: What child welfare professionals need to know. *Clinical Supervisor, 21*(1), 145–153.

Butler, C. (2009). Sexual and gender minority therapy and systemic practice. *Journal of Family Therapy, 31*(4), 338–358.

Butler, A. C., Chapman, J. E., Forman, E. M., & Beck, A. T. (2006). The empirical status of cognitive-behavioral therapy: A review of meta-analyses. *Clinical Psychology Review, 26*, 17–31.

Campbell, D. (2000). *The socially constructed organization.* London: Karnac Books.

Carmeli, A. & Freund, A. (2009). Linking perceived external prestige and intentions to leave the organization: The mediating role of job satisfaction. *Journal of Social Service Research, 35*(3), 236–250.

Carter, L. & Matthieu, M. (2010). *Developing skills in the evidence based practice process.* St. Louis, MO: Washington University in St. Louis. Presented March 12, 2010.

Casa de Esperanza. (n.d.). *History.* Retrieved from https://www.casadeesperanza.org

CHANGE, Inc. Community Action Agency. (n.d.). *County needs assessment.* Retrieved from http://www.virtualcap.org/downloads/VC/US_NA_Examples_CHANGE_Inc_Community_Needs_Survey.pdf

Chaskin, R., Brown, P., Venkatsh, S., & Vidal, A. (2009). *Building community capacity.* New York: Aldine de Gruyter.

Chaskin, R. J. (2010). The Chicago School: A context for youth intervention, research and development. In R. J. Chaskin (Ed.), *Youth gangs and community intervention: Research, practice, and evidence* (pp. 3–23). New York: Columbia University Press.

Chaskin, R. J. (2013). Theories of community. In M. Weil's (Ed.), *The handbook of community practice* (pp. 105–121). Thousand Oaks, CA: Sage.

Chen, E. C., Budianto, L., & Wong, K. (2011). Professional school counselors as social justice advocates for undocumented immigrant students in group work. In A. A. Singh & C. F. Salazar, *Social justice in group work. Practical interventions for change* (pp. 88–94). New York: Routledge.

Christiensen, D. N., Todahl, J., & Barrett, W. C. (1999). *Solution-based casework: An introduction to clinical and case management skills in casework practice.* New York: De Gruyter.

Chu, W. C. K. & Tsui, M. (2008). The nature of practice wisdom in social work revisited. *International Social Work, 51*(1), 47–54.

Chun-Chow, J. & Austin, M. J. (2008). The culturally responsive social service agency: The application of an evolving definition to a case study. *Administration in Social Work, 32*(4), 39–64.

City of Seattle, Washington. (2012). *A community assessment of need for housing and services for homeless individuals and families in the Lake City neighborhood.* Retrieved from http://seattle.gov/realestate/pdfs/Needs_Assessment_data_report.pdf

Clowes, L. (2005). *Crossing cultures in systems of care.* Presented at the 1st New England LEND Conference, Burlington, VT.

Cnaan, R. A. & Rothman, J. (2008). Capacity development and the building of community. In J. Rothman, J. Erlich, & J. Tropman (Eds.), *Strategies of community intervention* (7th ed.) (pp. 243–262). Peosta, Iowa: Eddie Bowers Publishing Co., Inc.

CNN Wire Staff. (2012, August 6). *Missouri mosque destroyed in second fire in a month.* Retrieved from http://articles.cnn.com/2012–08–06/us/us_missouri-mosque-burned_1_vandalism-and-anti-muslim-sentiment-mosque-islamic-center

Colangelo, L. L. (2009, July 12). Queens one of the most diverse places on earth, new figures show. *New York Daily News.* Retrieved from http://articles.nydailynews.com/2009–07–12/local/17929058_1_dominicans-hispanic-queens

Collins, D., Jordan, C., & Coleman, H. (2013). *An introduction to family social work* (4th ed.). Belmont, CA: Brooks/Cole.

Collins, K. S. & Lazzari, M. M. (2009). Co-leadership. In A. Gitterman & R. Salmon, *Encyclopedia of social work with groups* (pp. 299–302). New York: Routledge.

Comer, E. & Meier, A. (2011). Using evidence-based practice and intervention research with treatment groups for populations at risk. In G. L. Greif & P. H. Ephross (Eds.), *Group work with populations*

Conan, N. (2012, February 15). Providing therapy across different cultures. *Talk of the Nation, NPR.* Retrieved from http://www.npr.org/2012/02/15/146936181/providing-therapy-across-different-cultures

Congress, E. P. (2004). Cultural and ethical issues in working with culturally diverse patients and their families: The use of the culturagram to promote cultural competent practice in health care settings. In A. Metteri, T. Krôger, A. Pohjola, & P. Rauhala (Eds.), *Social work visions from around the globe* (pp. 249–262). Binghampton, NY: Haworth.

Congress, E. P. (2009). The culturagram. In A. R. Roberts, *Social workers' desk reference* (2nd ed.) (pp. 969–975). New York: Oxford Press.

Cooney, K. (2006). The institutional and technical structuring of nonprofit ventures: Case study of a U.S. hybrid organization caught between two fields. *Voluntas: International Journal of Voluntary and Nonprofit Organizations, 17*(2), 143–161.

Corcoran, J. (2009). Using standardized tests and instruments in family assessments. In A. R. Roberts, *Social workers' desk reference* (2nd ed.) (pp. 390–394). New York: Oxford Press.

Cordova, T. L. (2011). Community-based research and participatory change: A strategic multi method community impact assessment. *Journal of Community Practice, 19*(1), 29–47.

Council on Social Work Education (CSWE). (2012). *Educational policy and accreditation standards.* Washington, DC: Author.

Cox, C. (2008). Empowerment as an intervention with grandparent caregivers. *Journal of Intergenerational Relationships, 6*(4), 465–477.

Cox, D. & Pawar, M. (2013). *International social work: Issues, strategies, and programs.* Thousand Oaks, CA: Sage Publications, Inc.

Cross, T. L., Bazron, B. J., Dennis, K. W., & Isaacs, M. R. (1989). *Toward a culturally competent system of care.* Washington, DC: Georgetown University Development Center.

Cumming-Bruce, N. (2012, September 12). U.N. says Syrian refugee numbers are surging. *New York Times.* Retrieved from http://www.nytimes.com/2012/09/28/world/middleeast/un-says-syrian-refugee-numbers-are-surging.html?_r=0

Cummings, T. G. & Worley, C. G. (2009). *Organizational development and change.* Mason, OH: South-Western Cengage Learning.

DeFrain, J. & Asay, S. M. (2007a). Epilogue: A strengths-based conceptual framework for understanding families worldwide. In J. DeFrain & S. M. Asay, *Strong families around the world: Strengths-based research and perspectives* (pp. 447–466). New York: Haworth Press, Inc.

DeFrain, J. & Asay, S. M. (2007b). Family strengths and challenges in the USA. In J. DeFrain & S. M. Asay, *Strong families around the world: Strengths-based research and perspectives* (pp. 281–307). New York: Haworth Press, Inc.

De Jong, P. (2008). Interviewing. In T. Mizrahi & L. E. Davis (Eds.), *Encyclopedia of social work* (20th ed.) (pp. 2:539–542). Washington, DC and New York: NASW Press and Oxford University Press.

DeJong, P. (2009). Solution-focused therapy. In A. R. Roberts, *Social workers' desk reference* (2nd ed.) (pp. 253–258). New York: Oxford Press.

De Jong, P. & Cronkright, A. (2011). Learning solution-focused interviewing skills: BSW student voices. *Journal of Teaching in Social work, 31,* 21–37.

De Jong, P., & Berg, I. K. (2013). *Interviewing for solutions* (4th ed.). Belmont, CA: Brooks/Cole.

deShazer, S. (1984). The death of resistance. *Family Process, 23,* 11–21.

Detroit Area Food Council. (n.d.). *Homepage.* Retrieved from http://www.detroitfoodpolicycouncil.net/

Diller, J. (2011). *Cultural diversity: A primer for the human services.* Belmont, CA: Thompson/Brooks/Cole.

Dolgoff, R., Loewenberg, F. M., & Harrington, D. (2012). *Ethical decisions for social work practice.* Itasca, IL: F. E. Peacock.

Dombo, E. A. (2011). Rape: When professional values place vulnerable clients at risk. In J. C. Rothman (Ed.), *From the front lines: Student cases in social work ethics* (3nd ed.) (pp. 185–188). Boston: Allyn & Bacon.

Donaldson, L.P. (2004). Toward validating the thera-peutic benefits of empowerment-oriented social action groups. *Social Work with Groups, 27*(2), 159–175.

Dressler, L. (2006). *Consensus through conversation*. San Francisco, CA: Berrett-Koehler Publishers, Inc.

Drumm, K. (2006). The essential power of group work. *Social Work with Groups, 29*(2/3), 17–31.

Dudley, J. R. (2009). *Social work evaluation: Enhancing what we do*. Chicago, IL: Lyceum Books, Inc.

Dunst, C. J., Trivette, C. M., & Deal, A. G. (2003). *Enabling and empowering families: Principles and guidelines for practice*. Newton: MA: Brookline Books.

Dunst, C. J. & Trivette, C. M. (2009). Capacity-building family-systems intervention practices. *Journal of Family Social Work, 12*, 119–143.

Dybicz, P. (2012). The hero(ine) on a journey: A post-modern conceptual framework for social work practice. *Journal of Social Work Education, 48*(2), 267–283.

Earley, L. & Cushway, D. (2002). The parentified child. *Clinical Child Psychology & Psychiatry, 7*(2), 163–178.

Early, T. J. (2001). Measures for practice with families from a strengths perspective. *Families in Society, 82*(3), 225–232.

East, J. F., Manning, S. F., & Parsons, R. J. (2002). Social work empowerment agenda and group work: A workshop. In S. Henry, J. East, & C. Schmitz (Eds.), *Social work with groups: Mining the gold* (pp. 41–53). New York: Haworth Press.

Eaton, Y. M. & Roberts, A. R. (2009). Frontline crisis intervention. Step-by-step practice guidelines with case applications. In A. R. Roberts, *Social workers' desk reference* (2nd ed.) (pp.207–215). New York: Oxford Press.

Edwards, R. L. & Yankey, J. A. (2006). *Effectively managing nonprofit organizations*. Washington DC: NASW Press.

Ephross, P. H. (2011). Social work with groups: Practice principles. In G. L. Grief & P. H. Ephross, *Group work with populations at risk* (3rd ed.) (pp. 3–14). New York: Oxford University Press.

Ephross, P. H. & Greif, G. L. (2009). Group process and group work techniques. In A. R. Roberts, *Social workers' desk reference* (2nd ed.) (pp. 679–685). New York: Oxford Press.

Epstein, M. H. (2004). *Behavioral and emotional rating scale: A strengths-based approach to assessment* (2nd ed.). Austin, TX: PRO-ED.

Epstein, M. H., Mooney, P., Ryser, G., & Pierce, C. D. (2004). Validity and reliability of the Behavioral and Emotional Rating Scale (2nd ed.): Youth Rating Scale. *Research on Social Work Practice, 14*(50), 358–367.

Evans, S. D., Hanlin, C. E., & Prillehensky, I. (2007). Blending Ameliorative and transformative approaches in human service organizations: A case study. *Journal of Community Psychology, 35*(3), 329–346.

Finlayson, M. L. & Cho, C. C. (2011). A profile of support group use and need among middle-aged and older adults with multiple sclerosis. *Journal of Gerontological Social Work, 54*, 475–493.

Fischer, J. & Orme, J. G. (2008). Single-System Designs. In T. Mizrahi & L. E. Davis, *Encyclopedia of social work* (20th ed.) (pp. 4:32–34). Washington, DC and New York: NASW Press and Oxford University Press.

Fleming, J. (2009). Social action. In A. Gitterman & R. Salmon, *Encyclopedia of social work with groups* (pp. 275–277). New York: Routledge.

Freedenthal, S. (2008). Suicide. In T. Mizrahi & L. E. Davis, *Encyclopedia of social work* (20th ed.) (pp. 4:181–186). Washington, DC and New York: NASW Press and Oxford University Press.

Frey, B. A. (1990). A framework for promoting organizational change. *Families in Society, 71*(3), 142–147.

Fortune, A. E. (2009). Terminating with clients. In A. R. Roberts, *Social workers' desk reference* (2nd ed.) (pp. 627–631). New York: Oxford Press.

Franklin, C., Jordan, C., & Hopson, L. M. (2009). Effective couple and family treatment. In A. R. Roberts, *Social workers' desk reference* (2nd ed.) (pp. 433–442). New York: Oxford Press.

Freire, P. (1973). *Education for critical consciousness*. New York: Seabury Press.

Fuller-Thomson, E. & Minkler, M. (2005). American Indian/Alaskan Native grandparents raising grandchildren: Findings from the Census 2000 Supplementary Survey. *Social Work, 50*(2), 131–139.

Furman, R., Rowan, D., & Bender, K. (2009). *An experiential approach to group work.* Chicago, IL: Lyceum Books, Inc.

Gamble, D. N. & Hoff, M. D. (2013). Sustainable community development. In M. Weil (Ed.), *The handbook of community practice* (pp. 215–232). Thousand Oaks, CA: Sage Publications.

Gambrill, E. (2013). *Social work practice: A critical thinkers guide.* New York: Oxford University Press.

Garkovich, L. E. (2011). A historical view of community development. In J. W. Robinson, Jr. & G. P. Green (Eds.), *Introduction to community development* (pp. 11–34). Los Angeles, CA: Sage Publications, Inc.

Garland, J., Jones, H., & Kolodny, R. (1965). A model for stages of development in social work groups. In S. Bernstein (Ed.), *Explorations in group work: Essays in theory and practice* (pp. 12–53). Boston: Boston University School of Social Work.

Garvin, C. D. & Galinsky, M. J. (2008). Groups. In T. Mizrahi & L. E. Davis, *Encyclopedia of social work* (20th ed.) (pp. 2:287–298). Washington, DC and New York: NASW Press and Oxford University Press.

Garvin, C. (2009). Developing goals. In A. R. Roberts, *Social workers' desk reference* (2nd ed.) (pp. 521–526). New York: Oxford Press.

Gilligan, C. (1993). *In a different voice.* Cambridge, MA: Harvard University Press.

Gitterman, A. & Germain, C. B. (2008a). Ecological framework. In T. Mizrahi & L. E. Davis (Eds.), *Encyclopedia of social work* (20th ed.) (pp. 2:97–102). Washington, D.C. and New York: NASW Press and Oxford University Press.

Gitterman, A. & Germain, C. B. (2008b). *The life model of social work practice: Advances in theory and practice* (3rd ed). New York: Columbia Press.

Gonzales, J. (2009). Prefamily counseling: Working with blended families. *Journal of Divorce & Remarriage, 50,* 148–157.

Goode, E., & Kovalski, S. F. (2012, August 12). Wisconsin killer fed and was fueled by hate-driven music. *New York Times.* Retrieved from http://www.nytimes.com/2012/08/07/us/army-veteran-identified-as-suspect-in-wisconsin-shooting.html?pagewanted=allhttp://www.nytimes.com/2012/08/07/us/army-veteran-identified-as-suspect-in-wisconsin-shooting.html?_r=1&pagewanted=all

Goodman, H. (2004). Elderly parents of adults with severe mental illness: Group work interventions. *Journal of Gerontological Social Work, 44*(1/2), 173–188.

Grace, K. S., McClellan, A., & Yankey, J. A. (2009). *The nonprofit board's role in mission, planning and evaluation.* Washington DC: BoardSource.

Grant, D. (2008). Clinical social work. In R. Mizrahi & L. E. Davis (Eds.), *Encyclopedia of Social Work. National Association of Social Workers and Oxford University Press, Inc. Encyclopedia of Social Work: (e-reference edition).* Oxford University Press. Retrieved April 1, 2010 from http://www.oxford-naswsocialwork.com/entry?entry=t203.e63

Gray, M. (2011). Back to basics: A critique of the strengths perspective in social work. *Families in Society: The Journal of Contemporary Social Services, 92*(1), 5–11.

Gray, M., Coates, J., & Hetherington, T. (2012). *Environmental social work.* New York: Routledge.

Greene, G. J. & Lee, M. Y. (2011). *Solution-oriented social work practice.* New York: Oxford University Press.

Greenpeace. (n.d.). *About us.* Retrieved from http://www.greenpeace.org/usa/en/campaigns/

Gregg, B. (2012). *Human rights as a social construction.* New York: Oxford University Press.

Grieco E. M., Acosta, Y. D., de la Cruz, P., Gambino, C., Gryn, T., Larsen, L. J., Trevelyan, E. N., & Walters, N. P. (2012). *The foreign-born population in the United States: 2010.* Washington, D.C.: U.S. Census Bureau.

Grief, G. L. & Morris-Compton, D. (2011). Group work with urban African American parents in their neighborhood schools. In G. L. Grief & P. H. Ephross, *Group work with populations at risk* (3rd ed.) (pp. 385–398). New York: Oxford University Press.

Grief, G. & Ephross, P. H. (Eds.). (2011). *Group work with populations at risk* (3rd ed.). New York: Oxford University Press.

Hall, J. C. (2011). A narrative approach to group work with men who batter. *Social Work with Groups, 34,* 175–189.

Hamilton, B. E., Martin, J. A., & Ventura, S. J. (2012). Births: Preliminary data for 2011. *National vital statistics reports, 61*(5). Hyattsville, MD: National Center for Health Statistics.

Hanley, J. & Shragge, E. (2009). Organizing for immigrant rights. *Journal of Community Practice, 17*(1), 184–206.

Hardina, D. (2002). *Analytical skills for community organization practice.* New York: Columbia University Press.

Hardina, D., Middleton, J., Montana, S., & Simpson, R. A. (2007). *An empowering approach to managing social service organizations.* New York: Springer Publishing Company.

Hardina, D. (2012). *Interpersonal social work skills for community practice.* New York: Springer.

Hardy, K. V. & Laszloffy, T. A. (1995). The Cultural genogram: Key to training culturally competent family therapists. *Journal of Marital and Family Therapy, 21,* 227–237.

Hartman, A. & Laird, J. (1983). *Family-centered social work practice.* New York: Free Press.

Harrington, D. & Dolgoff, R. (2008). Hierarchies of ethical principles for ethical decision making in social work. *Ethics and Social Welfare, 2*(2), 183–196.

Hartman, A. (1994). *Reflection & controversy: Essays on social work.* Washington, DC: NASW Press.

Harvey, A. R. (2011). Group work with African American youth in the criminal justice system: A culturally competent model. In G. L. Grief & P. H. Ephross, *Group work with populations at risk* (3rd ed.) (pp. 264–282). New York: Oxford University Press.

Hasenfeld, Y. (2000). Social welfare administration and organizational theory. In R. J. Patti (Ed.) *The handbook of social welfare management* (pp. 89–112). Thousand Oaks, CA: Sage Publications.

Haynes, K. S. (1998). The one-hundred year debate: Social reform versus individual treatment. *Social Work, 43*(6), 501–511.

Haynes, K. S. & Mickelson, J. S. (2010). *Affecting change* (7th ed.). Boston: Pearson.

Hayslip, Jr., B. & Kaminski, P. L. (2005). Grandparents raising their grandchildren. A review of the literature and suggestions for practice. *The Gerontologist, 45*(2), 262–269.

Head, J. W. (2008). *Losing the global development war.* Leiden, The Netherlands: Martinus Nijhoff Publishers.

Healy, L. (2008). *International social work: Professional practice in an interdependent world.* New York: Oxford University Press.

Healy, L. M. & Hokenstad, T. M. C. (2008). International social work. In T. Mizrahi & L. E. Davis, *Encyclopedia of social work* (20th ed.) (pp. 2:482–488). Washington, DC and New York: NASW Press and Oxford University Press.

Healy, L. M. & Link, R. J. (2012). *Handbook of international social work: Human rights, development, and the global profession.* New York: Oxford.

Herbert, R. J., Gagnon, A. J., Rennick, J. E., & O'Loughlin, J. L. (2009). A systematic review of questionnaires measuring health-related empowerment. *Research and Theory for Nursing Practice: An International Journal, 23*(2), 107–132.

Hillier, A. & Culhane, D. (2013). GIS applications and administrative data to support community change. In M. Weil's (Ed.) *The handbook of community practice* (pp. 827–844). Thousand Oaks, CA: Sage.

Hodge, D. R. (2005a). Social work and the House of Islam: Orienting practitioners to the beliefs and values of Muslims in the United States. *Social Work, 50*(2), 162–173.

Hodge, D. R. (2005b). Spiritual life maps: A client centered pictorial instrument for spiritual assessment,planning, and intervention. *Social Work, 50*(1), 77–87.

Hohman, M. (2012). *Motivational interviewing in social work practice.* New York: The Guilford Press.

Holland, T. (2008). Organizations and governance. In T. Mizrahi & L. E. Davis (Eds.) *Encyclopedia of Social*

Work (pp. 3:329–333). Washington DC: NASW Press and Oxford University Press.

Holland, T. P. & Kilpatrick, A. C. (2009). An ecological system—social constructionism approach to family practice. In A. C. Kilpatrick & T. P. Holland, *Working with families. An integrative model by level of need* (5th ed.) (pp. 15–31). Boston: Pearson.

Hong, P. Y. & Song, I. H. (2010). Glocalization of social work practice: Global and local responses to globalization. *International Social Work, 53*, 656–670.

Hopson, L. M. & Wodarski, J. S. (2009). Guidelines and uses of rapid assessment instruments in managed care settings. In A. R. Roberts, *Social workers' desk reference* (2nd ed.) (pp. 400–405). New York: Oxford Press.

Hudson, R. E. (2009). Empowerment model. In A. Gitterman & R. Salmon (Eds.), *Encyclopedia of social work with groups* (pp. 47–50). New York: Routledge.

Hull, G. H. & Mather, J. (2006). *Understanding generalist practice with families.* Belmont, CA: Thomson Brooks/Cole.

Human Rights Education Association. (n.d.). *Simplified version of the University Declaration of Human Rights.* Retrieved from http://www.hrea.org/index.php?base_id=104&language_id=1&erc_doc_id=5211&category_id=24&category_type=q3&group=

Ife, J. (2000). Localized needs and a globalized economy. *Social Work and Globalization (Special Issue), Canadian Social Work, 2*(1), 50–64.

"Indicators for the Achievement of the NASW Standards for Cultural Competence in Social Work Practice." (2008). In T. Mizrahi & L. E. Davis (Eds.), *Encyclopedia of social work. National Association of Social Workers and Oxford University Press, Inc. (e-reference edition).* Retrieved from http://www.oxford-naswsocialwork.com/entry?entry=t203.e427

International Association for the Advancement of Social Work with Groups, Inc. (IASWG) (2006). *Standards for social work practice with groups* (2nd ed.). Alexandria, VA: AASWG, Inc.

International Federation of Social Workers (IFSW). (2012). *Ethics in social work: Statement of principles.* Retrieved from http://ifsw.org/policies/statement-of-ethical-principles/

International Institute St. Louis. (2013). *Economic development.* Retrieved from http://www.iistl.org/edintro.html

Interorganizational Committee on Guidelines and Principles for Social Impact Assessment (IOCPG). (2003). Principles and guidelines for social impact assessment in the United States. *Impact Assessment and Project Appraisal, 21*(3), 231–250.

Jackson, K. F. & Samuels, G. M. (2011). Multiracial competence in social work: Recommendation for culturally attuned work with multiracial people. *Social Work, 56*(3), 235–245.

Janzen, C., Harris, O., Jordan, C., & Franklin, C. (2006). *Family treatment: Evidence-based practice with populations at risk.* Belmont, CA: Thomson Brooks/Cole.

Jayartne, S., Croxton, T. A., & Mattison, D. (2004). A national survey of violence in the practice of social work. *Families in Society, 85*(4), 445–453.

Jenson, J. M. & Howard, M. O. (2008). Evidence-based practice. In T. Mizrahi & L. E. Davis (Eds.), *Encyclopedia of social work* (20th ed.) (pp.2:158–165). Washington, DC and New York: NASW Press and Oxford University Press.

Johnson, M. & Austin, M. J. (2006). Evidence-based practice in the social services: Implications for organizational change. *Journal of Evidence-Based Social Work, 5*(1/2), 239–269.

Joplin Area CART. (n.d.). Homepage. Retrieved from http://joplinareacart.com/

Jordan, C. (2008). Assessment. In T. Mizrahi & L. E. Davis, *Encyclopedia of social work* (20th ed.) (pp 1:178–180). Washington, DC and New York: NASW Press and Oxford University Press.

Jordan, C. & Franklin, C. (2009). Treatment planning with families: An evidence-based approach. In A. R. Roberts, *Social workers' desk reference* (2nd ed.) (pp. 429–432). New York: Oxford Press.

Jung, M. (1996). Family-centered practice with single parent families. *Families in Society, 77*(9), 583–590.

Kagle, J. D. (2008). Recording. In T Mizrahi & L. E. Davis, *Encyclopedia of social work* (20th ed.) (pp. 3:497–498). Washington, DC and New York: NASW Press and Oxford University Press.

Kagle, J. D. & Kopels, S. (2008). *Social work records* (3rd ed.). Long Grove, IL: Waveland Press, Inc.

Kalyanpur, M. & Harry, B. (1999). *Culture in special education*. Baltimore: Paul H. Brookes.

Kasvin, N. & Tashayeva, A. (2004). Community organizing to address domestic violence in immigrant populations in the U.S.A. *Journal of Religion and Abuse*, 6(3/4), 109–112.

Kelley, P. (2008). Narratives. In T. Mizrahi & L. E. Davis (Eds.), *Encyclopedia of social work* (20th ed.) (pp. 3:291–292). Washington, DC and New York: NASW Press and Oxford University Press.

Kelley, P. (2009). Narrative therapy. In A. R. Roberts (Ed.), *Social workers' desk reference* (2nd ed.) (pp. 273–277). New York: Oxford Press.

Kelly, T. B. & Berman-Rossi, T. (1999). Advancing stages of group development theory: The case of institutionalized older persons. *Social Work with Groups*, 22(2/3), 119–138.

Kelly, M. S., Kim, J. S., & Franklin, C. (2008). *Solution-focused brief therapy in schools. A 360-degree view of research and practice*. New York: Oxford University Press.

Kettner, P. M. (2002). *Achieving excellence in the management of human service organizations*. Boston: Allyn & Bacon.

Kilpatrick, A. & Cleveland, P. (1993). *Unpublished course materials*. University of Georgia School of Social Work.

Kilpatrick, A. C. (2009). Levels of family need. In A. C. Kilpatrick & T. P. Holland, *Working with families. An integrative model by level of need* (5th ed.) (pp. 2–14). Boston: Pearson.

Kim, J. S. (2008a). Strengths perspective. In T. Mizrahi & L. E. Davis (Eds.), *Encyclopedia of social work* (20th ed.) (pp. 4:177–181). Washington, DC and New York: NASW Press and Oxford University Press.

Kim, J. S. (2008b). Examining the effectiveness of solution-focused brief therapy: A meta-analysis. *Research on Social Work Practice*, 18, 107–116.

Kim, H., Ji, J, & Kao, D. (2011). Burnout and physical health among social workers: A three-year longitudinal study. *Social Work*, 56(3), 258–268.

Kisthardt, W. E. (2013). Integrating the core competencies in strengths-based, person-centered practice. In D. Saleebey (Ed.), *The strengths perspective in social work practice* (6th ed.), pp. 53–78. Boston: Allyn & Bacon.

Kleinkauf, C. (1981, July). A guide to giving legislative testimony. *Social Work*, 297–303.

Kohli, H. K., Huber, R., & Faul, A. C. (2010). Historical and theoretical development of culturally competent social work practice. *Journal of Teaching in Social Work*, 30, 252–271.

Kong, E. (2007). The development of strategic management in the non-profit context: Intellectual capital in the social service non-profit organization. *International Journal of Management Reviews*, 10(3), 281–299.

Koop, J. J. (2009). Solution-focused family interventions. In A. C. Kilpatrick & T. P. Holland, *Working with families. An integrative model by level of need* (5th ed.) (pp. 147–169). Boston: Pearson.

Koren, P. E., DeChillo, N., & Friesen, B. J. (1992). Measuring empowerment in families whose children have emotional disabilities: A brief questionnaire. *Rehabilitation Psychology*, 37, 305–310.

Kreider, R. M. & Ellis, R. (2011). Living arrangements of children: 2009. *Household Economic Studies. Current Population Reports*, P70–126. Washington, DC: U.S. Census Bureau.

Kretzmann, J. P. & McKnight, J. L. (1993). *Building communities from the inside out: A path toward finding and mobilizing a community's assets*. Evanston, IL: Center for Urban Affairs and Policy Research.

Kretzmann, J. P. & McKnight, J. L. (2005). *Discovering community power: A guide to mobilizing local assets and your organization's capacity*. Evanston, IL: Asset-Based Community Development (ABCD) Institute.

Kurland, R. & Salmon, R. (1998). *Teaching a methods course in social work with groups*. Alexandria, VA: Council on Social Work Education.

Kurland, R., Salmon, R., Bitel, M., Goodman, H., Ludwig, K., Newmann, E.W., & Sullivan, N. (2004). The survival of social group work: *A call to action. Social Work with Groups*, 27(1), 3–16.

Kurland, R. (2007). Debunking the "blood theory" of social work with groups: Groups workers are made and not born. *Social Work with Groups, 31*(1), 11–24.

Larson, K. & McGuiston, C. (2012). Building capacity to improve Latino health in rural North Carolina: A case study in community-University engagement. *Journal of Community Engagement and Scholarship, 5*(1), 14–23.

Lawler, J. & Bilson, A. (2004). Towards a more reflexive research aware practice: The influence and potential of professional and team culture. *Social Work & Social Sciences Review, 11*(1), 52–69.

Leahy, M. M., O'Dwyer, M., & Ryan, F. (2012). Witnessing stories: Definitional ceremonies in narrative therapy with adults who stutter. *Journal of Fluency Disorders, 37*, 234–241.

Lee, J. A. B. & Berman-Rossi, T. (1999). Empowering adolescent girls in foster care: A short-term group record. In C. W. LeCroy (Ed.), *Case studies in social work practice* (2nd ed.). Pacific Grove, CA: Brooks/Cole.

Lee, J. A. B. (2001). *The empowerment approach to social work practice* (2nd ed.). New York: Columbia University Press.

Lee, M. Y. (2009). Using the miracle question and scaling technique in clinical practice. In A. R. Roberts, *Social workers' desk reference* (2nd ed.) (pp. 594–600). New York: Oxford Press.

Lee, M. Y. & Greene, G. J. (2009). Using social constructivism in social work practice. In A. R. Roberts (Ed.), *Social workers' desk reference* (2nd ed.) (pp. 294–299). New York: Oxford Press.

Lesser, J. G., O'Neill, M. R., Burke, K. W., Scanlon, P., Hollis, K., & Miller, R. (2004). Women supporting women: A mutual aid group fosters new connections among women in midlife. *Social Work with Groups, 27*(1), 75–88.

Levy, R. (2011). Core themes in a support group for spouses of breast cancer patients. *Social work with groups, 34*, 141–157.

Lewin, K. (1951). *Field theory in social science.* New York: Harper and Row.

Library of Congress. (1996). *Defense of Marriage Act.* Retrieved from: http://www.govtrack.us/congress/bills/104/hr3396#summary/libraryofcongress

Locke, B., Garrison, R., & Winship, J. (1998). *Generalist social work practice: Context, story, and partnerships.* Pacific Grove, CA: Brooks/Cole.

Logan, S. L. M., Rasheed, M. N., & Rasheed, J. M. (2008). Family. In T. Mizrahi & L. E. Davis (Eds.), *Encyclopedia of social work* (20th ed.) (pp. 2:175–182). Washington, DC and New York: NASW Press and Oxford University Press.

López, L. M. & Vargas, E. M. (2011). En dos culturas: Group work with Latino Immigrants and Refugees. In G. L. Greif & P. H. Ephross, *Group work with populations at risk* (3rd ed.) (pp. 144–145). New York: Oxford University Press.

Lotze, G. M., Bellin, M. H., & Oswald, D. P. (2010). Family-centered care for children with special health care needs: Are we moving forward? *Journal of Family Social Work, 13*, 100–113.

Lovell, M. L., Helfgott, J. B., & Lawrence, C. (2002). Citizens, victims, and offenders restoring justice: A prison-based group work program bridging the divide. In S. Henry, J. East, & C. Schmitz (Eds.) *Social work with groups: Mining the gold* (pp. 75–88). New York: Haworth Press.

Lowery, C. T. & Mattaini, M. (2001). Shared power in social work: A Native American perspective of change. In H. E. Briggs and K. Corcoran (Eds.), *Social work practice: Treating common client problems* (pp. 109–124). Chicago: Lyceum Books.

Lum, D. (2004). *Social work practice and people of color: A process stage approach* (5th ed.). Belmont, CA: Thomson Brooks/Cole.

Lum, D. (2008). Culturally competent practice. In T. Mizrahi & L. E. Davis, *Encyclopedia of social work* (20th ed.) (pp. 2:497–502). Washington, DC and New York: NASW Press and Oxford University Press.

Lum, D. (2011). *Culturally competent practice: A framework for understanding diverse groups and justice issues.* Belmont, CA: Brooks/Cole Cengage Learning.

Lundahl, B. W., Kunz, C., Brownell, C., Tollefson, D., & Burke, B. L. (2010). A meta-analysis of motivational interviewing: Twenty-five years of empirical studies. *Research on Social Work Practice, 20*(2), 137–160.

Lundy, C. (2011). *Social work, social justice, and human rights: A structural approach to practice.* North York, Ont.: University of Toronto Press.

Macgowan, M. J. (1997). A measure of engagement for social group work: The Groupwork engagement measure (GEM). *Journal of Social Service Research, 23,* 17–37.

Macgowan, M. J. (2000). Evaluation of a measure of engagement for group work. *Research on Social Work Practice, 10,* 348–361.

Macgowan, M. J. & Levenson, J. S. (2003). Psychometrics of the Group Engagement Measure with male sex offenders. *Small Group Research, 34*(2), 155–169.

Macgowan, M. J. & Newman, F. L. (2005). Factor structure of the Group Engagement Measure. *Social Work Research, 29*(2), 107–118.

Macgowan, M. J. (2008). Group dynamics. In T. Mizrahi & L.E. Davis, *Encyclopedia of social work* (20th ed.) (pp. 2:279–287). Washington, DC and New York: NASW Press and Oxford University Press.

Macgowan, M. J. (2009a). Evidence-based group work. In A. Gitterman & R. Salmon (Eds.), *Encyclopedia of social work with groups* (pp. 131–136). New York: Routledge.

Macgowan, M. J. (2009b). Measurement. In A. Gitterman & R. Salmon (Eds.), *Encyclopedia of social work with groups* (pp. 142–147). New York: Routledge.

Mackelprang, R. W. & Salsgiver, R. O. (2009). *Disability: A diversity model approach in human service practice.* Chicago, IL: Lyceum Books, Inc.

MacNeill, V. (2009). Forming partnerships with parents from a community development perspective: Lessons learnt from Sure Start. *Health and Social Care in the Community, 17*(6), 659–665.

Madigan, S. (2011). *Narrative therapy.* Washington DC: The American Psychological Association.

Manning, T. (2012). The art of successful persuasion: Seven skills you need to get your point across effectively. *Industrial and Commercial Training, 44*(3), 150–158.

Manor, O. (2008). Systemic approach. In A. Gitterman & R. Salmon (Eds.) *Encyclopedia of social work with groups* (pp. 99–101). New York: Routledge.

Maramaldi, P., Berkman, B., & Barusch, A. (2005). Assessment and the ubiquity of culture: Threats to validity in measures of health-related quality of life. *Health & Social Work, 30*(1), 27–36.

Marguerite Casey Foundation. (2012). *Organizational capacity assessment tool.* Retrieved from http://caseygrants.org/resources/org-capacity-assessment/

Mason, J. L. (1995). *Cultural competence self-assessment questionnaire: A manual for users.* Portland, OR: Portland State University, Research and Training Center on Family Support and Children's Mental Health. Retrieved from http://www.racialequity-tools.org/resourcefiles/mason.pdf

McCullough-Chavis, A. & Waites, C. (2008). Genograms with African American families: Considering cultural context. In C. Waites (Ed.), *Social work practice with African-American families: An intergenerational perspective* (pp. 35–54). New York: Routledge.

McGoldrick, M., Gerson, R., & Petry, S. (2008). *Genograms assessment and intervention* (3rd ed.). New York: W.W. Norton & Company.

McGoldrick, M. (2009). Using genograms to map family patterns. In A. R. Roberts, *Social workers' desk reference* (2nd ed.) (pp. 409–423). New York: Oxford Press.

McGowan, B. G. & Walsh, E. M. (2012). Writing in family and child welfare. In W. Green and B. L. Simon, *The Columbia guide to social work writing* (pp. 215–231). NY: Columbia University Press.

McKnight, J. L., & Block, P. (2010). *The abundant community: Awakening the power of families and neighborhoods.* San Francisco, CA: Berrett-Koehler Publishers.

McKnight, J. L. & Kretzmann, J. P. (1996). *Mapping community capacity.* Evanston, IL: Institute for Policy Research. Retrieved from http://www.racialequitytools.org/resourcefiles/mcknight.pdf

McNutt, J. & Floersch, J. (2008). Social work practice. In T. Mizrahi & L. E. Davis (Eds.), *Encyclopedia of social work. National Association of Social Workers and the Oxford University Press, Inc.(e-reference edition).* Retrieved from http://www.oxford-naswsocialwork.com/entry?entry=t203.e375-s2

McWhirter, P. T., Robbins, R., Vaughn, K., Youngbull, N., Burks, D., Willmon-Haque, S., Schuetz, S., Brandes, J. A., & Nael, A. Z. O. (2011). Honoring the ways of American Indian women: A group therapy intervention. In A. A. Singh & C. F. Salazar, *Social justice in group work. Practical interventions for change* (pp. 73–81). New York: Routledge.

Meyer, C. (1993). *Assessment in social work practice*. New York: Columbia University Press.

Middleman, R. R. & Wood, G. G. (1990). *Skills for direct practice in social work*. New York: Columbia University Press.

Miley, K. K., O'Melia, M. W., & DuBois, B. L. (2013). *Generalist social work practice: An empowering approach*. Boston: Pearson Allyn & Bacon.

Miller, L. (2011). *Counselling skills for social work*. London, Thousand Oaks, CA: Sage.

Miller, W. R. & Rollnick, S. (2013). *Motivational interviewing: Helping people change* (3rd ed.). New York: The Guilford Press.

Minieri, J. & Getsos, P. (2007). *Tools for radical democracy*. San Francisco, CA: Jossey Bass.

Minuchin, S. (1974). *Families & family therapy*. Cambridge, MA: Harvard University Press.

Minuchin, P., Colapinto, J., & Minuchin, S. (2007). *Working with families of the poor* (2nd ed.). New York: The Guilford Press.

Mondros, J. & Staples, L. (2008). Community organization. In T. Mizrahi & L. E. Davis (Eds.), *Encyclopedia of social work* (pp.1:387–398). Washington DC and New York: NASW Press and Oxford University Press.

Morgan, A. (2000). *What is narrative therapy?* Adelaide, South Australia: Dulwich Centre Publications.

Moxley, D. (2008). Interdisciplinarity. In T. Mizrahi & L. E. Davis, *Encyclopedia of social work* (20th ed.) Washington, DC and New York: NASW Press and Oxford University Press. (e-reference edition). Accessed August 17, 2010 from: http:// www.oxford-naswsocialwork.com/entry?entry?t203.e200

Mulroy, E. (2008). Community needs assessment. In T. Mizrahi & L. E. Davis (Eds.), *Encyclopedia of social work* (pp. 1:385–387). Washington DC and New York: NASW Press and Oxford University Press.

Musick, K. & Meier, A. (2009). Are both parents always better than one? Parental conflict and young adult well-being. *Rural New York Minute, 28*, 1.

Nakhaima, J. M. & Dicks, B. H. (2012). A role for the religious community in family counseling. *Families in Society Practice and Policy Focus.*

National Association of Area Agencies on Aging. (2012). *National aging services network*. Retrieved from http://www.n4a.org/about-n4a/join/

National Association of Cognitive-Behavioral Therapists. (2013). *Cognitive behavioral therapy*. Retrieved from: http://www.nacbt.org/whatiscbt.aspx

National Alliance on Mental Illness (NAMI). (2013). *Cognitive behavioral therapy (CBT)?* Retrieved from http://www.nami.org/

National Association of Social Workers (NASW). (1996). *Code of ethics*. Washington, DC: NASW.

National Association of Social Workers (NASW). (2001). *NASW standards for cultural competence in social work practice*. Washington D.C.: NASW. Retrieved from http://www.naswdc.org/practice/standards/NAswculturalstandards.pdf

National Association of Social Workers. (2007b). *Indicators for the achievement of the NASW Standards for Cultural Competence in Social Work Practice*. Washington, DC: NASW.

National Association of Social Workers. (2007a). *Children and families*. Retrieved January 18, 2013 from: http://www.socialworkers.org/pressroom/features/issue/children.asp

National Association of Social Workers (NASW). (2008). *Code of ethics*. Washington, DC: NASW.

National Association of Social Workers (NASW). (2012). *Practice*. Retrieved from http://www.social-workers.org/practice/

National Association of Social Workers-California Chapter. (2012). *Online continuing education*. Retrieved from http://www.socialworkweb.com/nasw/

National Association of Social Workers. (2012–2014a). *Cultural and linguistic competence in the social work profession. Social work speaks: National Association* of Social Workers policy statements 2012–2014. Washington, DC: NASW Press.

National Association of Social Workers. (2012–2014b). *Professional self-care and social work. Social work speaks: National Association of Social Workers policy statements 2009–2012.* Washington, DC: NASW Press.

National Association of Social Workers. (2013a). *Draft NASW Guidelines for Social Worker Safety in the Workplace.* Washington, D.C.: NASW.

National Association of Social Workers. (2013b). *Standards for social work case management.* Washington, D.C.: NASW.

National Association of Social Workers (NASW). (n.d.) *NASW WebEd.* Retrieved from http://www.naswwebed.org/

National Conference of State Legislatures (NCSL). (2012). *Defining marriage: Defense of marriage acts and same-sex marriage laws.* Retrieved from: http://www.ncsl.org/issues-research/human-services/same-sex-marriage-overview.aspx

Netting, F. E., Kettner, P. M., & McMurtry, S. L., & Thomas, L. (2011). *Social work macro practice.* Boston: Pearson Allyn & Bacon.

Newhill, C. E. (1995). Client violence toward social workers: A practice and policy concern. *Social Work, 40,* 631–636.

New York Times. (2012, October 16). *Income inequality.* Retrieved from http://topics.nytimes.com/top/reference/timestopics/subjects/i/income/income_inequality/index.html

New Zealand Association of Social Workers (NZASW). (1993). *Code of ethics.* Aoteora, NZ: NZASW.

Nichols, M. P. (2011). *The essentials of family therapy* (5th ed.). Boston: Pearson.

Nissly, J. A., Barak, M. E. M., & Levin, A. (2005). Stress, social support, and worker's intentions to leave their jobs in public child welfare. *Administration in Social Work, 29*(1), 79–100.

North Central Regional Center for Rural Development, Iowa State University. (n.d.). *Community assessment.* Des Moines, IA: Author

Nowicki, J. & Arbuckle, L. (2009). The social worker as family counselor in a nonprofit community-based agency. In A. R. Roberts, *Social workers' desk reference* (2nd ed.) (pp. 45–53). New York: Oxford Press.

O'Connor, M. K. & Netting, F. E. (2009). *Organization practice: A guide to understanding human service organizations.* Hoboken, NJ: Wiley.

Ohmer, M. L. & Korr, W. S. (2006). The effectiveness of community practice interventions: A review of the literature. *Research on Social Work Practice, 16*(2), 132–145.

Ohmer, M. L. (2008). Assessing and developing the evidence base of macro practice: Interventions with a community and neighborhood focus. *Journal of Evidence-based Social Work, 5*(3/4), 519–547.

Ohmer, M. L. & DeMasi, K. (2009). *Consensus organizing: A community development workbook.* Thousand Oaks, CA: Sage Publications, Inc.

Ohmer, M. L., Sobek, J. L., Teixeira, S. N., Wallace, J. M. & Shapiro, V. B. (2013). Community-based research: Rationale, methods, roles, and considerations for community practice. In M. Weil's (Ed.), *The handbook of community practice* (pp. 791–807). Thousand Oaks, CA: Sage.

Ohmer, M. L. & Brooks, F. (2013). The practice of community organizing. In M. Weil (Ed.), *The handbook of community practice* (pp. 233–248). Thousand Oaks, CA: Sage Publications

Oregon Legislature. (n.d.). *How to testify before a legislative committee.* Retrieved from http://www.leg.state.or.us/comm/testify.html

Packard, T. (2009). Leadership and performance in human services organizations. In R. J. Patti (Ed.), *The handbook of social welfare management* (pp. 143–164). Thousand Oaks, CA: Sage Publications.

Papell, C. P. & Rothman, B. (1962). Social group work models: Possession and heritage. *Journal of Education for Social Work, 2*(2), pp. 66–77.

Papero, D. V. (2009). Bowen family systems theory. In A.R. Roberts, *Social workers' desk reference* (2nd ed.) (pp. 447–452). New York: Oxford Press.

Parsons, R. J. (2008). Empowerment practice. In T. Mizrahi and L. E. Davis (Eds.), *Encyclopedia of social work* (20th ed.) (pp. 2:123–126). Washington, DC and New York: NASW Press and Oxford University Press.

Pawelski, J. G., Perrin, E. C., Foy, J. M., Allen, C. E., Crawford, J. E., Del Monte, M. Kaufman, M., Klein, J. D., Smith, K., Springer, S. Tanner, J. L., & Vickers, D. L. (2006). The effects of marriage, civil union, and domestic partnership laws on health and well-being of children. *Pediatrics, 118*, 349–364.

Payne, M. & Askeland, G. A. (2008). *Globalizaiton and international social work: Postmodern change and challenge.* Burlington, VT: Ashgate Publishing Company.

Pfeffer, J. (1992). *Managing with power and politics: Influence in organizations.* Boston, MA: Harvard Business School Press.

Pippard, J. L. & Bjorklund, R. W. (2004). Identifying essential techniques for social work community practice. *Journal of Community Practice, 11*(4), 101–116.

Plitt, D. L. & Shields, J. (2009). Development of the policy advocacy behavior scale: Initial reliability and validity. *Research on Social Work Practice, 19*(1), 83–92.

Poole, D. L. (2009). Community partnerships for school-based services. In A. Roberts (Ed.), *Social workers desk reference* (pp. 907–912). New York: Oxford University Press.

Pope, N. D., Rollins, L., Chaumba, J., & Risler, E. (2011). Evidence-based practice knowledge and utilization among social workers. *Journal of Evidence-Based Social Work, 8*, 349–368.

Potocky, M. (2008). Immigrants and refugees. In T. Mizrahi & L. E. Davis, *Encyclopedia of social work* (20th ed.) (pp. 3:441–445). Washington, DC and New York: NASW Press and Oxford University Press.

Putnam, R. D. & Feldstein, L. M. (2003). *Better together: Restoring the American community.* York: Simon & Schuster.

Ramanathan, C. S. & Link, R. J. (2004). *All our futures: Principles and resources for social work practice in a global era.* Belmont, CA: Brooks/Cole.

Randall, A. C. & DeAngelis, D. (2008). Licensing. In T. Mizrahi & L. E. Davis (Eds.), *Encyclopedia of social work* (20th ed.) (pp. 3:87–91). Washington, DC and New York: NASW Press and Oxford University Press.

Rapp, C. A. & Goscha, R. J. (2006). *The strengths model: Case management with people with psychiatric disabilities.* New York: Oxford University Press.

Rawls, J. (1971). *A theory of justice.* Cambridge, MA: Harvard University Press.

Reamer, F. G. (2003). Boundary issues in social work: Managing dual relationships. *Social Work, 48*(1), 121–133.

Reamer, F. G. (2006). *Social work values and ethics* (3rd ed.) New York: Columbia University Press.

Reamer, F. G. (2008). Ethics and values. In T. Mizrahi & L. E. Davis (Eds.) *Encyclopedia of social work* (pp. 2:143–151). Washington DC: NASW Press.

Reamer, F. G. (2009). Ethical codes of practice in the US and UK: One profession, two standards. *Journal of Social Work Values & Ethics, 6*(2), 4.

Redevelopment Opportunities for Women. (n.d.). *Economic programs.* Retrieved from http://www.row-stl.org/content/REAP.aspx

Reid, K. E. (1997). *Social work practice with groups: A clinical perspective* (2nd ed.). Pacific Grove, CA: Brooks/Cole.

Reid, K. E. (2009). Clinical social work with groups. In A. R. Roberts, *Social workers' desk reference* (2nd ed.) (pp. 432–436). New York: Oxford Press.

Reichert, E. (2011). *Social work and human rights: A foundation for policy and practice.* New York Columbia Press.

Reisch, M. (2013). Community practice challenges in the global economy. In M. Weil's (Ed.), *The handbook of community practice* (pp. 47–71). Thousand Oaks, CA: Sage.

Ringel, S. (2005). Group work with Asian-American immigrants: A cross-cultural perspective. In G. L. Greif & P. H. Ephross, *Group work with populations at risk* (2nd ed.) (pp. 181–194). New York: Oxford University Press.

Roberts, A. R. (2005). Bridging the past and present to the future of crisis intervention and crisis management. In *Crisis intervention handbook: Assessment, treatment and research* (3rd ed.) (pp. 3–34). New York: Oxford University Press.

Roberts, A. R. (2008). Crisis interventions. In T. Mizrahi & L. E. Davis, *Encyclopedia of social work* (20th ed.)

(pp. 1:484–491). Washington, DC and New York: NASW Press and Oxford University Press.

Roberts-DeGennaro, M. (2008). Case management. In T. Mizrahi & L. E. Davis, *Encyclopedia of social work* (20th ed.) (pp. 1:222–227). Washington, DC and New York: NASW Press and Oxford University Press.

Robinson, J. W. & Green, G. P. (2011) *Introduction to community Development: Theory, practice, and service-learning.* Thousand Oaks, CA: Sage.

Roche, S. E. & Wood, G. G. (2005). A narrative principle for feminist social work with survivors of male violence. *AFFILIA*, *20*(4), 465–475.

Rogers, C. (1957). The necessary and sufficient conditions of therapeutic personality change. *Journal of Consulting Psychology*, *22*, 95–103.

Rogers, E. E. (1975). *Organizational theory.* Boston, MA: Allyn & Bacon.

Roosevelt, E. (1958). Presentation of *In your hands: A guide for community action for the tenth anniversary of the Universal Declaration of Human Rights* [online]. Available: www.udhr.org/history/inyour. htm

Roscoe, K. D., Carson, A. M., & Madoc-Jones, L. (2011). Narrative social work: Conversations between theory and practice. *Journal of Social work Practice*, *25*(1), 47–61.

Roscoe, K. D. & Madoc-Jones, L. (2009). Critical social work practice: A narrative approach. *International Journal of Narrative Practice*, *1*, 9–18.

Rostoky, S. S. & Riggle, E. D. B. (2011). Marriage equality for same-sex couples: Counseling psychologists as social change agents. *The Counseling Psychologist*, *39*(7), 956–972.

Rothman, J. (2008). Multi modes of community intervention. In J. Rothman, J. Erlich, & J. Tropman (Eds.), *Strategies of community intervention* (7th ed.) (pp.141–170). Peosta, Iowa: Eddie Bowers Publishing Co., Inc.

Rothman, J. C. (2009a). An overview of case management. In A. R. Roberts, *Social workers' desk reference* (2nd ed.) (pp. 751–755). New York: Oxford Press.

Rothman, J. C. (2009b). Developing therapeutic contracts with clients. In A. R. Roberts, *Social*

workers' desk reference (2nd ed.) (pp. 514–520). New York: Oxford Press.

Royse, D., Staton-Tindall, M., Badger, K., & Webster, J. M. (2009). *Needs assessment.* New York: Oxford University Press.

Rozakis, L. (1996). *New Roberts Rules of Order.* New York: Smithmark Reference.

Rubin, H. J. & Rubin, I. S. (2008). *Community organizing and development.* Boston: Pearson Allyn & Bacon.

Rutgers School of Social Work. (2007). *Continuing education.* Retrieved from http://socialwork. rutgers.edu/ContinuingEducation/ce.aspx

Sager, J. S. & Weil, M. (2013). Larger-scale social planning: Planning for services and communities. In M. Weil (Ed.), *The handbook of community practice* (pp. 299–325). Thousand Oaks, CA: Sage Publications

Sandfort, J. (2005). Casa de Esperanza. *Nonprofit Management & Leadership*, *15*(3), 371–382.

Saint Louis University Pius Library (n.d.). *Research guides.* Retrieved from http://libguides.slu.edu/index.php

Saleebey, D. (2013). *The strengths perspective in social work practice.* Boston: Allyn & Bacon.

Scherrer, J. L. (2012). The United Nations Convention on the Rights of the Child as policy and strategy for social work action in child welfare in the United States. *Social Work*, *57*(1), 11–22.

Schein, E. H. (1992). *Organizational culture and leadership.* San Francisco: Jossey-Bass.

Schiller, L. Y. (1995). Stages of development in women's groups: A relational model. In R. Kurland & R. Salmon (Eds.), *Group work practice in a troubled society: Problems and opportunities* (pp. 117–138). New York: The Haworth Press.

Schiller, L. Y. (1997). Rethinking stages of group development in women's groups: Implications for practice. *Social Work with Groups*, *20*(3), 3–19.

Schiller, L. Y. (2007). Not for women only: Applying the rlational model of group development with vulnerable populations. *Social Work with Groups*, *30*(2), 11–26.

Schiller, L. Y. (2003). Women's group development from a relational model and a new look at facilitator influence on group development. In. M. B. Cohen & A. Mullender, *Gender and group work* (pp. 16–31). New York: Routledge.

Schultz, D. (2004). Cultural competence in psycho-social and psychiatric care: A critical perspective with reference to research and clinical experiences in California, US and in Germany. In A. Metteri, T. Krôger, A. Pohjola, & P. Rauhala (Eds.), *Social work visions from around the globe* (pp. 231–247). Binghamton, NY: Haworth.

Schneider, R. L. & Lester, L. (2001). *Social work advocacy*. Belmont, CA: Brooks/Cole.

Schwartz, W. (1961). *The social worker in the group*. The Social Welfare Forum, 146–177.

Sebold, J. (2011). Families and couples: A practical guide for facilitating change. In G. J. Greene and M. Y. Lee, *Solution-oriented social work practice* (pp. 209–236). NY: Oxford University Press.

Seligman, M. & Darling, R. B. (2007). *Ordinary families, special children: A systems approach to childhood disability* (3rd ed.). New York: The Guilford Press.

Shakya, H. B., Usita, P. M., Eisenberg, C., Weston, J., & Liles, S. (2012). Family well-being concerns of grandparents in skipped generation families. *Journal of Gerontological Social Work, 55,* 39–54.

Shalay, N. & Brownlee, K. (2007). Narrative family therapy with blended families. *Journal of Family Psychotherapy, 18*(2), 17–30.

Shebib, B. (2003). *Choices.* New York: Allyn and Bacon.

Shelton, M. (2012, May 7). Tornado recovery offers Joplin students new lessons. *NPR.* Retrieved from http://www.npr.org/2012/05/07/151950143/tornado-recovery-offers-joplin-students-new-lessons

Sherraden, M. (1993). Community studies in the baccalaureate social work curriculum. *Journal of Teaching in Social Work, 7*(1), 75–88.

Shields, G. & Kiser, J. (2003). Violence and aggression directed toward human service workers: An exploratory study. *Families in Society, 84*(1), 13–20.

Shier, M. L. (2012). Work-related factors that impact social work practitioners' subjective well-being: Well-being in the workplace. *Journal of Social Work, 12*(6), 402–421.

Shin, J., Taylor, M. S., & Seo, M-G. (2012). Resources for change: The relationships of organizational inducements and psychological resilience to employees' attitudes and behaviors toward organizational change. *Academy of Management Journal, 55*(3), 727–748.

Shulman, L. (2009a). Developing successful therapeutic relationships. In A. R. Roberts (Ed.), *Social worker's desk reference* (pp. 573–577). New York, NY: Oxford University Press.

Shulman, L. (2009b). Group work phases of helping: Preliminary phase. In A. Gitterman & R. Salmon (Eds.), *Encyclopedia of social work with groups* (pp. 109–111). New York: Routledge.

Siebold, C. (2007). Everytime we say goodbye: Forced termination revisited, a commentary. *Clinical Social Work Journal, 35*(2), 91–95.

Simmons, C. S., Diaz, L., Jackson, V., & Takahashi, R. (2008). NASW Cultural Competence Indicators: A new tool for the social work profession. *Journal of Ethnic and Cultural Diversity in Social Work, 17*(1), 4–20.

Simon, B. (1990). Re-thinking empowerment. *Journal of Progressive Human Services. 1*(1), 29.

Sims, P. A. (2003). Working with metaphor. *American Journal of Psychotherapy, 57*(4), 528–536.

Singh, A. A. & Salazar, C. F. (2011). Conclusion: Six Considerations for Social Justice Group Work. In A. A. Singh & C. F. Salazar, *Social justice in group work.* Practical interventions for change. New York: Routledge.

Slade, E., McCarthy, J. F., Valenstein, M., Visnic, S., & Dixon, L. B. (2012). Cost savings from Assertive Community Treatment services in an era of declining psychiatric inpatient use. *Health Services Research.* doi: 10.1111/j.1475–6773.2012.01420.

Smith, B. D. (2005). Job retention in child welfare: Effects of perceived organizational support, supervisor support, and intrinsic job value. *Children and Youth Services Review, 27*(2), 153–169.

Sohng, W. S. L. (2008). Community-based participatory research. In T. Mizrahi & L. E. Davis (Eds.), *Encyclopedia of social work* (pp. 1:368–370). Washington DC and New York: NASW Press and Oxford University Press.

Sormanti, M. (2012). Writing for and about clinical practice. In W. Green and B. L. Simon, *The Columbia guide to social work writing* (pp. 114–132). NY: Columbia University Press.

Sowers, K. M. & Rowe, W. S. (2009). International perspectives on social work practice. In A. R. Roberts (Ed.), *Social workers' desk reference* (2nd ed.) (pp. 863–868). New York: Oxford University Press.

Specht, H. (1990). Social work and the popular psychotherapies. *Social Service Review, 64*, 345–357.

Speer, P. W. & Christens, B. D. (2011). Local community organizing and change: Altering policy in the housing and community development system in Kansas City. *Journal of Community & Applied Social Psychology, 22*(5), 414–427.

St. Anthony's Medical Center. (2010). *Family Intervention and Planning*. St. Louis, MO

Stempel, J. (2013). *Supreme Court to hear same-sex marriage cases in late March*. Retrieved from: http://www.reuters.com/article/2013/01/07/us-usa-court-gaymarriage-idUSBRE9060N820130107

Steger, M. B. (2009). *Globalization*. New York: Sterling Publishing.

Stevenson, M. (2010). Flexible and responsive research: Developing rights-based emancipatory disability research methodology in collaboration with young adults with Downs Syndrome. *Australian Social Work, 63*(1), 35–50.

Strand, V., Carten, A., Connolly, D., Gelman, S. R., & Vaughn, P. B. (2009). A cross system initiative sup- porting child welfare workforce professionalization and stabilization. A task group in action. In C. S. Cohen, M. H. Phillips, & M. Hanson (Eds.), *Strength and diversity in social work with groups* (pp. 41–53). New York: Routledge.

Streeter, C. (2008). Community: Practice interventions. In T. Mizrahi & L. E. Davis (Eds.), *Encyclopedia of social work* (pp. 1:355–368). Washington DC and New York: NASW Press and Oxford University Press.

Strom-Gottfried, K. J. (2000). Ensuring ethical practice: An examination of NASW Code violations, 1986–97. *Social Work, 45*(3), 251–261.

Strom-Gottfried, K. J. (2003). *Managing risk through ethical practice: Ethical dilemmas in rural social work*. Presentation at the National Association of Social Workers Vermont chapter, Essex, VT.

Strom-Gottfried, K. J. (2008). *The ethics of practice with minors*. Chicago, IL: Lyceum Books, Inc.

Swenson, C. R. (1998). Clinical social work's contribution to a social justice perspective. *Social Work, 43*(6), 527–537.

Tebb, S. C. (1995). An aid to empowerment: A caregiver well-being scale. *Health and Social Work, 20*(2), 87–92.

Tebb, S. C., Berg-Weger, M. & Rubio, D. M. (2013). The Caregiver Well-Being Scale: Developing a short-form rapid assessment instrument. In press, *Health and Social Work*.

Thomas, H. & Caplan T. (1999). Spinning the group process wheel: Effective facilitation techniques for motivating involuntary client groups. *Social Work with Groups, 21*(4), 3–21.

Thyer, B. (2008). Evidence-based macro practice: Addressing the challenges and opportunities. *Journal of Evidence-based Social Work, 5*(3/4), 453–472.

Thyer, B. A. (2009). Evidence-based practice, science, and social work. An overview. In A.R. Roberts, *Social workers' desk reference* (2nd ed.) (pp. 1115–1119). New York: Oxford Press.

Tolbert, P. S. & Hall, R. J. (2009). *Organizations structures, processes, and outcomes*. Upper Saddle River, New Jersey: Pearson Prentice Hall.

Tomasello, N. M., Manning, A. R., & Dulmus, C. N. (2010). Family-centered early intervention for infants and toddlers with disabilities. *Journal of Family Social Work, 13*, 163–172.

Toseland, R. W. & Horton, H. (2008). Group work. In T. Mizrahi & L. E. Davis, *Encyclopedia of social work* (20th ed.) (pp. 2:298–308). Washington, DC and New York: NASW Press and Oxford University Press.

Turner, H. (2011). Concepts for effective facilitation of open groups. *Social work with groups, 34*, 146–156.

UAW Global Organizing Institute. (2012). *Homepage*. Retrieved from http://www.uaw.org/page/uaw-global-organizing-institute–0

Uken, A., Lee, M.Y., & Sebold, J. (2013). The Plumas Project: Solution-focused treatment of domestic violence offenders. In P. De Jong & I.K. Berg, *Interviewing for solutions* (4th ed.) (pp. 333–345). Belmont, CA: Brooks/Cole.

United Nations. (1997). *Human rights at your fingertips.* United Nations Department Of Public Information, New York: Author. Retrieved from http://www.un.org/rights/50/game.htm#60

U.S. Census Bureau. (2010b). *Valentine's Day 2011: February 14.* Available at: https://www.census.gov/newsroom/releases/archives/facts_for_features_special_editions/cb11-ff02.html

U.S. Census Bureau. (2011a). *Current Population Survey, 2011 Annual Social and Economic Supplement.* Washington, D.C. Government Printing Office

U. S. Census Bureau. (2011b). *Census bureau releases estimates of same-sex married couples.* Retrieved from http://www.census.gov/newsroom/releases/archives/2010_census/cb11-cn181.html

U.S. Census Bureau. (2012a). *Current Population Survey, 2012 Annual Social and Economic Supplement.* Washington, D.C. Government Printing Office

U.S. Census Bureau. (2012b). *Most children younger than age 1 are minorities.* Retrieved from http://www.census.gov/newsroom/releases/archives/population/cb12-90.html

U.S. Department of Housing and Urban Development. (n.d.). *Connecting to success: Neighborhood networks asset mapping guide.* Retrieved from http://www.hud.gov/offices/hsg/mfh/nnw/resourcesforcenters/assetmapping.pdf

Van Den Bergh, N. & Crisp, C. (2004). Defining culturally competent practice with sexual minorities: Implications for social work education and practice. *Journal of Social Work Education, 40*(2), 221–238.

Van Hook, M. P. (2008). *Social work practice with families: A resiliency-based approach.* Chicago: Lyceum Books.

Van Soest, D. (2008). Oppression. In T. Mizrahi & L. E. Davis, *Encyclopedia of social work* (20th ed.) (pp. 3:322–324). Washington, DC and New York: NASW Press and Oxford University Press.

Van Treuren, R. R. (1993). Self-perception in family systems: A diagrammatic technique. In C. Meyer, *Assessment in social work practice* (p. 119). New York: Columbia University Press.

Van Wormer, K. (2009). Restorative justice as social justice for victims of gendered violence: A standpoint feminist perspective. *Social Work, 54*(2), 107–116.

Vinter, R. D. (1974). Program activities: An analysis of their effects on participant behavior. In P. Glassner, R. Sarri, & R. Vinter (Eds.), Individual change through small groups (pp. 233–243). New York: The Free Press.

Vodde, R. & Giddings, M. M. (1997). The propriety of affiliation with clients beyond the professional role: Nonsexual dual relationships. *Arete, 22*(1), 58–79.

Vodde, R. & Gallant, J. P. (2002). Bridging the gap between micro and macro practice: Large-scale change and a unified model of narrative deconstructive practice. *Journal of Teaching in Social Work, 38*(3), 439–458.

Wagner, E. F. (2008). Motivational interviewing. In T. Mizrahi & L. E. Davis, *Encyclopedia of social work* (20th ed.) (pp. 3:273–276). Washington, DC and New York: NASW Press and Oxford University Press.

Wahab, S. (2005). Motivational interviewing and social work practice. *Journal of Social Work, 5*(1), 45–60.

Walker, L. (2013). Solution-focused reentry and transition planning for imprisoned people. In P. De Jong & I. K. Berg, *Interviewing for solutions* (4th ed.) (pp. 318–328). Belmont, CA: Brooks/Cole.

Walz, T. & Ritchie, H. (2000). Gandhian principles in social work practice: Ethics revisited. *Social Work, 45*(3), 213–222.

Warde, B. (2012). The Cultural Genogram: Enhancing the cultural competency of social work students. *Social Work Education, 31*(5), 570–586.

Warren, R. L. (1978). *The community in America.* Chicago: Rand McNally.

Wayne-Metropolitan Community Action Agency (2007). *Wayne-Metropolitan Community Action Agency: Community Needs Assessment 2007.* Retrieved from http://infopeople.org/sites/all/files/past/2007/needs/needs_waynemetro_survey.pdf

Weick, A. (1999). Guilty knowledge. *Families in Society, 80*(4), 327–332.

Weick, A., Kreider, J., & Chamberlain, R. (2009). Key dimensions of the strengths perspective in case management, clinical practice, and community practice. In D. Saleebey (Ed.), *The strengths perspective in social work practice* (5th ed.) (pp. 108–121). Boston: Pearson.

Weil, M. & Gamble, D. N. (2009). Community practice model for the twenty-first century. In A. Roberts (Ed.), *Social workers' desk reference* (pp. 882–892). New York: Oxford University Press, Inc.

Weil, M. (2013). Community-based social planning. In M. Weil (Ed.), *The handbook of community practice* (pp. 265–298). Thousand Oaks, CA: Sage Publications.

Weil, M., Gamble, D. N., & Ohmer, M L. (2013). Evolution, models, and the changing context of community practice. In M. Weil (Ed.), *The handbook of community practice* (pp. 167–193). Thousand Oaks, CA: Sage Publications.

Weil, M., & Ohmer, M. L. (2013). Applying practice theories in community work. In M. Weil's (Ed.), *The handbook of community practice* (pp. 123–161). Thousand Oaks, CA: Sage.

Weil, M., Reisch, M., & Ohmer, M. L. (2013). Introduction: Contexts and challenges for 21st century communities. In M. Weil's (Ed.), *The handbook of community practice* (pp. 3–26). Thousand Oaks, CA: Sage.

West Virginia Board of Social Work Examiners. (n.d.). *Level D: LICSW: (Licensed Independent Social Worker) license.* Retrieved from http://www.wvsocialworkboard.org/licensinginfo/regular/licswlicense.htm

Wharton, T. C. (2008). Compassion fatigue: Being an ethical social worker. *The New Social Worker, 15*(1),4–7.

Wharton, T. C. & Bolland, K. A. (2012). Practitioner perspectives of evidence-based practice. *Families in Society: The Journal of Contemporary Social Services, 93*(3), 157–164.

Whitaker, T. & Arrington, P. (2008). *Social workers at work. NASW Membership Workforce Study.* Washington, DC: National Association of Social Workers.

Whitaker, T., & Wilson, M. (2010). *National Association of Social Workers 2009 compensation and benefit study: Summary of key compensation findings.* Washington DC: NASW.

Wheeler, W. & Thomas, A. M. (2011). Engaging youth in community development. In J. W. Robinson Jr. & G. P. Green (Eds.), *Introduction to community development: Theory, practice and service-learning* (pp. 209–227). Los Angeles, CA: Sage Publications.

Williams, N. R. (2009). Narrative family interventions. In A. C. Kilpatrick & T. P. Holland, *Working with families. An integrative model by level of need* (5th ed.) (pp. 199–223). Boston: Pearson.

Winship, K. & Lee, S. T. (2012). Using evidence-based accreditation standards to promote Continuous Quality Improvement: The experience of San Mateo County Human Services Agency. *Journal of Evidence-based Social Work, 9*(1–2), 68–86.

Wise, J. B. (2005). *Empowerment practice with families in distress.* New York: Columbia University Press.

Witkin, S. L. (2000). Ethics-R-Us. *Social Work, 45*(3), 197–212.

Wood, G. G. & Tully, C. T. (2006). *The structural approach to direct practice in social work: A social constructionist Perspective* (3rd ed.). New York: Columbia University Press.

Wood, G. G. & Roche, S. E. (2001). Representing selves, reconstructing lives: Feminist group work with women survivors of male violence. *Social Work with Groups, 23*(4), 5–23.

Work Group for Community Health and Development at the University of Kansas. (2012). *The Community Tool Box.* Retrieved from http://ctb.ku.edu/en/tablecontents/chapter_1033.aspx

World Health Organization. (2012). *Global democracy deficit.* Retrieved from http:// www.who.int/trade/glossary/story037/en/index/html

Yalom, I. D. & Leszcz, M. (2005). *The theory and practice of group psychotherapy* (5th ed.). New York: Basic Books.

Young, S. (2013). Solutions for bullying in primary schools. In P. De Jong & I. K. Berg, *Interviewing for solutions* (4th ed.) (pp. 308–318). Belmont, CA: Brooks/Cole.

Zandee-Amas, R. R. (2013). A good groups runs itself— and other myths. *The New Social Worker, 20*(1), 10–11.

Zur, O., & Lazarus, A. A. (2002). Six arguments against dual relationships and their rebuttals. In A. A. Lararus & O. Zur (Eds.), *Dual relationships and psychotherapy* (p. 3–24). New York, NY: Springer.

CREDITS

Photo 1-A: © Lisa F. Young

Ex 1.1: Copyrighted material reprinted with permission from the National Association of Social Workers, Inc.

Ex 1.2: Healy, L. M. & Link, R. J. (2012). Handbook of international social work: Human rights, developmen, and the global profession. Used by permission of Oxford University Press.

Photo 1-B: © Lisa F. Young

Ex 1.4: University Declaration of Human Rights used by permission of Human Rights Education Association.

Photo 2-A: © marekuliasz

Ex 2.1: Copyrighted material reprinted with permission from the National Association of Social Workers, Inc.

Ex 2.3: Copyrighted material reprinted with permission from the National Association of Social Workers, Inc.

Ex 2.4: International Federation of Social Workers (IFSW). (2012). Ethics in social work: Statement of principles. Retrieved October 14, 2012 from http://ifsw.org/policies/statement-of-ethical-principles/. Used by permission.

Ex 2.5: New Zealand Association of Social Workers (NZASW). (1993). Code of ethics. Used by permission.

Photo 2-B: © Mark Bowden

QG 3: From Dolgoff/Loewenberg/Harrington. Ethical Decisions for Social Work Praictce, 8E. © 2009 Wadsworth, a part of Cengage Learning, Inc. Reproduced by permission. www.cengage.com/permissions

Ex 2.7: From The Propriety of Affiliation with Clients beyond the Professional Role: Nonsexual dual relationships. Arete 22(1) by R. Vodde and M.M. Giddings. © 1997. Reprinted with permission.

Photo 3-A: © Yuri Arcurs

Ex 3.3: From Skills for Direct Practice in Social Work by R. R. Middleman and G.G. Wood. Copyright © 1990. Columbia University Press.

Ex 4.1: From Assessing strengths, Identifying acts of resistance to violence and oppression, by K.M. Anderson, C.D. Cowger and C.A. Snively. In The Strengths perspective in social swork practice (the d.), by D. Saleebey (Ed.). Copyright Allyn & Bacon, 2009.

Ex 4.2: From Assessing strengths, Identifying acts of resistance to violence and oppression, by K.M. Anderson, C.D. Cowger and C.A. Snively. In The Strengths perspective in social swork practice (the d.), by D. Saleebey (Ed.). Copyright Allyn & Bacon, 2009.

Photo 4-A: © fatihhoca

QG 8: Adapted from The Strengths perspective in social work (5th ed.), by D. Saleebey. Copyright © 2009, Allyn & Bacon.

Photo 4-B: © Lisa F. Young

QG 10: Kagle, J. D. & Kopels, S. (2008). Social work records (3rd ed.). Long Grove, IL: Waveland Press, Inc. Used by permission.

Ex 4.8: Adapted from St. Anthony's Medical Center, St. Louis, Missouri. Reprinted with permission.

Ex 4.9: Adapted from St. Anthony's Medical Center, St. Louis, Missouri. Reprinted with permission.

Ex 4.10: Adapted from St. Anthony's Medical Center, St. Louis, Missouri. Reprinted with permission.

QG 11: From Dejong/Berg. Interviewing for Solutions, 4E. © 2013 Wadsworth, a part of Cengage Learning, Inc. Reproduced by permission. Www.cengage.com/permissions

Photo 5-A: © Alexander Raths

Ex 5.1: Adapted from The structural approach to direct practice in social work: A social constructionist perspective (3rd ed.), by G.G. Wood and C.T. Tully. Copyright 2006, Columbia University Press. Reprinted with permission.

Photo 5-B: © Adam Gregor

QG 16: Sormanti, M. (2012). Writing for and about clinical practice. In W. Green and B. L. Simon, The Columbia guide to social work writing (pp. 114-132). NY: Columbia University Press.

Photo 6-B: © Rob Hainer

Ex 6.4: From Culture in special education, by M. Kalyanpur and B. Harry. Copyright 1999, Paul H. Brookes. Reprinted with permission.

Ex 6.5: Van Hook, M.P. (2008). Social work practice with families: A resiliency-based approach. Chicago: Lyceum Books.

Ex 6.6: Van Hook, M.P. (2008). Social work practice with families: A resiliency-based approach. Chicago: Lyceum Books.

Ex 6.7: From Self-perception in family systems: A diagrammatic technique, by R.R. Van Treuren. In assessment in social work practice, by C. Meyer. Copyright 1993, Columbia University Press. Reprinted with permission.

QG 18: Warde, B. (2012). The Cultural Genogram: Enhancing the cultural competency of social work students. Social Work Education, 31(5), 570-586. Used by permission.

Ex 6.8: From The Culturagram, by E. P. Congress. In Social Workers' desk reference (2nd ed.), by A.R. Roberts. Copyright 2009, Oxford Press. Reprinted with permission.

QG 19: Adapted from St. Anthony's Medical Center, St. Louis, Missouri. Reprinted with permission.

Ex 7.1: From Hull/Mather. Undertssanding Generalist Practice with Families, 1E. © 2006 Wadsworth, a part of Cengage Learning, Inc. Reproduced by permission. www.cengage.com/permissions

Ex 7.2: Sebold, J. (2011). Families and couples: A practical guide for facilitating change. In G. J. Greene and M. Y. Lee, Solution-oriented social work practice (pp. 209-236). NY: Oxford University Press.

Photo 7-A: © Lisa F. Young

Ex 7.3: Adapted from St. Anthony's Medical Center, St. Louis, Missouri. Reprinted with permission.

Ex 7.4: Adapted from St. Anthony's Medical Center, St. Louis, Missouri; Missouri Department of Social Services.

QG 22: From Enabling and empowering families: principles and guidelines for practice, by CX.J. dunst, C.M. Trivette and A.G. Deal. Copyright 2003, Brookline Books. Reprinted with permission.

QG 23: From Enabling and empowering families: principles and guidelines for practice, by CX.J. dunst, C.M. Trivette and A.G. Deal. Copyright 2003, Brookline Books. Reprinted with permission.

Photo 7-B: © Lisa F. Young

Photo 8-A: © Blaj Gabriel

Ex 8.6: From Teaching a methods course in social work with groups, by R. Kurland and R. Salmon. Copyright 1998, Council on Social Work Education.

Ex 8.7: Kurland, R. & Salmon, R. (1998). Teaching a methods course in social work with groups. Alexandria, VA: Council on Social Work Education.

Photo 8-B: © Yuri Arcurs

Ex 8.8: Adapted from St. Anthony's Medical Center, St. Louis, Missouri. Reprinted with permission.

Ex 8.9: Adapted from Women's Support and Community Services, St. Louis, Missouri.

Photo 9-A: © Glynnis Jones

QG 27: From Group Composition, diversity, the skills of the social worker, and group development, by T. Berman-Rossi and T.B. Kelly. Presented at the Council for Social Work Education Annual Meeting, Atlanta, February. Copyright 2003. Reprinted with permission.

Photo 9-B: © Blaj Gabriel

Ex 9.1: Comer, E. & Meier, A. (2011). Using evidence-based practice and intervention research with treatment groups for populations at risk. In G.L. Greif & P.H. Ephross (Eds.) Group work with populations at risk (3rd ed.) (pp. 459–488). New York: Oxford University Press

Ex 9.2: Greif, G. & Ephross, P.H. (Eds.). (2011). Group work with populations at risk (3rd ed.). New York: Oxford University Press.

QG 28: Berg, R.D., Landreth, G.L., & Fall, K.A. (2013). Group counseling concepts and procedures (5th ed.). New York: Routledge.

Photo 9-C: © vm

Photo 9-D: © Yuri Arcurs

QG 30: Berg, R.D., Landreth, G.L., & Fall, K.A. (2013). Group counseling concepts and procedures (5th ed.). New York: Routledge.

Ex 9.7: Berg, R.D., Landreth, G.L., & Fall, K.A. (2013). Group counseling concepts and procedures (5th ed.). New York: Routledge.

Photo 10-A: © vm

Ex 10.2: Adapted from Center of Organizational and Social Research, Saint Louis University.

Ex 10.3: Royse, D., Staton-Tindall, M., Badger, K., & Webster, J.M. (2009). Needs assessment. New York: Oxford University Press.

Photo 10-B: © CREATISTA

Ex 10.4: City of Seattle, Washington. (2012). A Community Assessment of Need for Housing and Services for Homeless Individuals and Families in the Lake City Neighborhood. Retrieved from http://seattle.gov/realestate/pdfs/Needs_Assessment_data_report.pdf

Ex 10.7: Kretzmann, J. P. & McKnight, J. L. (1993). Building communities from the inside out: A part toward finding and mobilizing a community's assets. Evanston, IL: Center for Urban Affairs and Policy Research. Used by permission.

Ex 10.8: McKnight, J. L., & Block, P. (2010). The abundant community: Awakening the power of families and neighborhoods. San Francisco, CA: Berrett-Koehler Publishers

Ex 10.9: McKnight, J. L., & Block, P. (2010). The abundant community: Awakening the power of families and neighborhoods. San Francisco, CA: Berrett-Koehler Publishers

Photo 10-C: © THEGIFT777

Ex 11.1: Netting, F. E., Kettner, P. M., McMurtry, S. L., & Thomas, L. (2011). Social work macro practice. Boston: Pearson Allyn & Bacon.

Ex 11.3: Source: 350.org

Photo 11-A: © 350.org

Photo 11-B: © 350.org

QG 35: Adapted from Organizing for social change, by K. Bobo, J. Kendall, and S. Max. Copyright 2010, The Forum Press. Reprinted with permission.

QG 36: Adapted from New Robert's Rules of Order by L. Rozakis. Copyright 1996, Smithmark Reference.

QG 37: Adapted from Consensus through conversation, by L. Dressler. Copyright 2006, Berrett-Koehler Publishers, Inc. All rights reserved. www.bkconnection.com

Ex 11.5: Kretzmann, J. P. & McKnight, J. L. (2005). Discovering community power: A guide to mobilizing local assets and your organization's capacity. Evanston, IL: Asset-Based Community Development (ABCD) Institute. Used by permission.

Ex 11.7: Ohmer, M.L. & DeMasi, K. (2009). Consensus organizing: A community development workbook. Thousand Oaks, CA: Sage Publications, Inc.

Ex 11.9: Ohmer, M.L. & Korr, W.S. (2006). The effectiveness of community practice interventions: A review of the literature. Research on Social Work Practice, 16(2),132–145. Used by permission.

Ex 11.10: From Localized needs and a globalized economy, by J. Ife in Social work and globalization (Special Issue), Canadian Social Work, 2(1). Copyright 2000.

Ex 11.11: From International social work: Issues, strategies and programs by D. Cox and M. Pawar. Copyright 2006, Sage Publications, Inc. Reprinted with permission.

Ex 11.14: Speer, P. W. & Christens, B. D. (2011). Local community organizing and change: Altering policy in the housing and community development system in Kansas City. Journal of Community & Applied Social Psychology, 22(5), 414-427. Used by permission.

Photo 12-A: © Digital Vision

Ex 12.1: National Association of Area Agencies on Aging. (2012). National aging services network. Retrieved from http://www.n4a.org/about-n4a/join/

Photo 12-B: © Chris Fertnig

Photo 12-C: © CandyBox Images

Ex 12.5: Gambrill, E. (2012). Social work practice: A critical thinkers guide. New York: Oxford University Press.

QG 39: From Locke/Garrison/Winship. Generalist Social Work Practice, 1E. © 1998 Wadsworth, a part of Cengage Learning, Inc. Reproduced by permission. www. Cengage.com/permissions

Ex 12.7: Larson, K., & McGuiston, C. (2012). Building capacity to improve Latino health in rural North Carolina: A case study in community-University engagement. Journal of Community Engagement and Scholarship, 5(1), 14-23.

QG 42: Plitt, D. L. & Shields, J. (2009). Development of the policy advocacy behavior scale: Initialreliability and validity. Research on Social Work Practice, 19(1), 83-92. Reprinted by permission.

Photo 13-A: © gosphotodesign

Ex 13.1: Evans, S. D., Hanlin, C. E., & Prillehensky, I. (2007). Blending Ameliorative and transformative approaches in human service organizations: A case study. Journal of Community Psychology, 35(3), 329-346. Used by permission.

Ex 13.2: Netting, F. E., Kettner, P. M., McMurtry, S. L., & Thomas, M. L. (2012). Social work macro practice. Boston: Pearson Allyn & Bacon.

Ex 13.4: Netting, F. E., Kettner, P. M., McMurtry, S. L., & Thomas, M. L. (2012). Social work macro practice. Boston: Pearson Allyn & Bacon.

QG 43: Manning, T. (2012). The art of successful persuasion: Seven skills you need to get your point across effectively.

Ex 13.6: O'Connor, M. K., & Netting, F. E. (2009). Organization practice: A guide to understanding human service organizations. Hoboken, NJ: John Wiley and Sons.

Ex 13.7: Winship, K. & Lee, S. T. (2012). Using evidence-based accreditation standards to promote Continuous Quality Improvement: The experience of San Mateo County Human Services Agency. Journal of Evidence-based Social Work, 9(1-2), 68-86.

GLOSSARY/INDEX

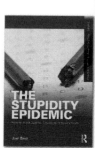

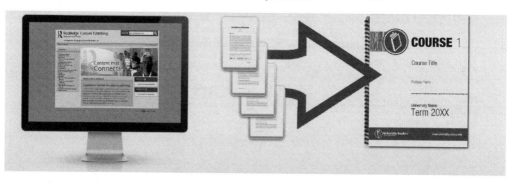

NEW DIRECTIONS IN SOCIAL WORK

SERIES EDITOR: ALICE LIEBERMAN, UNIVERSITY OF KANSAS

New Directions in Social Work is an innovative, integrated series offering a uniquely distinctive teaching strategy for generalist courses in the social work curriculum, at both undergraduate and graduate levels. The series integrates five texts with custom websites housing interactive cases, companion readings, and a wealth of resources to enrich the teaching and learning experience.

Research for Effective Social Work Practice, Third Edition

Judy L. Krysik, Arizona State University and Jerry Finn, University of Washington, Tacoma

HB: 978-0-415-52100-0
PB: 978-0-415-51986-1
eBook: 978-0-203-07789-4

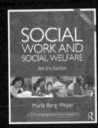

Social Work and Social Welfare, Third Edition

Anissa Taun Rogers, St. Louis University

HB: 978-0-415-52080-5
PB: 978-0-415-50160-6
eBook: 978-0-203-11931-0

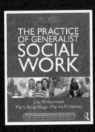

The Practice of Generalist Social Work, Third Edition

Julie Birkenmaier, Marla Berg-Weger, both at St. Louis University, and Martha P. Dewees, University of Vermont

HB: 978–0–415–51988–5
PB: 978–0–415–51989–2
eBook: 978–0–203–07098–7

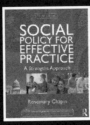

Social Policy for Effective Practice: A Strengths Approach, Third Edition

Rosemary Chapin, University of Kansas

HB: 978–0–415–51991–5
PB: 978–0–415–51992–2
eBook: 978–0–203–79476–0